高等教育管理科学与工程类专业

GAODENG JIAOYU GUANLI KEXUE
YU GONGCHENG LEI ZHUANYE 系列教材

国际工程合同管理

——FIDIC条款解析与案例

GUOJI GONGCHENG HETONG GUANLI
——FIDIC TIAOKUAN JIEXI YU ANLI

主 编/舒 畅

重庆大学出版社

内容简介

本书希望帮助读者了解 FIDIC 合同形式的各个方面,使其能够理解建设项目的合同条件。通过详细讲解 FIDIC 2017 版红皮书施工合同理论条款,帮助读者全面掌握 FIDIC 合同的实践应用及注意事项。逐条讲解合同条款,便于读者学习记忆,及时掌握对每一个小条款的运用,能够将掌握合同管理知识和进行工程管理实践应用有效地结合起来。

全书分为三大部分,共 6 章。第一部分(第 1 章—第 5 章)介绍了 FIDIC 组织,FIDIC 合同的演变和发展历程,产生的背景和前提,合同的特点、语言特色、相关合同系列、新旧版本的区别等内容。第二部分(第 6 章)详细分析了 FIDIC 红皮书施工合同条款。第三部分(附录 1—附录 12)对第二部分的知识点进行了总结和补充,包括工程师角色在条款中的定义、索赔条款与反索赔条款的总结、承包商责任和权力的对应条款和内容、通知条款的运用,以及支付条款的运用等内容。书中还附有重点词汇及常见专业术语的中文释义,便于读者自查。

本书适合作为高等教育管理科学与工程类等相关专业的教材和指导书,也可用作合同管理人员、工程管理人员的学习参考书。

图书在版编目(CIP)数据

国际工程合同管理:FIDIC 条款解析与案例/舒畅
主编. --重庆:重庆大学出版社,2023.3
高等教育管理科学与工程类专业系列教材
ISBN 978-7-5689-3749-8

Ⅰ.①国… Ⅱ.①舒… Ⅲ.①国际承包工程—经济合同—管理—中国—高等学校—教材 Ⅳ.①F752.68

中国国家版本馆 CIP 数据核字(2023)第 036787 号

国际工程合同管理——FIDIC 条款解析与案例
主 编 舒 畅
责任编辑:林青山 版式设计:夏 雪
责任校对:王 倩 责任印制:赵 晟
*
重庆大学出版社出版发行
出版人:饶帮华
社址:重庆市沙坪坝区大学城西路 21 号
邮编:401331
电话:(023)88617190 88617185(中小学)
传真:(023)88617186 88617166
网址:http://www.cqup.com.cn
邮箱:fxk@cqup.com.cn(营销中心)
全国新华书店经销
重庆市正前方彩色印刷有限公司印刷
*
开本:787mm×1092mm 1/16 印张:15.25 字数:509 千
2023 年 3 月第 1 版 2023 年 3 月第 1 次印刷
印数:1—2 000
ISBN 978-7-5689-3749-8 定价:42.00 元

本书是为了适应工程管理建设的需要，培养具有工程基础理论与专业知识，具有较强的工程实践能力的应用型高层次人才，以及适应国家的双语课程建设的需要，强化工程教育国际化意识而编写的。FIDIC 合同在国内外都有大量的研究和专著，但是适合本科生和研究生学习的教材还比较少。此书希望为高等教育管理科学与工程类等相关专业的学生，以及工程管理人员、合同管理人员等提供一个学习参考。

本书的编写促成原因包括国际工程管理和 FIDIC 战略性课程的设置及其相关课题。课程的教学理念在于"双语化，精品化，经典代表，典范树立"。工程教育观念国际化就是要将工程专业人才培养的改革和发展置于一带一路和世界经济发展的大背景之中，从国际化的视野而非单一地区的角度对工程人才培养的总体素质进行考查。FIDIC 合同条款是将最新的国外管理理念引进国内市场的典型课程范例，也是对学生进行国际化培养方案实施的最重要的课程基础之一。

2017 年 12 月 5—6 日，FIDIC 组织在伦敦正式发布 2017 年第 2 版 FIDIC 合同系列文件。历经 18 年的运用，FIDIC 对 1999 版合同条件进行了大幅修订，合同文本的字数、条款均有大幅增加，这使得 FIDIC 合同条件中的相应规定更加刚性化、程序化。2017 年第 2 版 FIDIC 合同对承包商的项目管理和合同管理提出了更严格和更高的要求，无疑会给业主、承包商和工程师等项目干系人带来巨大的挑战。

FIDIC 对中国的影响有以下几个方面：

（1）在国际工程方面

如前所述，对于中国工程界而言，FIDIC 就是"国际工程合同"的代名词。虽然 FIDIC 在国际工程中应用非常广泛，但论其影响力，恐怕在任何一个国家中都不及中国。尤其是在一些发达国家中，例如英国、美国、法国等，由于其现代化工程管理的发展历史比较长，早已形成了自己的工程合同范本体系，例如美国的 AIA 合同范本，英国的 JCT、ICE 合同范本等。在这些国家，FIDIC 的影响力比较有限。但是，由于 FIDIC 对中国建设工程根深蒂固的影响，其影响力又通过中国的工程公司进一步向外输出。

（2）对国内工程合同的影响

FIDIC 条款在我国建设上的使用，始于 20 世纪 80 年代中期的世界银行贷款项目。由于其具有条款严密，系统性和可操作性强，工程建设各方（业主、监理工程师、承包商）风险责任明确、权利义务公平的特点，逐步为我国所接受使用。在使用过程中，FIDIC 条款根据我国的具体情况不断加以调整（尤其是在监理工程师的职权上），极大地促进了我国建设管理模式的改革。例如，1999 年颁布的《建设工程施工合同（示范文本）》（GF-1999-0201），摒弃了多年来延用的模式，变为和 FIDIC 框架一致的通用条款与专用条款。住建部从 1999 年开始发布第一版《建设工程施工（合同范本）》，其基本框架和内容就是参考自 FIDIC 合同，目前这个范本几经更新,但基本框架并没有发生大的变化,且后来的工程总承包合同范本、咨询设计合同范本等,也是在参考 FIDIC 合同的基础上编制的。

全书分为三大部分。第一部分是前言介绍(第 1 章—第 5 章),包括了 FIDIC 组织介绍,合同的演变和发展历史,产生的背景和前提,合同的特点,合同的语言特色,合同系列介绍,FIDIC 新版与旧版的区别。第二部分(第 6 章)是红皮书的条款释义,并附有大量的讨论问题。针对法律、合同这类对文字性、理解性和应用能力要求很高的课程,这种条款与案例相结合的方法为学生所欢迎,可以帮助他们更深入地了解知识,理解条款的运用。第三部分是附加知识部分(附录 1—附录 12),是对第二部分知识的总结和小知识点的补充。

本书由舒畅老师完成,在课题的申请和材料的编写过程中,大量的专家、同行提出了宝贵的意见,校方、学院和系教研组提供了大力的支持,对此表示莫大的感谢。

由于编者水平与经验有限,书中难免存在疏漏之处,敬请广大读者批评指正。

编　者

2022 年 4 月

Contents

Chapter 1

FIDIC Introduction

Ⅰ Introduction of FIDIC history

FIDIC is indeed a short form of the French name "Fédération Internationale des Ingénieurs-Conseils".

FIDIC was founded in 1913. At the inception stage, there were only three member associations from the European countries, including France and Belgium.

In 1949, the British Civil Engineering Association joined and hosted the FIDIC seminar in London, which was described by historians as the birth of the contemporary FIDIC. In 1959, the USA, South Africa, Australia and Canada all came in, thus made the FIDIC break the limit of regional boundaries and become a real international organization. Its headquarter is located in Geneva, Switzerland.

In 1996, China also joined and became a member. Today, its members and associations come from 97 countries, spreading all over the world, representing more than 1 million professionals and most of the private practice consulting engineers in the world.

Ⅱ FIDIC objectives

(1) Be the recognised international authority on issues relating to consulting engineering best practice.

(2) Actively promote high standards of ethics and integrity among all stakeholders involved in the development of infrastructure worldwide.

(3) Maintain and enhance FIDIC's representation of the consulting engineering industry worldwide.

(4) Enhance the image of consulting engineering.

(5) Promote and assist the worldwide development of viable consulting engineering industries.

(6) Promote and enhance the leading position of FIDIC's Forms of Contract.

(7) Improve and develop FIDIC's training and publishing activities.

(8) Promote and encourage the development of young professionals in the consulting engineering industry.

Ⅲ Types of members

1) Member Association

A national association which is the largest association of firms providing technology-based intellectual consulting services for the built and natural environment in a country.

2) Affiliate Member

Any association, organization, firm or group of firms which is based in a country having or not having a Member Association, and which supports the objectives of the federation. This membership category is aimed at commercial organizations which aim to maintain a close contact with FIDIC and to support the federation's activities.

3) Associate Member

Any individual, organization, association, firm or group of firms which is based in a country not having a Member Association, and which has a major part of its activity in the engineering consulting industry. This membership category is aimed at organizations that aim to become a FIDIC national Member Association.

Ⅳ FIDIC publications

FIDIC, in the furtherance of its goals, publishes international standard forms of contracts for works and for clients, consultants, sub-consultants, joint ventures and representatives, together with related materials such as standard pre-qualification forms.

FIDIC also publishes business practice documents such as policy statements, position papers, guidelines, training manuals and training resource kits in the areas of management systems (quality management, risk management, business integrity management, environment management, and sustainability) and business processes (consultant selection, quality based selection, tendering, procurement, insurance, liability, technology transfer, and capacity building).

Ⅴ FIDIC vision

Enabling the development of a sustainable world as the recognised global voice for the consulting engineering industry.

Ⅵ FIDIC mission

To work closely with our stakeholders to improve the business climate in which we operate and enable our members to contribute to making the world a better place to live in, now and in the future.

Ⅶ FIDIC values

1) Quality

Quality has been one of FIDIC's fundamental principles ever since its establishment in 1913.

Quality is important both in the work undertaken by consulting engineers and in the way that they are selected, and it is very difficult to achieve the first of these if the second is not also implemented.

2) Integrity

The issue of integrity has always been important but has became even more so of late given the increased legislation in the UK and other countries and the anti-corruption procedures implemented by multinational development banks. FIDIC has responded to the changes by introducing its own updated integrity management system and has also drafted a government procurement integrity management system. It is essential that all integrity systems that are introduced are at least as comprehensive as those drafted by the federation.

3) Sustainability

Addressing sustainability is, of course, crucial to the survival of mankind. The problem is that in many parts of the world the issue is ill-defined or misunderstood.

Many people are totally confused by the range and variability of sustainability assessment tools available. FIDIC is therefore preparing a publication on this issue and this in turn will, it is hoped, lead to much more consistency between the tools being used (or abused) in different part of the world.

※ Vocabulary

1. associations *n.* 协会，[遗]关联(association 的复数)；关联分析，协会组织
2. historian *n.* 历史学家，史学工作者
3. actively promote 积极推动，积极促进
4. integrity *n.* 正直，诚实；完整，完全；职业操守；(电子数据的)集成度
5. associate member 协会成员；准会员
6. affiliate *v.* 使隶属，使紧密联系；<正式>加入；(组织)接纳……为成员
    n. 附属机构，分支机构
7. furtherance *n.* 促进；助成；助长
8. implemented *v.* 实施(implement 的过去分词)；执行
    adj. 应用的
9. addressing *n.* 寻址；定址；访问
    v. 在(信封上)写收件人姓名和邮址；对……讲话；致词；考虑处理(问题)；
    (高尔夫)就位击球(address 的现在分词)
10. conditions of contract 合同条件；[法] 契约条件

Chapter 2

FIDIC Contract Evolvement

In 1945, the Institution of Civil Engineer, with the joint efforts of the Federation of civil engineering contractor, unified various civil engineering contract forms which were adopted by different countries before World War II and promulgated a standard form which was widely recognized afterwards.

This standard form package is named as the General Conditions of Contract and Forms of Tender, Agreement and Bond for Use in connection with works of civil engineering construction, and abbreviated as ICE form.

In January of 1950, after the agreement of ACE (in London) who joined recently, the ICE form was promulgated again after some amendments. It's reprinted in March of 1951 (3rd edition), January of 1955 (4th edition), 1969 (with some supplements), June of 1973 (5th edition) and 1991 after repeated modifications.

Many professional associations imitated the ICE form and, after some adjustments, published their own contract conditions adapted to their national or regional legislation system. ACE associated with the British architecture export group to work on contract files that could be used elsewhere other than the U.K., as approved by ICE and in urgent need of the international construction industry. This contract file is called the Overseas (Civil) Conditions of Contract with the short name of ACE form and was published in August of 1956. ACE form varies slightly with ICE form as to formation and main text content, and is constituted by standard tendering letter, appendix to tendering latter, and contract agreement sample. In order to be distinguished from ICE, its cover was printed in blue. The ACE format is the first international standard conditions of contract for works of civil engineering construction and it's divided into two parts. The first part includes 68 clauses, called the general condition. The second part is the particular conditions of the contract, including the explanation for the first part and some new terms for selection.

After that, FIDIC worked with FIEC and published the construction contract conditions for the civil engineering in August of 1957 (1st edition) (CONS), often called FIDIC conditions, which was based on the formation of ACE. This FIDIC condition also consists of two parts.

After the recognition and approval of the FAWPC (International Federation of Asian and Western Pacific Contractor's Associations, Philippine, Rizal) in July of 1969, the 2nd edition was republished. The supplement part to the 2nd edition which is named as dredging and filling engineering particular conditions constitutes the 3rd part of the contract conditions. In 1973, it's reprinted after the recognition and approval of the AGCA (Associated General Contractors of America, Washington) and FIIC (Inter-American Federation for the Construction Industry, Panama).

There had been a big controversy about the 5th edition of the ICE form published in June of 1973, giving a chance for further amendment on FIDIC conditions. The 5th edition deviated from the civil engineering conventions embodied in the 4th edition in some important aspects, and was criticized of being ambiguous in language and structure. While it enlightened the editors of the FIDIC conditions and contributed to the publication of the 3rd edition in July of 1977.

Although not publicly acknowledged, the CONS dealt properly with the potential conflicts caused by different legislative systems. Many projects conducted world widely proved the success of its 2nd edition and 3rd edition, especially the latter, with the evidence of the escalated economic growth in the Middle East and Far East countries in the 1970s and 1980s. The 3rd edition was translated into German and Spanish. When coming into the late 80s, arbitration cases multiplied and the 3rd edition started to gain public criticism.

Thus the 3rd edition was critically examined by some lawyers sentence by sentence who were good at big term explanation, and the 4th edition was published in September of 1987. FIDIC conditions initially were drafted for international projects while later on they were found out to be adapted to domestic projects as well, thus the word "International" was removed from the 4th edition.

The second part of particular conditions of the 4th edition was expanded and published as a sole volume, whilst the clause number corresponds to the general parts and together constitute the contract conditions specifying the rights and obligation of each party.

In 1988, after some editorial amendments aiming to clarify the real intention rather than altering the meaning of the clauses, the CONS was republished.

Of the 1992's reprint, further amendment concerned only with punctuation and alteration of characters like "and", "or".

In November of 1996, FIDIC published the "1992 Fourth Edition Revised Reprint supplement to Contract Conditions for civil engineering construction in 1987", providing the readers conveniences in three controversial aspects: dispute resolution, payment, and prevention of delay of issuing payment certificate.

The above publications have been recognized and approved by AGCA, FIIC and IFAWPCA (International Federation of Asian and Western Pacific Contractor's Associations, Philippine, Rizal) and recommended as standard contract conditions to the International Association of Dredging Companies, international organizations like the World Bank, and so on.

International federation of consulting engineers in September of 1999 issued the 1st edition of FIDIC contract model, and in 1999 seminar on use of the new contract was held in London on September 27th.

After nearly two decades of development, a new FIDIC document was launched in 2017.

After years of practice, the new FIDIC on the basis of the original makes a lot of revisions, compared to the old version of 30,400 words, the 2017 version of FIDIC words have broken through 50,000 words due to the refinement and expansion of the content. The revised document also contains 174 articles, compared with 167 in the previous version. This also reflects a fact from the side: the content stipulated in the FIDIC contract document is more detailed and has a stronger procedural nature, which fully involves the specific links such as claims and arbitration.

Highlights of the FIDIC contract conditions are as follows:

(1) FIDIC contract conditions are drafted with reference to the British domestic contracts.

(2) The concept of FIDIC contract is rooted in British Common Law system.

(3) The wording is based on the principle of British law.

(4) The concept of FIDIC conditions of contract is established on the basis by appointing a mutually trusted engineer as to project design and construction supervision.

(5) Compensation concept is established on the basis of temporary B. Q. for final measurement and payment.

(6) Division of rights of obligations is about risk sharing.

※ Vocabulary

1. promulgated *v.* 发布,公布;宣传;散布(promulgate 的过去式和过去分词)

2. abbreviated *adj.* 简短的;小型的;服装超短的

　　　　　v. 缩写;节略(abbreviate 的过去分词)

3. deviated from 偏离;脱离

4. embodied in 在……体现, 使具体化

5. enlightened *adj.* 开明的;文明的;有知识的;觉悟的

　　　　　v. 启迪;解释;照亮(enlighten 的过去式和过去分词)

6. common law system 普通法(法)系

7. on the principle of 根据……的原则

8. with reference 参照,根据

Chapter 3

Characteristics of FIDIC Contract Language

1. Interestingly, a census used to be made by the University of Reading about the language characteristics of the "Red Book" and the data collected from 38 countries showed that 71% of the interviewees credited it with the advantage of "easily to understand" followed by another contradicting comment of "incomprehensible".

2. When reading the contract conditions, you may go through a lot of formal phrases like "notwithstanding" and technical terms like "force majeure". Because FIDIC contract originates from ICE, thus bearing the distinct features of British English and law language. Be that as it may, British English and law have always been retained as some of the best ways to study English, and FIDIC contract conditions for university students and readers with similar background to learn international contract traditions.

3. Long sentence structure, which probably turns out to be a barrier for most foreign language readers, especially Chinese readers with their reading. As shown by the selected sentence from the text "Notwithstanding any other provision of this clause, if any event or circumstances outside the control of the parties (including, but not limited to, Force Majeure) arises which makes it possible or unlawful…", the average length of the sentence is 17 words.

4. Aiming to provide high quality contract form ever since its birth, FIDIC has shared no efforts in refining its language in pursuit of accuracy and authentic wording in case of discrepancy.

5. You may notice that some words and expressions are identified by the use of Capital Initial Letters. Therefore, the General Conditions, the Particular Conditions and the standardized forms should all use capital initial letters for words and expressions which are intended to have defined meanings.

For example, "Base Day" means the date 28 days prior to the latest date for submission of the Tender, "Day" means a calendar day and "year" means 365 days and some defined words like Contract, Employer, Engineer and so on.

※Vocabulary

1. in pursuit of 寻求,追求
2. intended to 打算做……, 想要……(intended 是 intend 的过去式和过去分词)
3. calendar day 历日;[天] 日历日
4. prior to 在……之前;居先

Chapter 4

FIDIC Contract Series

In December 2017, the FIDIC issued the 2nd edition of the 1999 edition of the three conditions of the contract at the international user conference held in London, which are as follows: Conditions of Contract for Construction (the Red Book), Conditions of Contract for Plant and Design-Build (the Yellow Book) and Conditions of Contract for Design-Procurement-Construction Turnkey Projects (the Silver Book). This revision started from the Yellow Book. FIDIC launched the pre-release version of the Yellow Book as early as 2016. Based on the Yellow Book, the relevant design obligations were deleted to form the Red Book, and the risk allocation was adjusted to form the Silver Book. During the revision process, FIDIC solicited and incorporated the views and suggestions of various users and relevant organizations in the international engineering industry, including contractor associations such as CICA (Confederation of International Contractor's Associations), EIC (European International Contractors), ICAK (International College of Applied Kinsiology) and OCAJI (Overseas Construction Association of Japan, Inc.).

The 2017 version series of contract conditions seek clarity, transparency and certainty, so as to reduce the disputes between the two parties and make the project more successful. The 2017 version series of terms of contract enhances the use of project management tools and mechanisms. It further balances the risk and responsibility distribution between the two parties and emphasizes the reciprocal relationship between the two parties. To reflect current international engineering practices and solve the problems arising from the use of the 1999 version, it also draws on experience of the Conditions of Contract for Plant and Design-Build-Operation (DBO) published by FIDIC in 2008.

The application scope, duties and obligations of the Owner and the Contractor, especially the principle of risk allocation, are basically the same as those in the 1999 version. The overall structure of the conditions of the contract remains largely unchanged, but the general conditions distinguish claims from disputes and a dispute warning mechanism is added. Compared with the 1999 version, the 2017 version of the general conditions significantly increase in length, more project management thinking is taken into account, the relevant provisions are more detailed and clearer, and more operational. The 2017 version strengthens and expands the position and role of engineer, while at the same time emphasizing the neutrality of engineer. It emphasizes more on allocation of risk and responsibility and handling of the owner and contractor's equal relationship in all procedures.

I Scope of application of 2017 version

The scope of appplication of 2017 version is the same as 1999 version. The first three books were initially published as Test Edition in 1998, and the many reactions to them were renewed before the first edition was published in 1999.

(1) For Construction, abbreviated as "CONS", which is recommended for building engineering works designed by the Employer by its representatives, the Engineer. Under the usual arrangement for this type of contract, the Contractor works in accordance with a design provided by the Employer. However, the Works may include some elements of Contractor-design civil mechanical, electrical or construction works.

As shown below, Figure 4.1 is about the whole procedure of the old CONS and Figure 4.2 is about the new CONS.

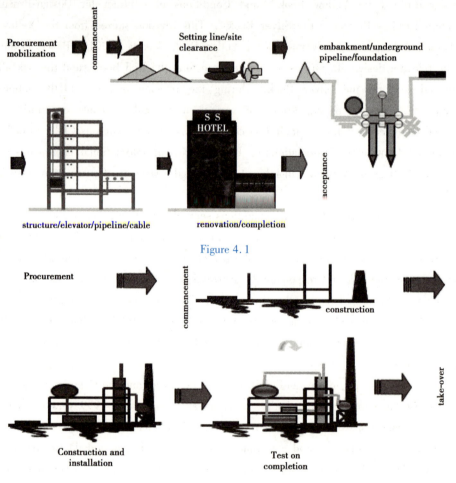

Figure 4. 1

Figure 4. 2

（2）For P&DB, which are recommended for the provision of electrical or mechanical plants, and for the design and execution of building or engineering works. Under the usual arrangements for this type of contract, the Contractor designs and provides, in accordance with the Employer's requirements, plant, or other works, which may include any combination of civil, mechanical, electrical or construction works. Figure 4.3 shows the procedure of the new P&DB.

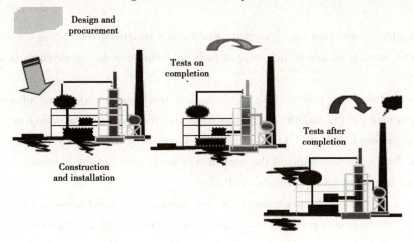

Figure 4.3

（3）For EPC, which are recommended for the provision on a turnkey basis of a process or power plant, and which may also be used where one entity takes total responsibility for the design and execution of a privately financial infrastructure project which involves little on no work underground. Under the usual arrangements for this type of contract, the entity carries out all the Engineering, Procurement and Construction (EPC), providing a fully-equipped facility, ready for operation at the turn of the key. Figure 4.4 shows the procedure of the new EPC.

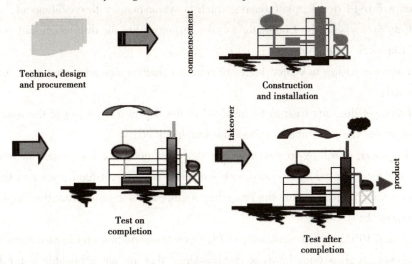

Figure 4.4

Ⅱ Selection of 2017 version

The selection of 2017 version is the same as the 1999 version.

(1) If only the following requirements have been met:

①for large and complex projects;

②projects are of traditional kind projects (e. g. infrastructure, building, hydropower, etc.), the Employer did nearly all the design;

③the Engineer administered the Contract, monitored the construction works and certified payment;

④the Employer was kept fully informed, could make variations, etc;

⑤with payment according to bills of quantities or lump sums for approved work done, then choose CONS.

(2) If in a traditional project, like electrical and mechanical works, including erection on site, the Contractor did the majority of the design, so that the plant met the outline or performance specification prepared by the Employer. The Engineer (or Employer's representative) administered the Contract, monitored the construction works and certified payment, and payment was paid on a lump sum basis, then choose P&DB.

(3) If it's a privately financed project of the Building-Operate-Transfer (BOT) or similar type, and the concessionaire probably requires to have a contract with the construction Contractor, i. e. an EPC (Engineering Procurement Construct) Contract, where the Contractor takes total responsibility for the design and construction.

If it is a process plant or a power plant where the Employer wishes the Contractor to take total responsibility for the design and construction, and hand it over ready to operate "at the turn of key", without an "Engineer" being involved.

If it's an infrastructure project (i. e. road, rail work, bridge, water or sewage treatment plant, transmission line, even dam or hydropower plant) where the Employer wishes to implement the project on a Fixed-Price Turnkey Basis, which is synonymous with conditions of:

①the Employer wishes the Contractor to take responsibility for the design and construction, without an "Engineer" being involved;

②the Employer wishes to higher degree of certainty that the agreed contrat price and time will not be exceeded;

③the Employer does not wish to be involved in the day-to-day project of the work, provided the end result meets the performance criteria he has specified;

④the Employer is willing to pay more for the construction of his project in return for the contract bearing the extra risks associated with enhanced certainty of final price and time.

If it's a building project, where the preceding requirements are also what the Employer wishes here, then choose EPC.

(4) BOT and PPP projects often adopt EPC in the construction and implementation phase.

(5) However, it gives three kinds of circumstances that are not applicable to the EPC:

①if the bidder does not have enough time or information to carefully study and verify the client's requirements, or carry out their design, risk assessment and estimation;

②if the works involve considerable amount of underground works, or if the bidder fails to investigate the works in the area (unless unforeseen conditions are stated in special terms);

③if the Owner wishes to closely supervise or control the Contractor's works or to audit a large part of the construction drawings.

Ⅲ Comparison of Contract Conditions Structure of 2017 version

The terms and conditions of these three contracts include three parts of General Conditions, Guidelines for Preparation of Special Conditions and Attachment (Letter of Guarantee, Letter of Tender, Letter of Acceptance (Silver Cover Letter does not have the Letter of Acceptance, FIDIC considers Silver Cover Letter to be more suitable for bidding negotiation), Contract Agreement and Dispute Adjudication/Arbitral Agreement Format). The general conditions and conditions of this contract are all 21 first-class terms. The overall structure is basically the same, but it is slightly adjusted according to its different application scope. Particular conditions are divided into two parts: contract data and special terms. The form of the guarantee of the three contracts remains the same and it is based on the Uniform Rules for Demand Guarantees of the International Commerce Council.

As can be seen from Table 4.1 and Table 4.2, of the three contracts, only Article 3 (Red and Yellow Book for the Engineers, Silver Book for the Owner's management), Article 5 (Red book as "subcontractor", Yellow Book and Silver Book for "design") and Article 12 (Red book for the measurement and valuation, Yellow Book and Silver Book for "inspection after the completion of") theses three first-class terms are different. The names of the other clauses remain the same. It can be seen that although the scope of application of the 2017 version of contract conditions is different, the general conditions still maintain a unified and standardized structure system, which will be conducive to the use of users.

Table 4.1

Number	CONS	P&DB	EPC
1	General provisions	General provisions	General provisions
2	The Employer	The Employer	The Employer
3	The Engineer	The Engineer	Owner's management
4	The Contractor	The Contractor	The Contractor
5	Subcontracting	Design	Design
6	Staff and labor	Staff and labor	Staff and labor
7	Equipment, materials and workmanship	Equipment, materials and workmanship	Equipment, materials and workmanship
8	Commencement, Delays and Suspension	Commencement, Delays and Suspension	Commencement, Delays and Suspension
9	Test on completion	Test on completion	Test on completion
10	Employer's taking-over	Employer's taking-over	Employer's taking-over
11	Defects after taking-over	Defects after taking-over	Defects after taking-over
12	Measurement and valuation	Test after completion	Test after completion

Continued

Number	CONS	P&DB	EPC
13	Variation and adjustment	Variation and adjustment	Variation and adjustment
14	Contract Price and Payment	Contract Price and Payment	Contract Price and Payment
15	Termination by Employer	Termination by Employer	Termination by Employer
16	Suspension and termination by Contractor	Suspension and termination by Contractor	Suspension and termination by Contractor
17	Care of the Works and Indemnities	Care of the Works and Indemnities	Care of the Works and Indemnities
18	Exceptional Events	Exceptional Events	Exceptional Events
19	Insurance	Insurance	Insurance
20	Employer's and Contractor's claims	Employer's and Contractor's claims	Employer's and Contractor's claims
21	Disputes and arbitration	Disputes and arbitration	Disputes and arbitration

Table 4. 2

CONS	P&DB	EPC
1.9 Delayed Drawings or Instructions	1.9 Error in owner's request	—
3.1 The Engineer	3.1 The Engineer	3.1 The Employer's personnel
3.2 Engineer's Duties and Authority	3.2 Engineer's Duties and Authority	3.2 Other Employer's personnel
3.3 The Engineer's Representative	3.3 The Engineer's Representative	3.3 The trustee personnel
3.4 Delegation by the Engineer	3.4 Delegation by the Engineer	—
3.5 Engineer's Instructions	3.5 Engineer's Instructions	3.4 Instruction
3.6 Replacement of the Engineer	3.6 Replacement of the Engineer	—
3.7 Agreement or Determination	3.7 Agreement or Determination	3.5 Agreement or Determination
3.8 Meetings	3.8 Meetings	3.6 Meetings
4.4 Contractor's Documents	5.2 Contractor's Documents	5.2 Contractor's Documents
4.5 Training	5.5 Training	5.5 Training

Continued

CONS	P&DB	EPC
4.12 Unforeseeable Physical Conditions	4.12 Unforeseeable Physical Conditions	4.12 Unforeseeable Physical Conditions
5.1 Subcontractors	4.4 Subcontractors	4.4 Subcontractors
5.2 Nominated Subcontractors	4.5 Nominated Subcontractors	4.5 Nominated Subcontractors
10.4 Surfaces Requiring Reinstatement	10.4 Surfaces Requiring Reinstatement	—
14.6 Issue of IPC	14.6 Issue of IPC	14.6 IPC

Engineers are involved in the Red Book and Yellow Book, while the Silver Book is the Owner's Representative. The Red book Client undertook most or all of the design work, while the Beige Book and Silver Book Contractor undertook most or all of the design, so the Beige Book and Silver Book specify the design in detail. The Red Book is a unit price contract, so it has detailed provisions in terms of measurement and valuation, while the Yellow Book and the Silver Book are total price contracts, so there are no corresponding provisions. At the same time, because the Yellow Book and the Silver Book are general contract/turnkey projects, they have more details on post-operation tests. However, because these three contract conditions apply to different situations, the adjustment range of the secondary sub-clauses is relatively large. Although some clauses have the same title, their specific contents may be different. The italicized part of the terms is different in position but basically the same in content, while the other parts are different in content.

※ Vocabulary

1. reciprocal *adj.* 相互的,互惠的,报答的;(路线,方向)反向的;(代词,动词)互相的;
    (量,函数)倒数的
    n. 反身代词,相互动词;倒数,乘法逆元素;互相起作用的事物
2. warning mechanism 预警机制
3. procurement *n.* (尤指为政府或机构)采购,购买;取得,获得
4. concessionaire *n.* 特许权获得者,受让人
5. synonymous *adj.* 紧密联系的,引起联想的;(词,短语)同义的
6. letter of acceptance 中标通知书;接受函
7. letter of guarantee 保证书;[贸易]信用保证书
8. demand guarantee 即期担保,见索即付保函
9. conducive to 有益于……
10. adjustment range 调整幅度

Chapter 5

FIDIC（2nd Edition 2017）Main Changes in Contract Conditions

FIDIC officially released on 5—6 December 2017 in London the Second edition FIDIC contract series documents. After 18 years of application, FIDIC 1999 new version of the Rainbow contract conditions were substantially revised, contract text number increased to over 50,000 words from 23,600 in 1987 and 30,400 in 1999. The terms also increased from 167 in the 1999 edition to 174, making the FIDIC contract Conditions of the corresponding provisions more rigid, procedural. More clear provisions are made on claims, dispute awards and arbitration. The application of the second edition FIDIC contract in 2017 will undoubtedly bring great challenges to project stakeholders such as owners, contractors and engineers, putting forward stricter and higher requirements for project management and contract management of contractors.

The main changes of the second edition 2017 of the contract are as follows.

Ⅰ Comparison of the number of words

Figure 5.1 shows the comparision of number of words between different book, and Figure 5.2 shows the comparision of number of words between 2017 version and 1999 version of Red Book by chapters.

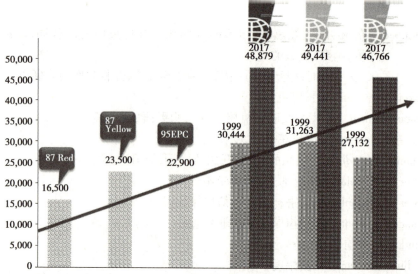

Figure 5.1

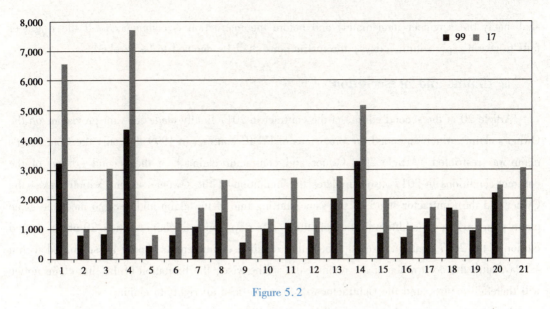

Figure 5.2

Ⅱ **Engineers**

In the FIDIC contract system, the status and role of the Engineers have changed greatly. In the second edition of 2017, the FIDIC contract still favors the role of Engineers in making decisions in Section 3.7, but the following requirements are put forward for engineers. Firstly, neutrality should be maintained when making decisions on any matter or claim. In addition to paragraph 3.7 of the 2017 second edition contract, Engineers are still Employees of the Owners.

On the other hand, whether the addition of a "neutral" word could truly change the professional ethics and standards of Engineers, particularly national consultants in international engineering projects, could not reach an accurate conclusion or be of great doubt.

Secondly, negotiate with the Owners and Contractors individually or jointly, encourage Owners and Contractors to discuss, as far as possible, to agree on claims. Thirdly, strict compliance with deadlines for reaching agreements or decisions. If an Engineer cannot give notice of consent or decision within the prescribed time limit, it shall be considered that the Engineer has made a decision to reject any matter or claim.

The second edition of the 2017 contract provides for "Notification of Discontent" (NOD) requiring the Owner or Contractor to give notice of discontent within 28 days of the Engineer's decision, otherwise it shall be deemed to be the Parties that the Owner and the Contractor have accepted the Engineer's decision in the final and complete manner.

In the second edition of the contract in 2017, Engineers are required to perform their duties "with appropriate qualifications, experience and ability in the main engineering fields corresponding to the implementation of the project". This requirement may cause problems when the Owner's project manager performs his responsibilities as an Engineer.

A new provision was added to the new paragraph 3.5 in the second edition of 2017, which provides that if the Contractor considers that an instruction constitutes a change, the Contractor shall notify the Engineer immediately and before the instruction is commenced. If the Engineer fails to give a reply within 7 days, the instructions shall be deemed to be revoked.

Ⅲ Claims and prescription

Article 20 of the second edition of the contract in 2017 finally made relevant provisions on the Owner's claim, which amended the provisions of FIDIC contract in 1999 that only the Contractor's claim was restricted. Article 20 〔Owner and contractor claims〕 of the second edition of the contract conditions in 2017 also stipulates the limitation of the Owner's claim, which makes the Owner and the Contractor stand on the same starting line of the claim and need to meet the same claim prerequisite. In addition to the limitation of 28 days' notice of claim, Article 20 of the second edition of the 2017 contract also stipulates that detailed claim reports should be submitted within 42 days after the occurrence of the claim event. Otherwise, the limitation of the first claim notice will therefore expire, and the Contractor will therefore lose all rights to claim.

In the claim notice, the second edition of the 2017 contract requires the Contractor to issue a "valid" claim notice. Therefore, for the Contractor, within 28 days after the claim event, issuing the title "claim notice" or "claim intention notice" is the most appropriate solution to avoid the future occurrence of claims.

Whether the provisions of the second edition of the "double limitation" in 2017 would give rise to additional claims by Contractors, approximately 24% of experts considered that claims would decrease, 26% of experts considered that there would be no change in the increase or decrease of claims, and 50% of experts considered that claims would increase.

Ⅳ Payment of contract prices

In 2017, the second edition of the contract stipulates that "cost plus profit" is 5 %. In addition, Sub-Clause 13.6 of the 2017 second edition of the contract is not only a change of law, but also includes any changes in licence, permit and approval. What's more, the Contract also stipulates that the unit price table can be used as the basis for changing the valuation.

Ⅴ Interim Certificate of payment

Sub-Clause 14.6 of the second edition of 2017 revised the 1999 edition of the Contract as an Engineer who can consider the amount payable to the Contractor fairly, and the Engineer can suspend any amount he thinks there are obvious errors or contradictions, but the Engineer must calculate the suspension in detail and give the reasons for the suspension. Sub-Clause 14.6.3 of the second edition of 2017 stipulates that Engineers and Contractors can amend or modify the interim payment certificate, and Contractors should mark those controversial amounts in payment applications so that Engineers can make decisions according to the provisions of Sub-Clause 3.7.

Ⅵ **Dispute Avoidance / Adjudication Board（DAAB）**

Article 21 of the 2017 second edition of the contract introduced the Dispute Avoidance / Adjudication Board in order to avoid disputes more effectively and resolve disputes more effectively. And it emphasizes the role of DAAB pre-warning mechanism. DAAB protocol templates and rules of procedure also increased from 6 pages in 99 to 17 pages.

The 2017 edition requires the establishment of DAAB as soon as possible after the start of the project, and emphasizes that DAAB is a permanent institution（the 1999 edition only requires DAAB to be a permanent institution, and neither the Yellow Book nor the Silver Book）. It also makes detailed provisions on the failure of the parties to appoint DAAB members. DAAB meets regularly with the Parties and conducts on-site inspections. The 2017 edition puts forward and emphasizes the role of DAAB in informal dispute avoidance. DAAB can informally participate in or attempt to deal with potential problems or differences between the Parties to the Contract at the common request of both Parties. FIDIC expects all Parties to avoid and reduce major disputes with this proactive attitude.

The relevant provisions of Article 21 DAAB are as follows：

①DAAB is a permanent DAAB rather than a temporary DAAB；

②both Parties may request assistance or formal consultation.

However, the issues that failed to reach an agreement can be jointly submitted to DAAB. If DAAB understands any problem or fails to reach an agreement, DAAB may invite the Parties to jointly submit the dispute to DAAB for settlement.

If a Party is dissatisfied with the DAAB decision, he may give notice of dissatisfaction 28 days after receipt of the decision, otherwise the DAAB decision will be legally binding on both Parties. The Parties are required to start arbitration within 182 days after issuing or receiving a dissatisfaction notice. If the Parties fail to commence arbitration within 182 days, the notice of dissatisfaction will be invalidated and no longer valid.

Ⅶ **Risk-sharing and liability limits**

Sub-Clause 17. 4 of the second edition of 2017 extended the Contractor's indemnity to "design work and other professional services that led to the inability of the project to meet the functional requirements", which would allow the Contractor's indemnities to exceed the contractual liability limits. Therefore, many international Contractors expressed dissatisfaction with FIDIC.

Sub-Clause 17. 1 of the second edition of 2017 provides that "all risks other than Sub-Clause 17. 1" are borne by the Contractor, which places the Contractor in all uncertain risks and residual risks other than those borne by the Owner, which undoubtedly increases the risk of uncertainty for the Contractor.

Ⅷ **Progress plan requirements and common delays**

Section 8. 3 of the second edition of 2017 puts forward multiple requirements for the progress plan provided by the Contractor, including the need to provide key lines and other information. In paragraph 8.5, FIDIC contract introduces the concept of common delay which may cause great controversy, but FIDIC does not give a clear provision.

And the problem is introduced into the special clause, and the special clause is to solve the problem of common delay, or, if the special clause does not stipulate common delay, it should consider all the relevant circumstances.

It should be noted that, according to the general practice of international engineering, when the delay of the Owner's responsibility and the delay of the Contractor's responsibility are competing, the Contractor can only request the extension of the construction period without claiming any additional costs, that is, the time is money principle.

IX 2017 Differentiated treatment of 2017 Series Conditions of Contract between Claims and Disputes

In order to effectively avoid and reduce disputes between Owners and Contractors, the 2017 edition adopts the following measures: differentiate claims and disputes; changes the role of Engineers; emphasizes the role of DBA in dispute avoidance; introduces a pre-warning mechanism.

Claims and disputes are the main "friction" in the process of project contract execution. Therefore, FIDIC takes claims and disputes as important issues in the revision process of the 2017 edition series of contract conditions, hoping to deal with claims reasonably and timely, so as to avoid claims upgrading to disputes.

X Project management thinking

The 2017 series of contract conditions incorporate more project management thinking.

FIDIC recognizes that although the engineering contract is a legal document, the engineering contract is not only for lawyers, but also for project managers. Therefore, the 2017 edition of the series of contract conditions incorporates more project management thinking. Drawing on the best practice of project management in the international engineering community, many more detailed and clear project management regulations are added to the provisions of the general conditions, which is also the main reason for the content increase of the 2017 edition of the general conditions.

The 2017 edition of the progress plan, progress report requirements are clearer, the content increased significantly, such as requirements for each progress plan must include logical relationship and critical path, the use of what version of the progress plan software and other details are required in the contract in details. More specific provisions are made as to how to modify and adjust the progress plan in the process of project implementation.

The Contractor is also requested to submit a detailed schedule of the completion test 42 days before the start of the completion test. The 2017 edition draws on some of the mature concepts of project management in the NEC (New Engineering Contract) Contract by adding a provision to the "extension of the duration" clause aimed at addressing "common delays".

The 2017 edition stipulates that Contractors need to prepare and implement a Quality Management System (QMS) and Compliance Verification System (CVS). In addition, the Contractor is required to conduct an internal audit of QMS and report the audit results to the Engineer and submit a complete set of CVS records according to the engineer's requirements. The book stipulates that contractors need to prepare and implement a QMS and CVS.

The 2017 edition introduces the " Advance Warning " pre-warning mechanism used in the 2008 FIDIC gold book, requiring the Parties to the Contract to inform the Parties in advance of the known or possible events or situations that they are aware of, which will seriously affect the works of the Contractor personnel, seriously affect the future engineering performance and raise the Contract Price or delay the construction period, so as to minimize the loss. This provision aims to make the Parties to the Contract communicate effectively in advance and solve the problem at the initial stage, so as to reduce the occurrence of disputes.

The book also reflects the importance attached to project managers from all Parties, such as the addition of provisions on qualification requirements for key Contractors and the appointment of Contractors' Representatives as a prerequisite for all payments. The Silver Book stipulates that unless the Owner agrees, the Contractor's Representative should stay at the site. (1999 version of the Silver Book does not have this requirement). And there are requirements for key personnel in the owner requirements' document. The Yellow Book and Silver Book on the qualifications of designers put forward more specific, strict requirements. More specific requirements are also put forward for the qualifications of Engineers (the Silver Book are representatives of Owners).

XI **Reciprocity relationship**

On the basis of the 1999 edition, the 2017 edition series emphasizes more on the reciprocal relationship between the Owners and Contractors in the allocation of risks and responsibilities and in the processing procedures. Article 15 [Termination by Employer] and Article 16 [Termination by Contractor] of the 1999 edition of the generic terms are the best examples of FIDIC's desire for reciprocity between the Parties to the Contract. This concept has been strengthened again in the revision process of the 2017 edition, making it clearer that FIDIC has always emphasized and respected the principle of risk and liability equivalence between the Parties to the Contract, mainly in the following areas:

(1) Emphasize that the Owner's financial arrangements need to include the contract data that if there is a substantial change, the Owner shall immediately notify the Contractor and provide detailed support information, and that if the Owner fails to comply with this provision, the Contractor may even terminate the Contract, that provision is equivalent to the performance guarantee provided by the Contractor to the Owner;

(2) A lot of provisions on notice about the requirements of both Parties of the Contract are equivalent, such as Owners and Contractors have the obligation to give early warning notice to the other Party (and Engineers) for known or possible future events;

(3) Owners and Contractors should abide by the same confidentiality provisions;

(4) Owners and Contractors should abide by all the contract applicable law;

(5) Owners and Contractors should assist each other to obtain the corresponding license;

(6) More specific requirements are put forward on the qualifications of Engineers and their representatives (Owners' representatives of the silver Book), which are equivalent to the detailed and strict requirements for the qualifications of Contractors;

(7) Both Owners and Contractors should take corresponding responsibilities for the design part they are responsible for;

(8) Owners and Contractors are not allowed to hire each other's employees;

(9) When there is a common delay in the construction period, the Owner and the Contractor shall bear the corresponding responsibilities, and the reference solution is given in the description of the special conditions;

(10) The security clause separates the Owner's security to the Contractor from the Contractor's security to the Owner and adds a cross-liability clause;

(11) Include Owners' and Contractors' Claims in the same process and require both Parties to comply with the same DAAB procedure;

(12) The termination clauses of the Owners' and Contractors' Contracts also include non-compliance with the final binding decisions of the Engineer, non-compliance with the DAAB decisions, fraud and corruption as triggers for termination.

XII FIDIC proposes five gold principles for the drafting of special conditions

FIDIC has always been known for the fair and balanced distribution of risks and responsibilities between Owners and Contractors (even if most of the risks are handed over to the Contractor's Silver Book, FIDIC also clearly illustrates the scope and circumstances of its non-applicable), each FIDIC contract conditions have its specific scope of application.

With the increasingly widespread use of FIDIC contract conditions in the industry, some users have taken FIDIC contract conditions as the blueprint, but directly or unlimitedly modified the content of general conditions through special conditions. The final contract documents have seriously deviated from the drafting principles of FIDIC corresponding contract conditions, disrupted the industry order, and seriously damaged the reputation of FIDIC. In view of the problem that more and more FIDIC contract conditions are abused in the industry, FIDIC first proposed the five golden principles for the drafting of special conditions (FIDIC Golden Principles) when issuing the series of contract conditions in the 2017 edition, so as to remind users to consider carefully when drafting special conditions. These five principles are as follows:

(1) The responsibilities, rights, obligations, roles and responsibilities of all participants in the Contract are generally implied in the general conditions and adapt to the needs of the project;

(2) The drafting of special conditions must be clear and clear;

(3) Dedicated conditions do not permit a change in the balance between risk and return distribution in general conditions;

(4) The time required for the parties to fulfil their obligations under the Contract must be reasonable;

(5) All formal disputes must be submitted to DAAB for temporary binding decisions before being submitted to arbitration.

FIDIC emphasizes that the general conditions provide a benchmark for both Parties of the Contract, and the drafting of the special conditions and the modification of the general conditions can be regarded as a deviation from the benchmark through the game playing between the Parties in a specific situation. The five golden principles given by FIDIC try to ensure that there is no serious deviation from the risk and responsibility allocation principle of general conditions and the provisions in the drafting process of special conditions.

※Vocabulary

1. project stakeholders 项目关系人，项目利益利害关系者，关系人
2. substantially *adv.* 大量地，可观地；大体上，基本上；很坚固地
3. strict compliance 严格相符，严格一致
4. prescribed time 法定期间
5. interim certificate 临时证书；中期证明书
6. amount payable 应付金额
7. adjudication board 裁决委员会，裁判团
8. resolve disputes 解决争端
9. stipulated *adj.* 规定的
   v. 规定；保证（stipulate 的过去分词）
10. residual risk 剩余风险
11. in dispute 在争论中
12. compliance verification［审计］依从性审核
13. engineering performance 工程性能标准
14. advance warning 事前警告（警报）
15. key personnel *n.* 主要工作人员；关键员工
16. performance guarantee［法］履行合同保证人；［法］履约保证
17. reference solution 参考解决方案
18. balanced distribution 均衡分布
19. submitted to 均衡分布
20. game playing 博弈

Chapter 6

Contract Provison Interpretation and Cases

1   General Provisions

1.1   Definition

◆Discussion:

Why should these phrases and terms be defined prior to the beginning of contract conditions?

On the one hand, contracts identified as legal documents are to confine the rights and obligations of both parties, abiding by the principle of accuracy and strictness. On the other hand, civil engineering projects usually go through complex procedures, which have to be administrated through the instrument of contract. It's a highly laudable thing for all people to work together towards a common goal, while problems of coordination may arise in different situations, especially when the interests of different parties are concerned, not to mention under such circumstances as complex as international projects.

For example, Contractor is entitled to claim for "Cost" under certain circumstances as specified in the contract, and lacking of definition will cause great difficulties to reach common understanding on its calculation method.

1.1.1   Accepted Contract Amount

The Accepted Contract Amount is indeed the tender price offered by the Contractor. Another possibility is that if there's something wrong with the tender price calculation which is discovered during the period of tender valuation, the Employer can modify the price. And the tender price will become effective with the confirmation from the Contractor.

1.1.2 Advance Payment Certificate

This was never the case in previous versions of the FIDIC Conditions of Contract 2017. Under the previous FIDIC conditions, the Employer shall pay the Contractor the advance payment immediately after the Contractor has submitted the Performance Security and the Advance Payment Guarantee of the same amount in accordance with the Contract. However, in the actual implementation process, after the Contractor has completed the relevant provisions of the contract, the Owner still insists on requiring the Contractor to submit the payment certificate as the proof of the advance payment.

There is a problem here. There is no provision in the contract for an advance payment certificate, and the advance payment is not an interim payment certificate. If the interim bill is submitted to the Owner, then the relevant contract provisions of the interim bill are also applicable to the advance payment, but the Owner is difficult to accept, so it is easy to cause contract disputes.

Therefore, FIDIC 2017 directly defines the advance payment certificate, thus differentiating the advance payment certificate from other interim payment certificates, and making the advance payment and contract provisions more specific. In Article 14.2.2, there are detailed advance payment provisions (which will be explained in details in later articles), avoiding the disputes between the Owner and the Contractor.

After the responsibilities and rights of the Contractor and the Owner concerning the advance payment have been made clear, both parties shall carry out the relevant work in accordance with the provisions of the contract, so as to facilitate the contract management personnel to manage the contract.

1.1.3 Advance Payment Guarantee

Although the terms of advance payment and advance payment guarantee exist in each version of FIDIC, the Owner will also include different forms of advance payment guarantee (conditional and unconditional) in the contract documents prepared. However, the reader will notice that previous versions of FIDIC only have a definition of a Performance Security or Performance Security. Therefore, the 2017 edition of FIDIC completes the definition of advance payment guarantee in this respect, which is also a measure to avoid contract disputes.

1.1.4 Base Date

Base Date is a new term in 1999 version and mainly used for price adjustment.

1.1.5 Bill of Quantities

They're comprised in the "schedule", and some specific works allow the possibilities without Daywork Schedule, which circumstances are specified with "if any".

1.1.6 **Claim**

Claims are common for people working on overseas projects, and there is no project without claims. Meanwhile, each version of FIDIC elaborates on the procedure but does not give a clear definition of claims. However, the 2017 edition of FIDIC completes the definition, and makes it clear that claim is "in any of the conditions of the contract under the terms, or other relevant provisions in the contract, or the terms of the contract to produce, or associated with the execution of engineering, or in the execution of engineering, by a party to the other party about lifting or entitled to claim or demand."

Here are two key words to grasp: The notion of entitlement and relief is related to our claim. If the reader is a person engaged in FIDIC contract management, it is not difficult to find from various versions of FIDIC that in the case that the time period or cost of the Contractor's project is extended or increased, the Contractor is entitled to a period or cost, and the FIDIC contract clause uses the word entitle.

In addition, where the Contractor's obligations are concerned, for example, if part of the work requires a design by the Contractor, the Contractor's design is usually approved by the Supervising Engineer/Owner's Representative. It is stated in the contract that the approval of the Supervising Engineer/Owner's Representative does not relieve the Contractor of the relevant responsibilities.

Therefore, FIDIC 2017 makes it clear that the claim is related to the rights and obligations, whether it is the claim of the Owner or the claim of the Contractor, all follow this principle.

1.1.7 **Commencement Date**

Administration of the Contract may be facilitated by redefining the Base Date and Commencement Date as particular calendar dates in the Contract Agreement.

1.1.8 **Compliance Verification System**

This definition and provision is a new addition to the 2017 edition of FIDIC and will be detailed in Sub-Clause 4.9.2. In fact, although the written definition and regulations are new to us, who are engaged in overseas engineering projects will be familiar with them. Before the Contractor starts to perform any procedure, the Contractor generally gives 24 hours' notice in advance to the supervision Engineer/Owner's representative. Such notice is in writing. The format of the notice shall be agreed upon by the Supervising Engineer/Owner's representative and the Contractor during the start-up period and then be implemented.

In addition, during the start-up period of the project, the Contractor needs to submit the project construction programme. In the part of the construction scheme of this programme, the Contractor should clarify its construction scheme and inspection application procedure, which coincides with this new clause in FIDIC 2017 edition. This also indicates that the FIDIC drafters will also project the actual implementation process into the FIDIC contract conditions to make it complete.

1.1.9 Conditions of Contract or these Conditions

FIDIC 2017 clarifies that contract conditions include general and special conditions, avoiding disputes in contract management. When we use other versions of FIDIC contract conditions for contract management, we often mention these two words in the correspondence with the Supervision Engineer/Owner's Representative and Owner, which is tacitly understood and accepted as general conditions and special conditions.

1.1.10 Contract

The "Contract" hereto is the sum-up of all contract documents which means the Contract Agreement, the Letter of Acceptance, the Letter of Tender, these Conditions, the Specification, the Drawings, the Schedules, and the further documents (if any) which are listed in the Contract Agreement or in the Letter of Acceptance.

Different from the domestically-used contracts, FIDIC requires all contract documents complied to be a "contract package", including the Letter of Acceptance and Letter of Tender.

Sub-Clause of "Contract" lists the documents which together comprise the Contract in the same sequence as the order specified in Sub-Clause 1.5 of Priority of Documents. Any letter of Acceptance or Contract Agreement will typically contain a list of documents which comprise the Contract, and any such priority over Sub-Clause "Contract".

◆ **Discussion:**

How to determine whether a contract file can be incorporated into a contract package?
Subject to its "legal effectiveness".

A stamped file can't be regarded as an effective contract file before delivery is achieved. Legal proofs are needed on completion of tasks like fax record, sign on receipt certificate, courier receipt, etc.

1.1.11 Contract Agreement

◆ **Discussion:**

Is a Contract Agreement necessary to be included in Contract files?
Even if the applicable law does not necessitate a Contract Agreement, the latter is often considered advisable, in order to record what constitutes the Contract under CONS.

1.1.12 Contract Data

Part A is the original Appendix to Tender of Version 1999, hereafter referred to as "Contract Data", and the original Particular Conditions of Version 1999 are part B of the Particular Conditions of Version 17.

1.1.13 Contract Price

We can learn from the definition that rather than a "static" procedure, the final price is the settlement price calculated upon the completion of the Works which has taken into account the accumulated adjustments of price during the execution of the Works.

◆ **Discussion:**

What is the difference between "Accepted Contract Amount" and "Contract Price"?

More than often, the amount stated in the Letter of Acceptance and hereby accepted by the Employer is the modified price. This amount is rather than the effective contract price which can only be determined after the Works is completed but just the contract price by name.

Rather than a "static" procedure, the final price is the settlement price calculated upon the completion of the Works which has taken into account the accumulated adjustments of price during the execution of the Works.

1.1.14 Contractor

Party B referred to as in Contract.

1.1.15 Contractor's Documents

◆ **Discussion:**

Under CONS, the Contractor undertakes the construction referring to the design provided by the Employer, what kind of documents do they have to prepare by themselves?

Referring to Sub-Clause 4.1 [Contractor's General Obligations].

1.1.16 Contractor's Equipment

◆ **Discussion:**

Does the Contractor's equipment include the equipment used or owned by the Subcontractor?

1.1.17 Contractor's Personnel

The Contractor's Personnel include all Subcontractors' employees on the Site, and others assisting the Contractor's execution of the Works.

1.1.18 Contractor's Representative

The Contractor's Representative is often included in the key staff list, which is annexed to the Letter of Tender and submitted to the Employer.

In China, this address is often replaced by "project manager", who is assigned by the Contractor.

1.1.19 Cost

Refer to the interpretation herein.

1.1.20 Cost Plus Profit

In previous versions of FIDIC, cost and profit were separated, that is, cost is cost, profit is profit, and the Contractor claims the cost to the Owner. The 2017 edition of FIDIC added cost and profit, namely "cost plus profit as a percentage, right stipulated in the contract data (if not specify, 5%), according to the contract conditions, if the Contractor has cost plus profit, this percentage should just add in the cost, cost plus profit and then added to the contract price."

In previous versions of FIDIC, the Contractor could claim costs under certain contract terms, and in some cases, the Contractor could claim both costs and profits. Therefore, it was necessary to explain costs and profits clearly so as to avoid disputes arising from ambiguities in the actual operation. Especially when changing new unit price, cost and profit must be divided clearly, otherwise, may produce dispute because of this.

1.1.21 Country

Some "linear" shape projects like pipe or road projects may cross over some countries borderlines.

◆ **Discussion:**

Will the country in which the Site is located always be the country of the Employer?

1.1.22 DAAB

DAAB is a new dispute resolution method introduced into FIDIC in 2017, which includes dispute prevention and dispute mediation. Dispute prevention is a completely new concept. One of the most familiar Dispute mediation methods in the execution of overseas engineering projects is Dispute Review Expert (DRE), or Dispute Review Board (DRB), or the Dispute Adjudication Board (DAB), or Arbitration.

Here, in the previous FIDIC, no matter the DRE, DRB or DAB, its members were either one or three, and the emphasis was on dispute resolution. Therefore, in the past FIDIC version, when there was a dispute in the execution of the contract, the solution we thought of was mediation and reconciliation between the two parties. We ask for the appointment of a DRE, DRB or DAB in order to protect or, in the case of mediation, maximize our own interests.

With the emergence of DAAB in FIDIC 2017, we have a new solution in dispute resolution. In fact, the most novel place is dispute prevention, which is the new role of DAAB. That is to say, no matter it is a one-person DAAB or a three-person DAAB, it should provide the owner and contractor with the function of dispute prevention during the project execution. We can prevent disputes from happening.

1.1.23 DAAB Agreement

The definition and conternt have been clearly explained herein.

1.1.24 Date of Completion

This is a very important concept, which involves the interests of both the Owner and the Contractor. If the Contractor's completion date exceeds the contract period, the Contractor will face the penalty for breach of contract from the Owner, while the Owner will enjoy liquidated damages. If the Contractor's completion date is within the contract period, the risk of being fined by the Owner will be exempted, and the Owner will be able to use the completed project on time. In practice, it is impossible for the Supervising Engineer/Owner's Representative to issue the handover certificate to the Contractor on the exact day of completion. That is to say, the actual date of issuance of the handover certificate is usually after the completion date. Therefore, it becomes complicated to determine the completion date. The 2017 version of FIDIC specifies the completion date here and avoids the contractual risk.

1.1.25 day

It is defined as a calendar day.

1.1.26 Daywork Schedule

"Day work Schedule" means the documents so named (if any) which are comprised in the Schedules.

1.1.27 Defects Notification Period

(1) The expression recognizes the most significant aspect of this period, the notifying If defects by the Engineer to the Contractor.

(2) "the Works" here means the Works or a Section which has been taken over by the Emplotyer and a Taking-Over Certificate has been issued to the Contractor.

(3) Length of the "Period" is specified in the Appendix to Tender.

(4) It can be extended under 11.3 extension of Defects Notification Period.

(5) The period commences on the completion of the Works or a Section, and the completion date is subject to the date in the Taking-Over Certificate.

1.1.28 Delay Damages

It is defined here in the 2017 edition of FIDIC, and its details are the same as the 1999 edition of FIDIC Red Book.

1.1.29 Dispute

In the previous version of FIDIC, we learned about the dispute resolution procedure. However, the 2017 version of FIDIC defines a dispute for the first time. In simple terms, a dispute means that one party makes a claim against the other party, and the other party rejects the claim in whole or in part, but the party who initiated the claim disagrees and sends a notice of dissatisfaction. In addition, if the party being claimed remains silent about the claim, it means that the claim is rejected. In both cases, it's called a dispute.

According to this definition, both the Contractor and the Owner have the flexibility to deal with contractual claims and disputes arising during the execution of the project in accordance with the provisions of this clause.

1.1.30 Drawings

Specification and Drawings are the documents where the Employer specifies all matters not covered by the Conditions of Contract, including the location of the Site, the scope of the Works, details of how each part of the Works is required to be constructed, and (possibly) a program of work.

Drawings mentioned hereafter are those specified in the contract, and amendment or supplement provided by the Employer in execution of the works.

FIDIC clearly states that for the Employer, whether to provide basic design drawings or working drawings depends on the requirements in other specifications of the Contract.

1.1.31 Employer

Is it right to call a manager or a boss of real estate company "Employer"? No, he is one of the Employer Personnel.

1.1.32 Employer's Equipment

In the Specification, details of the equipment like type, brand, specification, origin of fuel shall be specified. On the contrary, if such things haven't been mentioned at all, the implication of this is that the Employer won't provide the Contractor any equipment.

1.1.33 Employer's Personnel

The Employer's personnel would include those involved in inspection and testing, but would typically not include all the Employer's other Contractors on the Site. The Engineer is clearly defined to be the Employer's personnel, hereby alter the qualities of "independence" and "impartiality" which are embodied in the definition and description of the previous editions.

1.1.34 Employer-Supplied Materials

The 2017 edition of FIDIC adds a new definition of materials to be supplied by the Owner as "materials (if any) to be supplied by the Owner to the Contractor under Sub-Clause 2.6 (Materials to be supplied by the Owner and Owner's Equipment)".

1.1.35　Engineer

The Engineer acts in a special way, "person" herein as it's so named, but refers to a consulting company in the majority of the cases. "Person" can be either a natural person or legal person, and includes corporations. In western countries, the Engineer can be either a corporation or a person. Under the current circumstances in China, the "Engineer" refers to the superintendence company and the authorized representative from the company is called chief engineer. The Engineer is the real administrator of the Works and the most important role of all.

1.1.36　Engineer's Representative

In FIDIC 2017, the definition of a Supervising Engineer Representative is added as "a natural person appointed by the Supervising Engineer in accordance with Sub-Clause 3.3 [The Engineer's Representative]".

1.1.37　Exceptional Event

The definition of an abnormal event has been added to FIDIC 2017 as "an event or circumstance defined in Sub-Clause 18.1 [Exceptional Events]". After a detailed interpretation of Sub-Clause 18.1 of the 2017 version of FIDIC, it can be found by comparing the 1999 version of FIDIC that in the 1999 version of FIDIC, the title of this provision is Force Majeure and it is Sub-Clause 19.1. As force majeure has been defined in the laws of some countries, there may be disputed events during the execution of the Contract. In 2017 edition of FIDIC, with the replacement of unusual events to force majeure, we can find that the scope of its coverage is greater and the contract disputes are reduced, to some extent in the day to day management of contracts, encountered such incident, managers are more likely to make judgments, according to the provisions of the Contract at the same time, and take the corresponding measures.

1.1.38　Extension of Time or EOT

The definition of deferrals has been added to FIDIC 2017 version. In other versions of FIDIC, we are very familiar with the events in which you can apply for an extension, but none of the versions defines an extension, and this is the first time.

1.1.39　FIDIC

The English name: the International Federation of Consulting Engineers.

1.1.40　Final Payment Certificate or FPC

The Final Payment Certificate is one of the payment certificates, which is issued under Sub-Clause 14.13. The issue of this certificate means the due payment to the Contractor will be paid soon.

1.1.41　Final Statement

In fact, the final statement draft is an application submitted to the Engineer by the Contractor, inquiring the Engineer to issue the Final Payment Certificate. After the approval from the Engineer, the draft effectively turns into a Final Statement. On such premise that the Engineer has issued to the Employer the Final Payment Certificate based on the Final Statement will the Contractor receive the final payment (Figure 6.1).

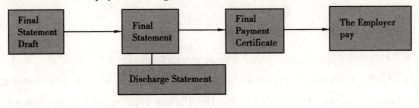

Figure 6.1

1.1.42　Foreign Currency

In order to differentiate it from local currency, so it is named foreign currency.

1.1.43　General Conditions

For the documents above, both the Contractor and the Employer share the same, while for the documents below, they follow the principle that Employer's documents should have priority over the Contractor's documents.

1.1.44　Goods

Goods almost covers all things needed in construction.

1.1.45　Interim Payment Certificate

There're basically two sorts of payment certificates, one is the Interim Payment Certificate, the other is the Final Payment Certificate.

1.1.46　Joint Venture

Refer to the interpretation herein.

1.1.47　JV Undertaking

There is a new definition of FIDIC in 2017 edition, which is the first time in the FIDIC contract conditions. In the bidding of overseas projects, the bidder can be a joint venture or an independent company. In the bidding documents issued by the Owner, the joint venture is generally described in details. This definition is added in the FIDIC contract conditions, indicating that the influence of the FIDIC contract conditions is expanding in the use.

1.1.48　Key Personnel

2017 edition of FIDIC adds a new definition of key personnel. In overseas engineering bidding, we can make a clear request asking bidder to provide key personnel information, the key personnel, including the project manager, key positions and personnel information in the qualification requirements of bidding documents. For example, the project manager, construction manager, structural engineers, materials engineers, and so on.

1.1.49　Laws

Refer to the interpretation herein.

1.1.50　Letter of Acceptance

Letter of Acceptance is the document which would typically have brought the Contract into effect. Under CONS, the Contract typically becomes legal biding when the Contractor receives the Letter of Acceptance, as stated in CONS 1.6: The Parties shall enter into a Contract Agreement within 28 days after the Contractor receives the Letter of Acceptance, unless they agree otherwise.

During the process of tendering, 4 ~ 5 times of tendering clarifications or more will be executed and correspondingly, many letters addressed as "letter of acceptance" will be issued.

Highlight: this letter of an acceptance is the acceptance to that corresponding letter of tender rather than any other.

We accept the offer contained in your Letter of Tender dated _____ to (design), execute and complete the above-named Works and remedy any defects therein, for the Accepted Contract Amount of _____ Unless and until a formal Agreement is prepared and executed…

◆**Discussion:**

Comparision between "the letter of acceptance" and "the notice of the site id ready by the Employer to the Contractor"

The Letter of Acceptance can be defined as formal acceptance in reply to the Letter of Tender from Employer to Contractor and comes into effect only when bearing a signature. More than which, it also includes the negotiations on issues like the clarification and confirmation to the ambiguous part and correction of mistakes, which are attached as memoranda with signatures of both parties.

However, CONS allows for the possibility that there may be no such the Letter of Acceptance. For example, the Parties may sign a Contract Agreement which brings the Contract into effect, but without a "A Letter of Acceptance", the signing date of which will be the reference for the Letter of Acceptance, and the Accepted Contract Amount must be defined in the Contract Agreement.

1.1.51　Letter of Tender

In the "Letter if Tender", the tenderer offers to enter into a legally-binding contract. It's called a "Letter of Tender", so as to differentiate it from the overall package of documents called the "Tender". "Tender" comprises two parts, one is the core called the "Letter of Tender", the other includes all kinds of schedules to be filled in by tenderer and tender securities. "Letter of

Tender" is not a lengthy document, but is important under CONS because when the Letter of Tender is accepted in the Letter of Acceptance, these two letters will typically create a legally-bidding Contract.

1.1.52 Local Currency

Local currency means the currency of the country where the project locates.

1.1.53 Materials

The materials here exclude those used in the "Temporary Works". "Supply-only-materials" mean the Contractor provides only supply according to the Contract, excluding any "processing" after procurement which will change the materials into part of the Permanent Works.

1.1.54 month

In the 2017 edition of FIDIC, the definition of month has been added. In general, we often do not use months. However, in special cases, we will also use months.

1.1.55 No-objection

In the process of project contract management, this word appears most frequently, especially in the letter from the Supervision Engineer to the Contractor, which is generally the reply of the Supervision Engineer to the documents submitted by the Contractor.

1.1.56 Notice

In the process of contract management, the frequency of notice is a direct reflection of the smooth execution of the project. In fact, we are all well aware that in most cases, the term is used by the Contractor to send notice of claim to the Supervision Engineer/Owner. We also found that the more smoothly the project was executed, the fewer contract claims were reported and the better the relationship between the Owner and the Contractor.

1.1.57 Notice of Dissatisfaction or NOD

In the 1999 version of the FIDIC Conditions of Contract, the term is used primarily to refer to the fact that either party is dissatisfied with the award of the DAB and shall, within 28 days of receipt of the award of the DAB, give notice of the dissatisfaction to the other party before proceeding further. However, the 1999 version of FIDIC does not have similar requirements, or provisions, for the supervision of the award. This new definition has been added to FIDIC in 2017. From the definition, we can see that the notice of dissatisfaction can be used for both the DAAB's decision and the Supervision Engineer's decision. Therefore, the scope of use is wider and more practical.

1.1.58 Part

In the terms of the handover of the Project, we can see the word "part". According to the

2017 FIDIC Conditions of Contract, part means part of a paragraph or part of the Works used and deemed to have been handed over by the Employer in accordance with Clause 10. 2 (handover portion) of the 2017 FIDIC Conditions of Contract. That is, whenever any part of the Works is used by the Employer, that part shall be deemed to have been handed over to the Employer, as described in further detail in Clause 10. 2.

1. 1. 59 Particular Conditions

The Contract documents consist of general conditions and particular conditions.

1. 1. 60 Party

The Parties to the Contract are defined to be the Employer and the Contractor only. All other persons or units whoever might get involved in the Works are regarded as either the Employer's personnel or the Contractor's personnel. The Engineer is also sort of special personnel of the Employer.

1. 1. 61 Payment Certificate

Payment certificate includes the interim payment certificate and the final payment certificate.

1. 1. 62 Performance Certificate

(1) It's to certify that the Contractor has fulfilled all his contract obligations. The receipt of this certificate to Contractor means the Works is completed.

(2) To help the Contractor get the Performance Security back.

1. 1. 63 Performance Security

Possibilities remain that there may be several performances securities or no performance securities at all. It's defined as, giving consideration to some Employers have no requirements on performance securities.

1. 1. 64 Permanent Works

Permanent Works will be handed over to the Employer after the Works have been completed and thus is listed under the glossary of the Employer's belongs.

1. 1. 65 Plant

"Vehicles" usually belongs to the "Contractor's Equipment" and "vehicles" here means those which form part of the permanent works.

For example, in a petrol pipe project, the measurement station of which needs water-supply during the operation, a scheme is devised to transport water from places far away by lorry with water tank. This lorry with water tanks provided by the Contractor is regarded as sort of Plant and forms part of the Permanent Works.

1.1.66 Programme

Time limits in connection with program are specified:

(1) The Contractor shall submit time programme to the Engineer within 28 days after receiving the notice.

(2) The Engineer shall, within 21 days after receiving a programme, gives notice to the Contractor stating the extent to which it does not comply with the Contract (Figure 6.2).

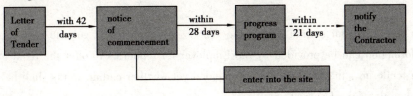

Figure 6.2

Contractor should revise the program whenever the previous program is inconsistent with: ①actual progress; ②the Contractor's obligation; ③his intention.

◆ **Discussion:**

Program verse Contract documents?

No. Program is drafted and submitted by the Contractor to the Engineer after the Contract is signed. And program is more of reference document, the provision of which will be invoked by the Contractor in execution of the Works; It doesn't alter the role of either Party, nor relieve either Party from their responsibility under the Contract.

If the specific date of hand-over of Site is neglected in the Appendix to Tender, then the program provides a reference time schedule for the Employer to make arrangement until the hand-over of the Site to the Contractor.

Besides, it may also works as criteria for the works of the Engineer, whether to issue instructions or drawings.

◆ **Discussion:**

How if the Contractor fails to submit the program in time?

This Sub-Clause doesn't provide a solution if the Contractor fails to submit it in time. On the whole, the delay of submission of program won't cause a big problem to the Employer. While in order to simulate the Contractor to act properly in submitting program, it's advisable to add one more condition for payment, which is that the Employer needn't pay the Contractor before the Contractor submit the program.

1.1.67 Provisional Sums

The sum is often shown in fixed number or sometimes in the form of the percentage of the tendering price, and it's usually embodied in the Bill of Quantities.

◆ Discussion：

Does the provisional price constitute part of the Contract Price?

After the study of the definition of "Contract Price", we can be sure that the provisional sum does account for part of the Contract Price.

The provisional sum is prepared for as follows：

(1) Contingency costs may occur in the execution of the Works. i. e. costs related to the Daywork.

(2) In tendering, for certain part of the Works, research hasn't gone to such an extent that detailed information can be provided by the Employer for tenderers to offer the fixed unit price.

(3) In tendering, the Employer hasn't decided yet whether certain works shall be included in the work schedule of the Contract.

1.1.68　QM System

Quality is the reputation of contractors, especially international contractors. Quality is also related to reputation and can even determine the survival of contractors. The definition of quality management system has been added to FIDIC 2017 edition. It simply outlines the terms of the Contract and the documents to be submitted by the Contractor to ensure the quality of the work. In addition, during the execution of the project, especially in the construction plan submitted by the Contractor, the Contractor shall specify the measures taken to ensure the quality of the project, which shall be approved by the Supervision Engineer.

Article 4.9 of the 2017 FIDIC Contract Conditions describes the measures the Contractor needs to take to control the project quality in a more detailed way, and directly clarifies the responsibility of the Contractor. In other words, the control of the project quality is more strict. The Contractor cannot control the quality of the project as he wishes, but must strictly comply with the contract requirements.

1.1.69　Retention Money

Actually it's a sort of cash deposit, which shares the same virtues with the Performance Security, aiming to provide the guarantee that Contractors will fulfill his obligations in execution of the Works, otherwise the Employer will be entitled to draw the money and complete the work, which was supposed to be done by the Contractor, to remedy the defects during the Defects Notifying Period. Meanwhile, if the account is overdrawn for interim payment, the Employer can compensate it with that from the Retention Money.

The Retention Money together with the Performance Security will be legally binding to the Contractor.

Up to 50% of retention money shall be returned to the Contractor when the Works is taken over.

1.1.70　Review

The definition of review has been added to FIDIC 2017. In nutshell, the Supervision Engineer gives inspection and consideration to what the Contractor submit. In the process of project implementation, without approval of Supervision Engineer, the Contractor can't according to their wishes to perform the Contract, the main purpose is to ensure that the Contractors will abide by the Contract, to prevent the Contractor not to perform in accordance with the Contract, and ensure that the interests of the Owners are protected.

1.1.71　Schedule

Refer to the interpretation herein.

1.1.72　Schedule of Payments

Payment schedule is a plan that shows the amount and manner of payment to the Contractor. The Contractor does the work for the owner according to the Contract, and the Owner shall pay the Contractor according to the plan and method, and make the payment clear to ensure the interests of the Contractor are protected.

1.1.73　Section

◆ **Discussion**:

What's the meaning of section in these conditions?

1.1.74　Site

Sites include as follows:
(1) Sites used for the Permanent Works and the Temporary Works;
(2) Sites where the Plant and the Materials are stored and warehouses;
(3) Sites for office and living;
(4) Others so named as "sites" stipulated by the Contact.

1.1.75　Special Provision

In Particular Conditions.

1.1.76　Specification

Specification is to describe the Employer's tendering projects in technical language, and propose technical standards and procedures during execution. Contractor's engineers of cost need to study the Specification when calculate the tendering price, so do Contractor's procurement personnel before procurement of materials as well as project managers and technicians in charge of construction.

Employer's management staff shall know more about specifications so as to ensure their ends to be met.

◆**Discussion**：

How to apply this Sub-Clause into Chinese projects?

When applying FIDIC into domestic projects, domestic compulsory "legal regulation" shall be differentiated from the specification.

For example, if the Works include work on an existing facility, the Contractor might be required to phase the work in a particular way in order to minimize the disruption to the continuing operation of the facility.

The specification may include the matters referred to some or all of the followings：

(1)Requirements for Contractor's Documents；

(2)Permissions being obtained by the Employer；

(3)Phased possession of foundations, structures, plant or means of access；

(4)Contractor's designs；

(5)Other Contractors (and others) on the Site；

(6)Setting-out points, lines and levels of reference；

(7)Third Parties；

(8)Environmental constraints；

(9)Electricity, water, gas and other services available on the Site；

(10)Employer's Equipment and free-issue material；

(11)Nominated Subcontractors；

(12)Facilities for Personnel；

(13)Samples；

(14)Testing during manufacture and/or construction；

(15)Tests on Completion；

(16)Provisional Sums.

1.1.77　Statement

Statement includes the monthly statement, statement upon the completion of the Works and the final statement.

1.1.78　Subcontractor

Different from that of the Contractor, the performance of the Sub-contractor directly affect the whole Works. Four factors have to be taken into consideration when evaluating the candidates of subcontractor：reasonableness of offer, technical competence, financial background and reputation.

Highlights：The Contractor shall be liable for all the behavior and default of the subcontractor.

◆ **Discussion**:

Does the Contractor need the agreement of the Engineer before appointing subcontractor?

Other Subcontractors need to be approved by the Engineer, except for the material supplier and the appointed Subcontractors in the Contract.

1.1.79　Taking-Over Certificate

Usually, the Contractors wish to receive the certificate as soon as possible, after which the responsibility of custody of the Works will be passed to the Employer, and Retention Money can also be refund. Hereafter, the Works comes to the stage of defect notification period.

The general sequence of events is as follows:

(1) the Contractor completes the Section or Works;

(2) the Contractor carries out tests defined as the Tests on Completion;

(3) the Employer takes over the Section or Works; and

(4) the Tests after Completion are carried out, if any.

1.1.80　Temporary Works

The temporary works include: houses and offices on construction site, construction pavement, temporary bridge, cofferdam in hydro-projects, labour sandstone system, concrete mixture, processing workshops, experiment rooms, facilities for security and lightening, etc.

Generally, after the completion of the Works, all temporary works need to be dismantled, though some may be preserved for usage during the operation of the Works.

1.1.81　Tender

In the "Letter of Tender", the tenderer offers to enter into a legally-binding contract. It's called a "Letter of Tender", so as to differentiate it from the overall package of documents called the "Tender". "Tender" comprises two parts, one is the core called the "Letter of Tender", the other includes all kinds of schedules to be filled in by tenderer and tender securities.

"Letter of Tender" is not a lengthy document, but is important under CONS because when the Letter of Tender is accepted in the Letter of Acceptance, these two letters will typically create a legally-bidding Contract.

1.1.82　Tests after Completion

(1) It has to be clearly specified in the Contract otherwise it can be ignored.

(2) If any, they shall be carried out according to the specifications in the Particular Conditions.

(3) It shall be carried out as soon as the Works or a Section is completed.

(4) Tests after Completion are rarely spoken of under CONS.

1.1.83　Tests on Completion

（1）It's conducted before the whole Works or a Section is taken over by the Employer. Time needed for tests on completion shall be included in the time for completion.

（2）Its content and procedures are illustrated in the specifications.

（3）Additional tests agreed by both parties or required by the Employer shall be instructed as a Variation.

（4）Tests shall be carried out under Clause 9.

1.1.84　Time for Completion

（1）Time means a period of time rather than a fixed point of time.

（2）It's calculated from the Commencement of Date.

（3）It's the time specified until the completion of the Works.

（4）It's specified in the Appendix to Tender.

（5）It's related to either the whole Works or a Section.

（6）If the Contractor acquires any extension, the Time for Completion will be extended for a similar period of time.

1.1.85　Unforeseeable

If a Contractor wants to demonstrate something is unforeseeable, he/she will have to demonstrate these things beforehand：

（1）It's possible to foresee it before submission of the tender documents, which means unforeseeable during the preparation of tender.

（2）He must be an experienced Contractor, which means whatever he does, be it before the award of contract or after that, shall be regarded as behaviour of Contractor with rich experience, i. e. by putting forward questions, undertaking site survey, reading through tender documents, etc. Put it in another word, "failure of foreseeing" is caused by objective reasons but not lacking of experience.

It's reasonably unforeseeable. It's always difficult to get a full appreciation of what "reasonable" means. When encounter such a reasonably unforeseeable matter, the Employer will often attribute this to the Contractor's lacking of experience. And the phrase "reasonably unforeseeable" often relates to affairs such as natural conditions, extrinsic impediment, contamination, etc.

1.1.86　Variation

Referring to Clause 13［Variations and Adjustments］.

1.1.87　Works

Including the temporary works and the permanent works.

1.1.88 **Year**

Refer to the interpretation herein.

※ **Vocabulary**

1. coordination *n.* 协调,配合;身体的协调性;配位;同一等级(或类别)
2. advance payment guarantee 预付款保证金;预付款保函
3. contract disputes 合同纠纷
4. bill of quantities 工程量清单;工程量表;数量清单;工料清单;建筑工料清单
5. entitlement *n.* 有权得到的东西,应得的数额;权力;权利感,特权感;政府津贴
6. engaged in 从事
7. clarifies *v.* 澄清,阐明;(通过加热)使净化,使纯净
8. necessitate *v.* 使成为必需,需要;迫使
9. taken into account 考虑;重视;体谅
10. ambiguity *n.* 模棱两可,不明确;含混不清的语句;一语多义;暧昧,难以理解的感情(或想法)
11. dispute mediation 争议调解
12. dispute review 争议评审
13. cross over 横渡;压步;交叉点
14. reconciliation *n.* 和解,复交;协调,和谐一致;对账
15. date of issuance 签发日期
16. embodied in 在……体现,使具体化
17. chief engineer 总工程师;轮机长;主任工程师;总技师
18. force majeure [保险]不可抗力
19. due payment 到期付款
20. in connection with 与……有关;与……相连
21. inconsistent with 与……不一致;与……相矛盾
22. provisional price [物价]临时价格
23. provisional sum 备用款
24. contingency *n.* 可能发生的事,不测事件;应急措施,应急储备;应急开支;可能性,意外
25. precautionary *adj.* (计划或措施)未雨绸缪的,应急的
26. environmental constraints 环境限制
27. monthly statement 银行每月结单
28. reasonableness *n.* 合理;妥当
29. the appointed 指定,被任命的人
30. sequence of events 事件顺序,作业顺序;事故顺序记录,事情的进展
31. award of contract 授予合同;[经]签订合同

1.2　Interpretation

Gender, when these languages are used as contract languages, disputes concerning about "gender" may occur, thus does it specifically indicate one gender include all genders. It also indicates that different meaning may be expressed when in different forms of either singular or plural. i. e. damage, damages. The former means loss, injury, but the latter means money asked from or paid by a person causing loss or injury.

Thus, important documents are seldom "electronically made" in prevention of disputes.

1.3　Notices and Communications

Through comparison, we can find that the title of the 2017 edition of the FIDIC Red Book has been changed, and the statement of notice has been added on the original basis. In the definition of section, we have learned that the definition of notice has been added in the 2017 FIDIC Red Book, and the terms of notice have also been added here, which shows how important the requirement of notice is in the 2017 Red Book.

In this article, the requirement of giving notice is made clear. If a notice is involved in the communication with the Supervision Engineer and the Owner, the relevant document must be confirmed as notice. Meanwhile, the document confirmed as notice shall take effect immediately after receiving it.

In general, in the process of project implementation, if the Contractor sends Supervision Engineer and the Owner notice, which also proves urgency and significance of the event, this requires the Supervision Engineer and the Owner to solve the problem as soon as possible, if not solved, may cause delay to the Contractor, and (or) generate additional cost, this is the first purpose of issuing notice. Secondly, the notice is to comply with the contract provisions, according to the contract implementation procedures, this is the procedure to deal with contract issues, and must be followed. Finally, if the Supervision Engineer and the Owner fail to solve the problem in time, according to the Contract, the notice is a necessary condition for the Contractor to carry out the next step of the work and also one of the measures to safeguard the interests of the Contractor. Otherwise, the Contractor will lose his contract rights and interests, or there will be a contract dispute.

1.4　Law and language

The law governing the Contract must be stated. The law typically will affect the interpretation of these Conditions, such that some provisions may have different consequences in different jurisdictions.

The ruling language only relates to a part of the Contract for which different versions have been written in different languages.

The language for communications should be stated in the Appendix to Tender, if there's no such statement, then the language used to write the Contract will be taken as the communication language.

It's common for a contract to be in two language versions, i. e. the middle-east countries regard Arabic as the official language but also use English in their daily lives. And in a Contract, Arabic is usually defined as the ruling language and English is for communication.

1.5 Priority of Documents

Contract Documents-as referred to 1. 1. 1. 1 are a package of documents including the Contract Agreement, the Letter of Acceptance, the Letter of Tender, these Conditions, the Specification, the Drawings, the Schedules, and the further documents (if any) which are listed in the Contract Agreement or in the Letter of Acceptance.

◆**Discussion**:

The necessity of setting the priority of documents.

The interrelationship of the above documents shall be complementary to each other rather than being contradictory to each other. While actually, the compilation of contract documents takes long time and wide participation of a large number of editors, which will unavoidably result in inconsistency or contradiction. In order to resolve these problems, in cases where the same subject matter is covered several times in different parts of the Contract, this Sub-clause provides an order of precedence of the documents.

The priority of the documents is shown in Table 6. 1.

Table 6. 1

①	Contract Agreement	constituted by both offer and acceptance
②	Letter of Acceptance	replace the contract agreement when the it's absent
③	Letter of Tender	need to be confirmed by the Letter of Acceptance
④	Particular Conditions	Part A—Contract Data
⑤	Particular Conditions	Part B—Special Provisions
⑥	General Conditions	
For the documents above, both of the Contractor and the Employer share the same, while for the documents below, they follow the principle that Employer's documents should have priority over the Contractor's documents.		
⑦	Specifications	basic technical data which are the reference used for the compilation of the drawings and the schedules
⑧	Drawings	
⑨	Schedules	the Works starts when all the above documents have been well prepared and noticed to be ready for use
⑩	The JV Undertaking	
⑪	any other documents forming part of the Contract	

If there's an ambiguity or discrepancy within a particular contract document, Sub-Clause 1. 5 and Sub-Clause 3. 3 empower the Engineer to issue as clarification or instruction.

For instance, in an oversea construction project, white cement is preferred in the work of mosaic joint pointing in wash rooms as specified in the B. Q. , while it's replaced by Portland cement in the Specifications and the Drawings.

Disputes occurred as to which kind of cement should be used. The Employer voted for white cement, but the Contractor intended to use Portland cement in order to economize the project costs. Also, different sets of documents applied for each option. In the last resort, the Engineer proceeded to make decisions, and the principle of the Priority of Documents was quoted and supports went to the Contractor, because the Specifications and the Drawings prevailed over the B. Q. In the Employer insisted on using white cement, the Engineer would instruct variations based on the Clause 13 "Variation and Adjustment" requiring the contractor to make a new offer, taking into account the extra costs. Finally, the Employer compromised the aesthetic standard for the saving of cost, and the use of Portland cement was determined. This enabled a save of at least $100,000 to the Contractor.

1.6 Contract Agreement

The Contract agreement consists of 3 parts as follows:

(1) All the terminologies to be used in the Contract documents that have been defined in a particular way.

(2) All the schedules to be used in the Contract documents.

(3) Clarification of the offers and acceptances from the Parties, i. e. the Contractor promises to carry on the Works in accordance with the Contract, the Employer guarantee that the payment will be paid to the Contractor as stated in the Contract.

Structure analyzed	
The Parties shall enter into a Contract Agreement within 28 days after the Contractor receives the Letter of Acceptance, unless they agree otherwise. The Contract Agreement shall be based upon the form annexed to the Particular Conditions.	第一句话：签订合同协议书的时间
	第二句话：合同协议书的格式
The costs of stamp duties and similar charges (if any) imposed by law in connection with entry into the Contract agreement shall be borne by the Employer.	第三句话：确定承担印花税和类似费用的承担者

1.7 Assignment

◆**Discussion：**

What are the reasons for the 2nd type of assignment?

As we well know, a large-scale project demands huge amount of expenditures at the early stage, often enough, the advance payment of the Employer is insufficient for this amount of expenditure and the Contractor may need to finance the difference by applying for loan from the banks. Generally, banks or financial institutes will require the Contractor to secure their loans with the due payment or those which will become due, and sometimes even to open a new account for the remittance of the due moneys.

1.8   Care and Supply of Documents

If a Party becomes aware of an error or defect of a technical nature in a document which was prepared for use in executing the Works, the Party shall promptly give notice to the other Party of such error or defect.

◆**Discussion:**

If some problems occur to the technical documents of one party, which results in the failure of the execution of part of the Works, is it possible for the party to shirk the responsibility and shift the blames to the other party, with the excuse that they're not notified by the errors or defects?

We can rather regard the notification as one of the operation procedure specified for the purpose of "effective management", advocating the relationship of cooperation and team spirit.

1.9   Delayed Drawings or Instructions

The procedure is displayed as Figure 6.3.

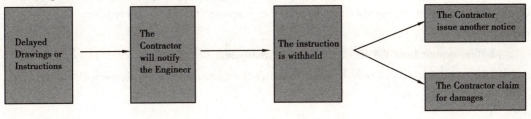

Figure 6.3

The Contractor should be reminded:

(1) to take the initiatives to give notice to the Engineer rather than wait positively. The notice should include details of the drawings or instructions and the reasons why they're needed, with the supporting details of the construction plans and arrangements approved by the Engineer, and the requirements of the Engineer on the Site.

(2) their works should be in compliance with the contract requirements and make sure not to grant the Engineer chances to find any excuses and show disapproval of the claims.

1.10   Employer's Use of Contractor's Documents

Contractor's Documents include a variety of design documents including computer software, models, operations and maintenance manuals and other manuals and information of a similar nature.

After sign on the Contract, permission will be granted to the Employer for use of the Contractor's documents. The Employer will be entitled to use the Contractor's documents during the working life of the Works and even communicate with the third parties about these documents.

◆ **Discussion**:

Copyrights

The Contractor shall be deemed (by signing the Contract) to give to the Employer a non-terminable transferable non-exclusive royalty-free license to copy, use and communicate the Contractor's Documents, including making and using modifications of them.

Highlight: The Employer is entitled to use the Contractor's Documents for the Works, but he is not entitled to use them for other purposes.

1.11　Contractor's Use of Employer's Documents

The Employer's consent must be given in writing, and is not to be unreasonably withheld or delayed, in accordance with Sub-Clause 1.3. It may be reasonable for the Employer to withhold consent if the Contractor declined to accept reasonable conditions in respect of secrecy or of restriction on use.

1.12　Confidential Details

In order to protect the Contractor's rights, and prevent the Engineer from demanding too much, this provision is specified by asking the Engineer to act in accordance with following requirements:

(1) the request from the Engineer must be reasonable;

(2) the information can only be used to verify the Contractor's compliance with the Contract.

◆ **Discussion**:

What kind of information shall be kept as confidential?

As far as civil engineering industry in concerned, they can be unique processes (which are gained by the construction companies through years of experiences and used to improve the work efficiency and add to competence in the industrial circles. Such processes are called "know-how", which is different from patent and not under the protection of laws. Once published, these processes will no longer be of any value to their companies.

1.13　Compliance with Laws

Abiding by the Contract is also within the scope of abiding by the law. Sub-Clause 1.13 of the 2017 edition of the FIDIC Red Book explains in detail the contractual provisions of abiding by the law. Regarding this contract clause, compared with the previous FIDIC, the 2017 edition of FIDIC Red Book has added about the consequences arising from breach of contract. Subject to this

Clause, the Contractor shall be entitled to claim against the Owner for the construction period and the cost plus profit in the event of any cost and/or delay incurred by the Contractor as a result of the Owner's delay or failure to obtain a permit, authority, license or consent on time. On the other hand, if the Contractor's non-cooperation results in the Employer incurring additional costs, the Contractor shall pay the relevant costs to the Employer.

This has created the FIDIC contract conditions precedent in this regard, under normal circumstances, the Contractor often meet additional costs and delays resulted due to any reason attributable to the Owner, however, the Contractor has to undertake the consequence by himself, the Owner's responsibility is not clear in the Contract. At the same time, the responsibility of the Contractor is not clear neither, which will eventually lead to contract disputes. Through such a clear stipulation of rights and responsibilities of both Parties, both Parties have clear rights and responsibilities in the process of implementing the project, which can avoid contract disputes and protect the interests of both Parties so long as they act in accordance with the Contract.

1.14　Joint and Several Liability

There may be pros and cons considering constituting a joint venture, consortium or other incorporated grouping. The united forces may turn out to be a great advantage when their roles are complementary to each other, hence making it easier for them to win the Contract. While therein lie also disadvantages that there may be conflicts between the members and difficulties in project management.

1.15　Limitation of Liability

This contract clause is a new contract clause in the 2017 FIDIC Red Book. Through this contract clause, the scope of liability of both parties is determined in the form of words. The scope shall not exceed the total amount stated in the contract data or the accepted contract price, so as to reduce disputes. In addition, even if there is a dispute, the relevant liability scope has been fixed and will not exceed the provisions of the Contract.

1.16　Contract Termination

The 2017 FIDIC Red Book specifies the scope of limitation of the Parties, followed by the scope of liability of the Parties with respect to the termination of the Contract. Specifically, according to Sub-Clause 1.16, neither Party shall take action against the other Party if the Contract is terminated in accordance with applicable law. In other words, if the Contract is terminated not by default of either Party, but is required by law, then neither the Contractor nor the Owner shall be allowed to take contractual measures against the other Party, such as claims for costs and damages, under the terms of this contract.

In fact, this is also an additional clause based on actual needs. According to Sub-Clause 1.13, both the Owner and the Contractor must abide by the applicable laws during the project execution. Any party who commits any illegal act will be subject to the jurisdiction of the laws.

Therefore, both the Owner and the Contractor must comply with the law to perform the provisions of the Contract, where the law requires that the performance of the Contract be terminated.

※Vocabulary

1. gender *n.* 可变名词性;性别

2. singular *adj.* 形容词单数的;单数形式的

3. plural *adj.* 形容词复数的;复数形式的

4. consortium *n.* (若干人或公司组成的)财团,联合企业

5. complementary *adj.* 相互补充的;相辅相成的

6. patent *n.* 专利权

7. entitled *v.* 给予……权利;给予……资格

8. withhold *v.* 拒绝给予;扣留

9. delay *v.* 使延期;使延迟;推迟

　　　 n. 延期;延迟;推迟

10. terminable *adj.* 有期限的,可终止的

11. transferable *adj.* 可转让的;可转移的

12. non-exclusive *adj.* 非独家的

13. shirk the responsibility 逃避,规避(责任、义务);偷懒

14. shift the blames to the other party 推卸,推诿,转嫁(责任)

15. notify *v.* 通知;告知

2　The Employer

In general, the obligations of the Employer specified in the Contract include:

(1)To appoint an Engineer to oversee the daily operation of the Works, who acts impartially and complies with the criteria of professional ethics. Under 3.4 if the Employer intends to replace the Engineer, notice is required to be given to the Contractor. And the Employer shall not replace the Engineer without the consent from the Contractor. The degree of the Engineer's independence is one of the risk factors that the Contractor has to take into consideration in tendering. And normally the replacement of the Engineer is not encouraged.

(2) To provide all the information needed in the design and the construction to the Contractor, and ensure the authenticity of the information.

(3)To hand-over the site to the Contractor. Site is defined in the Specifications or the Drawings. Without the handover of the site, the contractor won't be able to proceed to work.

(4)Not to interfere in the construction of the Works. For instance, the Employer entrusts the Engineer to give instructions which are not specified in the Contract and lead to the change (increase or decrease) of the amount of work. This shall be regarded as sort of interference and enable the Contractor to claim for extension or compensation.

(5) To nominate a Subcontractor. If the Subcontractor who is nominated by the Employer has interfered with the construction of the Works, it's the Employer who shall take the responsibility and compensate for the loss.

(6) To make sure that due payment will be paid in time. What tops the list of all the obligations for the Employer is to pay the Contractor, which is also the basic requirement to the Employer in FIDIC. And what accounts is to "be in time".

2.1 Right of Access to the Site

For the Employer, he is deemed to provide the Site and the facilities in time, otherwise the Contractor shall be compensated for the loss he has suffered.

For the Contractor, if he wants to claim for compensation, he must give notice in time and make sure that the Employer's failure was not caused by an error or delay by the Contractor.

The Employer is required to make the Site available to the Contractor within a prescribed time. In additional to that, the Employer is also required to give processions of any foundation, structure, plant or means of access, also in the time and manner stated in the Specification.

But the second sentence of the Sub-Clause states that other Parties may also have right of access to, and procession of, the Site.

Highlight: The Employer is only required to grant the Contractor the "right" of access to the Site, it being that there is a route along which access either is already physically practicable or can be constructed by the Contractor. In other words, the practicable difficulties is getting to and from the Site are to be solved by the Contractor.

2.2 Assistance

It's the Contractor who owes the liability to the Employer for obtaining all permits, permissions, licenses or approvals. And the Employer is required to provide reasonable assistance, the extent of which depend upon the relationship between the Employer and the Contractor and how the Works goes on. This "reasonable assistance" may, for example, comprise the authentication of the Contractor's application documentation, but it would not be reasonable for the Contractor to expect the Employer to do anything which the Contractor can do himself.

The Employer has no obligation under Sub-Clause 2.2 to provide any "reasonable assistance" unless and until he receives the Contractor's request, which must be in writing in accordance with Sub-Clause 1.3.

Two words have been added, one is that copies of the laws of the country need to be provided by the Employer, the other is that permissions have been added in addition to permits, licenses or approvals. Permit means more in legal proceedings or permitted by regulations, and nouns mean permits, as above. Permission means permission. It can be used in the part of speech to act with subjective will.

2.3 Employer's Personnel and other Contractors

Requirement of two C——"Cooperation" and "Compliance with regulations".

Cooperation: The Employer's personnel and other Contractors are required to cooperate with the Contractor's coordination efforts, and take actions in respect of safety procedures and environmental protection.

Compliance with regulations: For example, anyone on site must put on safety helmet, or 50 yuan will be fined, irrespective of being the personnel of the Employer, the Contractor or the third Party. Under Article 4, there're also similar requirements imposed on the Contractor. The restrictive stipulations conform to the standpoint of impartiality of FIDIC.

2.4 Employer's Financial Arrangements

The Employer is required to provide reasonable evidence of financial arrangements when requested. The "reasonable evidence" means bank certificates and the like. Nowadays, it's frequent for the Employer to withhold the project payments against the Contractor, which often results in the default on the obligation of the Contractor This provision is specified in order to diminish the happening of such cases and perfect the management of obligation fulfillment.

The evidence is required to demonstrate the Employer's ability to pay the Contract Price, which typically would be the estimated final Contract Price at the time of the request but excluding the effect of adjustment which have not yet become available. For example, it would usually be unreasonable to add a contingency to allow for the possibility of a future event resulting in an adjustment.

Tenderers would be entitled to be concerned at such deletion of this Sub-Clause, especially if the Employer has been unable to replace it by some other form of assurance (e.g. GPPC's Annex G). The Contractor will be entitled to (after 21 days' notice) to suspend work, or reduce the rate of work, if the Employer fails to submit the evidence requested under Sub-Clause 2.4. Termination provides the ultimate remedy.

2.5 Site Data and Items of Reference

All of these shall be provided by the Employed to the Contractor.

2.6 Employer-Supplied Materials and Employer's Equipment

Similar to 1999 version Sub-Clause 4.20 [Employer's Equipment and Free-Issue Material] except that materials are stated to be provided in accordance with rates and prices. The provisions entitle the Contractor to use whichever of these things are described as being available, in CONS' Specifications. This Sub-Clause refer to the possibility of two categories of items being made available to the Contractor: self-supplied materials and equipment.

The Employer will provide to the Contractor the equipment under the conditions that rates will be charged, which has an equal effect of renting. The details are included in the CONS'

Specification such as: rates charged by the Employer, equipment specification and status, calculation of operation time, which party is responsible for equipment maintenance and providing operators, fuel and equipment. Typically, the Employer rents out the equipment with more favorable conditions comparing.

For free-issue materials, you can also find details of the materials availability, arrangements and particular requirements in the CONS' Specifications. Sensitive issues include the place for delivering the materials and time arrangement.

※Vocabulary

1. authenticity *n.* 真实性,可靠性
2. safety procedures 安全规程
3. contingency *n.* 可能发生的事,不测事件;应急措施,应急储备;应急开支;可能性,意外
   adj.(计划或措施)未雨绸缪的,应急的

3　The Engineer

The role of the Engineer is described as follows:

(1)he's employed by the Employer to undertake the administration of the Works;

(2)he's one of the Employer's personnel, rather than an impartial intermediary;

(3)he exercises the authority attributable to the Engineer as specified in or necessarily to be implied by the Contract;

(4)he exercises a special authority as approved by the Employer.

In general, the obligations of the Employer specified in the Contract include:

(1)To appoint an Engineer to oversee the daily operation of the Works, who acts impartially and complies with the criteria of professional ethics.

(2) To provide all the information needed in the design and the construction to the Contractor, and ensure the authenticity of the information.

(3)To hand-over the site to the Contractor.

(4)Site is defined in the Specifications or the Drawings. Without the handover of the Site, the Contractor won't be able to proceed to work.

(5)Not to interfere in the construction of the Works.

(6)To nominate a Subcontractor.

(7)To make sure that due payment will be paid in time.

For instance, the Employer entrusts the Engineer to give instructions which are not specified in the Contract and lead to the change (increase or decrease) of the amount of work. This shall be regarded as sort of interference and enables the Contractor to claim for extension or compensation.

3.1　The Engineer

Sub-Clause 3.1 of the FIDIC Red Book 2017 specifies all rights required to grant the Supervising Engineer to act as the Supervising Engineer in the Contract. If the Supervising Engineer is an entity, a natural person shall be authorized to act on behalf of the Supervising Engineer. In the actual execution, the Supervision Engineer is generally an entity, and it is impossible for the entity to perform the duties of the Supervision engineer. It is a natural person who performs the duties. Therefore, it is necessary to specify clearly who is the authorized natural person who plays the role of the Supervision Engineer.

There is a problem here. The Supervision Engineer is an entity. Can the general manager of this entity exercise his rights on behalf of the Supervision Engineer without authorization? Now, the FIDIC Red Book 2017 gives us a standard answer: the general manager appointed as the Supervision Engineer entity is not able to exercise his authority on behalf of the Supervision Engineer without authorization, and the letters and documents issued by him to the Contractor are invalid (Figure 6.4).

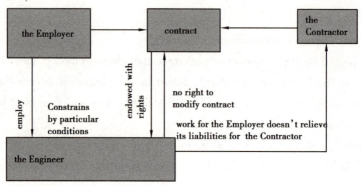

Figure 6.4

The Engineer should carry out his duties and exercise his authority in professional manner, utilizing the "suitable quality engineers and other professionals".

When examining the tender documents and considering the role of the Engineer, tenderers may take account of such matters as:

(1) the Engineer's technical competence and reputation particularly in relation to reviewing Contractor's Documents;

(2) the degree of independence indicated by the status of the appointed Engineer, namely whether he is an independent consulting engineer;

(3) the practical consequences of any constraints on the Engineer's authority.

And in the B.Q., there's an item named "the Engineer's preliminaries", specifying that the Contractor has to provide the Engineer with things like vehicles, fuel, fax machine, telephone, etc. and bear all the relevant costs. All these (excluding those which have been consumed) will be reverted to the Contractor after the accomplishment of the Works.

◆**Discussion**:

What's the role of an Engineer?

Making a figurative illustration: if a project is, say, a particular "product", then the Engineer is identified with the supervisor of the manufacture of this "product", and his approval can be taken as a permission to enter into the next working procedure and an acknowledgment of what have already been done. It is to ensure that the manufacture procedure of the "product" will be in compliance with the Contract specifications and industrial conventions. The Contractor has to guarantee the hand-over of a qualified final product to the Employer, the Employer is the purchaser of the product, and the Engineer is employed to ensure the qualification of the product. The Engineer is in no way under the obligation to the Contactor, but they two may be in frequent contact with each other in work, and probably, the Contractor may think of it the most difficult to cope with the Engineer.

Consultancy work is of high technical value added and consultancy engineer is the talent with expertise of technical management.

Ever since the contract has been signed, both of the Employer and the Contractor will be obliged to follow the instruction of the Engineer as far as the instructions are workable. Until and unless they can no longer put up with the contract obligations, the case will be submitted for international arbitration. The Engineer has to explain his instructions in the arbitration, and all the previous decisions may be questioned, examined or modified, which forces the Engineer to make sensible decisions.

In international projects, the consultancy fees account for about 10% of the total project investment, which is inversely proportional to the Contract Price, much higher than that in domestic projects, which is around 1%~4%.

For example, as described by a piece of article, in a World Bank project, all that the Engineer has done is as simple as to sign his name on the working drawings and issuing a confirmation letter to the Contractor which won't relieve the Contractor from any responsibility except as otherwise stated in some Condition.

Any approval, check, certificate, consent, examination, inspection, instruction, notice, proposal, request, test, or similar act by the Engineer (including absence of disapproval) shall not relieve the Contractor from any responsibility he has under the Contract, including responsibility for errors, omissions, discrepancies and non-compliances.

3.2 Engineer's Duties and Authority

The FIDIC Red book 2017 adds a very important new authority for the Supervisor, that is, the Supervisor does not need the consent of the Owner before exercising his authority under Clause

3.7 [Agreement or Determination]. Why is this an important license? We all know that the Supervision Engineer is appointed by the Owner and exercises the authority delegated by the Owner on behalf of the Owner. It is clear that the Supervision Engineer is the Owner's personnel. This is the premise, so when the Owner and the Contractor have an event to be adjudicated by the Supervision Engineer, if the supervision project needs to get the consent of the Owner before making a decision, the Supervision Engineer may not stand in a neutral perspective, but make a decision in favor of the Owner. Therefore, the new authorization of FIDIC in 2017 directly amplifies the rights of the Supervision Engineer, and at the same time ensures that the Supervision Engineer can at least maintain a reasonable neutral attitude when making decisions, and the interests of the Contractors will be guaranteed.

3.3 The Engineer's Representative

The Supervision Engineer's Representative, according to the provisions of Article 3.3, the Supervision Engineer may appoint a representative of Supervision Engineer, and entrust him on behalf of the Supervision Engineer on site Supervision Engineer's authorization. Here is very clear, the Supervision Engineer's Representative's work place is the site of the project. He will be based at the site of the project, in case of temporary leave, the Supervising Engineer shall appoint a replacement with the same qualifications and experience, who is competent for his position, and shall notify the Contractor. This is also an important addition. Why? We often encounter this kind of situation, the Supervision Engineer appoints a representative to be resident on the spot, in case of his temporarily leaves, this representative can entrust another person to exercise his right. Does this kind of practice accord with the contract provision? Similarly, the FIDIC Red Book 2017 also provides the standard answer that if the Supervision Engineer Representative leaves the project site temporarily, the Supervision Engineer should appoint a person to replace him, rather than find someone himself to delegate his responsibilities.

3.4 Delegation by the Engineer

Delegation procedure is displayed in Figure 6.5.

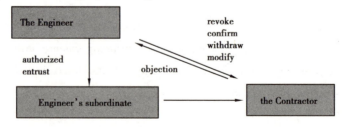

Figure 6.5

Under CONS, the Engineer is empowered by the Employer to administer the whole Works. In some complex projects, the Engineer may need to delegate the authority to his assistants and let the Contractor know about to what extent the assistant had been allowed to issue instructions.

The Employer should ensure that there are sufficient assistants and that they comply with the criteria in the second-paragraph of this Sub-Clause. They're included within the definition of "Employer Personnel". If the assistants have issued instructions beyond the authority they have been delegated to, the Contractor is entitled to reject such kind of instructions, failing which the Contract has to undertake the consequences themselves.

◆ **Discussion**:

An assistant has finished this examination of the work of the Contractor, and the Contractor has proceeded on to the next working procedure, while later on, the Engineer rejects the works when he arrives at the construction site. Is the Engineer entitled to act like this?

Yes, because he has right to reject the works which the assistant fails to disapprove. Any failure to disapprove any work, Plant or Materials shall not constitute approval, and shall therefore not prejudice the right of the Engineer to reject the work, Plant or Materials.

3.5 Engineer's In structions

Under CONS, the Contractor executes the Works in accordance with the Engineer's instructions, and with designs which has been carried out by (or on behalf of) the Employer. The Engineer is empowered to issue instructions, and the Contractor is generally obliged to comply.

The Contractor is especially concerned whether the instructions issued but by the Engineer are beyond what's specified in the Contract. Theoretically, if the instructions do go beyond the limits, they constitute Variations, and Article 13 applies. While in practice, the Engineer often instructs the Contractor to do certain work without indicating whether the instruction should be treated as Variation or not.

Under such circumstances, the Contractor should be able to distinguish the Variations from the instructions and raise a protest against the unfair judgment of the Engineer.

It may even be necessary for immediate oral instructions to be given, although they should be avoided wherever possible, in case the Contractor will be exposed to various kinds of risks. So detailed procedures are specified for an instruction which is no immediately confirmed in writing.

The procedure requires prompt confirmation or denial and alleged oral instruction, in order that its validity or invalidity can be established as soon as possible.

3.6 Replacement of the Engineer

Under CONS, the Engineer has a major role in the administration of the Contract, particularly with respect to issuing Variations and Payment Certificate, and reviewing any Contractor's Documents.

◆**Discussion：**

If the Employer considers the Engineer is incompetent，does he has the right to replace the Engineer？

Employers understandably consider that there should be no restriction imposed on replacing the Engineer. While tenderers may not want the Employer to be replaced because the replacement of the Engineer often will interrupt the continuity of the operation of the Works，thus cause the Contractor to suffer delay or incur cost.

Sub-Clause 3.4 provides a fair and reasonable compromise between the conflicting desires of the Parties. In the first paragraph of this provision，we can clearly see that the supervise.

3.7　Agreement or Determination

The engineer shall remain neutral between the Owner and the Contractor and shall not play the role of the Owner when performing his duties in accordance with this Article. This provision directly requires the Supervision Engineer to be fair when making decisions according to this Article. Then，in the following paragraphs，the Contract also sets out the procedures for the Supervision Engineer to make the decision.

The first is consultation to reach an agreement. On this point，during the execution of overseas projects，especially when the Supervision Engineer is making a decision，the Contractor and the Owner should be consulted first，either at the same time or separately. If an agreement is reached within the time specified in the Contract（42 days），the two Parties will sign an agreement，indicating that the problem has been solved. If the parties cannot reach an agreement within the time specified in the Contract，the Supervising Engineer shall exercise his rights in accordance with the Contract to make a fair decision within the time specified in the Contract and then notify the Contractor and the Owner. The purpose here is not only to give the authority to the Supervision Engineer，but also to provide a clear procedure to restrict the behavior of the Supervision Engineer，so as to ensure that the Supervision Engineer exercises the rights according to the Contract，rather than abusing the power granted by the Contract. This is a new feature of the FIDIC contract conditions in 2017 regarding the decision of the Supervision Engineer.

On this basis，the 2017 FIDIC contract conditions added a time limit，that is to say，the Supervision Engineer should solve the problem within the time specified in the Contract，rather than remain silent，do nothing，no matter what decision，or claim，must notify the Contractor and the Owner within 42 days. Failure to make a decision within 42 days，or silence，means that the Supervisorn Engineer rejects the claim and the matter to which the decision was made becomes a dispute. In the second case，either party may submit the dispute to the DAAB for adjudication without the need to submit a notice of dissatisfaction and Clause 21.4.1 shall cease to apply. Therefore，no matter it is a claim or any other thing，if the Supervision Engineer needs to make a decision，the Supervision Engineer should act in a fair manner according to the Contract to ensure that the interests of the Contractor and the Owner will not be damaged.

Secondly, since the Supervision Engineer can make decisions and facilitate mutual agreement, how effective is it? The 2017 FIDIC Conditions of Contract also have detailed provisions in this regard. That is, the decision of the Supervision Engineer shall be binding on both parties, unless the decision is modified in accordance with Article 21, that is, the decision of the Supervision Engineer shall be valid and executed by both parties. However, if either party finds any error in the decision or agreement made by the Supervision Engineer, it shall notify the Supervision Engineer within 14 days after receiving the decision of the Supervision Engineer. If the Supervision Engineer considers no error, it shall notify both Parties. If the Supervising Engineer himself discovers an error, he shall immediately notify both Parties. The Supervision Engineer shall correct the error within 7 days after receiving the notice and notify both Parties that the decision after modification is final.

Finally, with regard to the decision of the Supervision Engineer, if either Party is not satisfied with it, the dissatisfied Party shall send a notice of dissatisfaction to the other Party with a copy to the Supervision Engineer stating the reasons for the dissatisfaction. The notice of dissatisfaction shall be sent within 28 days after the receipt of the decision of the Supervision Engineer or his revised decision. If the Supervision Engineer fails to make a decision on the claim within the prescribed time, he shall give notice of dissatisfaction within 28 days after the expiration of the prescribed time. Then it is reported to the DAAB for adjudication according to the procedure decided by the DAAB. However, if both Parties fail to give notice of dissatisfaction within 28 days after receiving the Engineer's decision, the Engineer's decision shall be final and binding on both Parties. If either Party is dissatisfied with only one part of the decision, it may refer that part to the DAAB for adjudication. If the decision of the Supervising Engineer is final and either Party does not implement the decision of the Supervising Engineer, or the agreement brought about by the Supervising Engineer, then either Party may submit it to arbitration.

3.8 Meetings

The Engineer, the Contractor's Representative, the Employer's other Contractors, Personnel and Subcontractors may all attend such meetings.

※ Vocabulary

1. delegate *n.* 代表;(尤指)会议代表

   v. 授(权);把(职责、责任等)委托(给)

2. preliminary *adj.* 预备的;初步的

3. protest *v.* 抗议;提出异议;反对

4. amend *v.* 修改;修订

5. revocation *n.* 废止,撤回

6. reverse *v.* 逆转,彻底改变(决定、政策、趋势等)

7. dispute *n.* 争吵;吵闹

8. proceed *v.* 接下来做;接着做

4　The Contractor

4.1　The Contractor's General Obligations

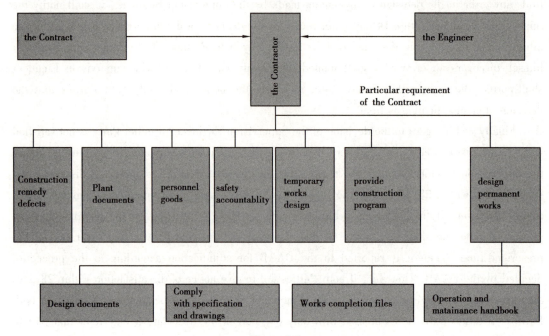

Figure 6.6

With regard to the Contractor's responsibility for design, the FIDIC Red Book 2017 provides a separate and detailed explanation of this obligation (Figure 6.6). In accordance with Sub-Clause 4.1, if the Contract specifies that the Contractor shall design any part of the Permanent Works, the Contractor shall perform his design obligation in accordance with this provision. Without rules, the Contractors don't have to do the design. In the actual project execution process, although the Employer has completed the design of the project, it is inevitable that there may be part of the project design that needs to be completed by the Contractor. The 2017 FIDIC Red Book is not one-size-fits-all. It only stipulates that the Contractor is only responsible for the construction and does not do any design. On the contrary, the 2017 edition of the FIDIC Red Book has added more detailed provisions. For example, the design of the Contractor should be reviewed and approved by the Supervision Engineer before the Contractor can start the construction of that part of the project. If the Contractor is responsible for the design changes, the Supervision Engineer also need to review and approve before the Contractor can start construction. In addition, the Contractor shall provide training to the Employer's personnel in the operation and maintenance of the Works designed by the Contractor, if required by the Contract.

Although the 1999 FIDIC Red Book also addresses design and construction, the 2017 FIDIC Red Book is novel in that it specifies the contractor's construction and design obligations separately, rather than together in the 1999 Red Book. Therefore, compared with the 1999 FIDIC

Red Book, the 2017 FIDIC Red Book has more realistic guiding significance. The main obligation of the Contractor is to perform the works in accordance with the Contract, not the design. The design is only part of the Contractor's obligation (if any) and the Contractor is only responsible for the design he makes. From a practical point of view, FIDIC 2017 is more practical.

4.2 **Performance Security**

The general obligation of the Contractor also includes the provision of the performance security to ensure the performance of the Contract. It can be said that the performance security is the initial obligation of the Contractor (Figure 6.7). After the submission of the performance security, the Parties can sign the Contract and reach the cornerstone of the rights and obligations of both Parties. 2017 edition of FIDIC Red Book adds content related to increase or decrease of Contract Price. During the execution of the project, changes may occur, which may increase or decrease the Contract Price. So, in this case, how should the amount of the performance security be handled? In the event of an increase of 20% in the original Contract Price under this Clause, the Owner may require the Contractor to increase the amount of the Performance Security and the Contractor's expenses thus incurred shall be treated in accordance with Article 13. In the event of a reduction in the Contract Price, the Contractor may, with the consent of the Owner, reduce the amount of the Performance Security.

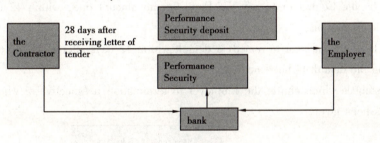

Figure 6.7

In international contracts, where the Employer may wish to anticipate the potential problems of default by the Contractor, a security is a common requirement for the protection of the Employer and of the project financial institution. The amount of Performance Security must be special in CON's Appendix to Tender, either as a sum or as a percentage of the Accepted Contract Amount.

There're many types of Performance Security, of which the most popular is the security issued by banks, hence have the name of the Performance Bank Guarantee. This security is usually 10% ~ 15% of the Accepted Contract Amount. This type of security can be subdivided into two:

(1) A "conditional" security requires certain conditions to be satisfies before it may be called (cashed), the conditions typically being an arbitral award or evidences like: the Contractor has been notified, reasons have been stated, agreement of the Contractor has been obtained, etc. This type of performance security provides less scope for unfair calls, and is typically preferred by the Contractors.

(2) An "unconditional" or "on-demand" security without pre-conditions, which can be directly called on banks if only the Employer considers it to be appropriate.

FIDIC used to adhere to the principle of using "conditional" security, while the example form annexed to the Contract Conditions in the new edition is proved to be of the "unconditional" type, reflecting its concept revolution.

In practice, the Contractor needs to be attentive to the specific stipulations in the Performance Security concerning amount, validity period and conditions, under which the Employer is entitled to claim.

Speaking of the Performance Security, usually, the Employer will make some improvements on the standard form which is annexed to the GPPC, in different aspects as follows:

(1) Deleting the passage from the example form that requires the Employer to make explanation on their default, so as to make it applicable for the security to be called on demand.

(2) Banks are not supposed to provide answers to any queries from the Contractor.

(3) No acts under the Contract or any illegal provisions will relieve the Contractor from their responsibilities under the Performance Security.

The Employer shall not make a claim under the Performance Security, except for amounts to which the Employer is entitled under the Contract in the event of:

①failure by the Contractor to extend the validity of the Performance Security as described in the preceding paragraph, in which event the Employer may claim the full amount of the Performance Security;

②failure by the Contractor to pay the Employer an amount due, within 42 days after this agreement or determination;

③failure by the Contractor to remedy a default within 42 days after receiving the Employer's notice requiring the default to be remedied; or

④circumstances which entitle the Employer to termination irrespective of whether notice of termination has been given.

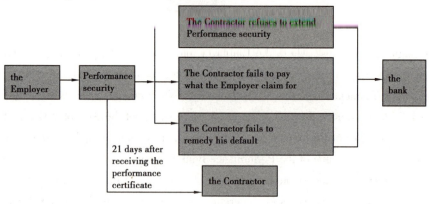

Figure 6. 8

4.3　Contractor's Representative

The role of the Contractor's Representative is of great importance and essential to the final success of the project. It's called "project manager" of the Contractor in China. The Contractor's Representative is the individual responsible for the performance of the Contractor's obligation under the Contract, including directing the Contractor's personnel and Subcontractors.

There're some basic criteria to judge whether the provisions are effective or not, one of which depends upon whether it's favorable to the smooth operation of the project and the improvement of work efficiency.

The last sentence specifies that the Representative and all these persons shall be fluent in the communication language. Undoubtedly, if only people from different parties could be able to communicate with one language, we can reasonably expect great improvement in the work efficiency.

4.4　**The Contractor's Documents**

In the 1999 FIDIC Red Book and the 2017 FIDIC Red Book, the Contractor's Documents are mentioned many times. Although the 1999 FIDIC Red Book and the 2017 FIDIC Red Book both have a description of the Contractor's Documents, the 2017 FIDIC Contract Conditions have a more detailed explanation, including the content, requirements and provisions, as well as the requirements for the Supervision Engineer. We can start from two aspects, one is in the actual construction, according to the Contract and the Supervision Engineer's requirements; Secondly, the answer can be found in the 2017 edition of the FIDIC Red Book.

First of all, in the process of the implementation of overseas projects, the Supervision Engineer has great power, documents related to the project construction are all prepared by the Contractor, reviewed and approved by the Supervision Engineer, then the Contractor will be able to conduct the construction according to the documents. This is indeed a very rigorous audit process, which can strictly control every construction activity of the project and ensure that the implementation of the project is carried out according to the Contract. If the Supervision Engineer thinks inappropriate, it is necessary to modify according to the requirements of Supervision Engineer, until he is satisfied, and the Supervision Engineer also can find fault at his will, which are unfair for the Contractors. Since there is no provision in the Contract in this respect, the Contractors can only accept it and find no contractual basis to defend their own interests.

Secondly, the Clause 4.4 of the Contract Conditions in the FIDIC Red Book of 2017 provides detailed provisions on the Contractor's Documents. During the execution of the Contract, the Contractor can act in accordance with the Contract Provisions and defend his own interests. With regard to the preparation of the Contractor's Documents, it specifies what the Contractor's Documents shall include and the language in which they shall be written. The Owner's personnel shall have the right to inspect the documents prepared by the Contractor. With regard to the audit of the Contractor's Documents, if the specifications or conditions of the Contract specify that the Contractor's Documents are required to be submitted to the Supervision Engineer for review, then the Contractor shall submit its prepared documents to the Supervision Engineer for review. If there is no such provision, there is no need.

The Supervision Engineer shall, within 21 days after receiving the documents, give the Contractor a reply without objection, which may include some minor opinions that do not affect the project substantially. Or the Supervision Engineer shall give a reason if the Contractor's Documents are not in accordance with the Contract. If the Supervision Engineer does not give a reply within 21 days after receiving the documents, he shall be deemed to have no objection. If the Supervision Engineer points out that the Contractor's Documents do not conform to the provisions of the Contract, the Contractor shall revise the documents according to the Contract and submit them to the Supervision Engineer for review again. After receiving the revised documents, the Supervision Engineer shall reply to the Contractor within 21 days in accordance with the above procedures.

Sub-Clause 4.1 of the 1999 FIDIC Red Book has a simple explanation for the completion documents and the operation and maintenance manual, while the 2017 FIDIC Red Book has detailed requirements for the content and format of the completion records. The Contractor shall prepare and update operations and maintenance manuals in accordance with the specifications if required. In addition, after the Contractor has prepared the Completion Records and the Operations and Maintenance Manual, it shall be submitted to the Supervision Engineer for review, and unless the Supervision Engineer agrees, it shall be deemed that the Works have not been handed over and completed in accordance with the Works and Paragraphs.

The 2017 edition of FIDIC Red Book has systematic and procedural provisions on the Contractor's Documents, which prevents the Supervision Engineer from abusing his power and imposing his own requirements on the Contractor when carrying out the rights granted by the Contract. At the same time, it is also stipulated that the Contractor should strictly abide by the provisions of the Contract and strictly control the preparation of his own documents in accordance with the provisions of the Contract. This can not only reduce the randomness of the provisions on this aspect, but also reduce the possibility of disputes in the process of contract execution. If the Contractor has any objection to the audit of the Supervision Engineer, the Contractor may also defend its own interests according to this Clause.

Based on a detailed interpretation of the Contract Documents, we have learned the new requirements for the Contractor's Documents in the FIDIC 2017 Red Book. These requirements include the content, preparation, audit, completion records and operation and maintenance manuals of the Contractor's Documents. With detailed explanation, the Contractor will have a clearer idea in preparing the documents. At the same time, it also stipulates the Supervision Engineer's behavior, which has more practical guidance to the actual work.

4.5　Training

The Contractor shall provide training to the Employer's employees.

4.6　Co-operation

For some large-scale or expansion projects, the Contractor may not have the exclusive right of access to, and possession of, the Site. In addition to the Employer's Personnel, the Contractor must also allow the Employer's other Contractors to carry out their works.

Several Subcontractors and Contractors carry out their works simultaneously on the same Site, and sometimes the Employer's personnel also join, which unavoidably lead to chaos. In such cases, cooperation is needed in order to maintain high efficient works on the Site. "Cooperation" is also specified to be one of the Contractor's obligations in the Contract considering promoting the cooperation between the Parties (Figure 6.9).

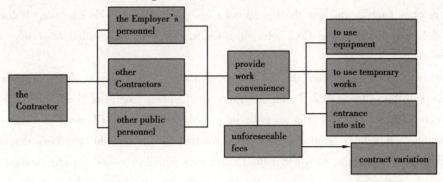

Figure 6.9

If instructions are given under the first sentence of this Sub-Clause, the Contractor is expected to have allowed in his Tender for Cost which an experienced contractor would reasonably have foreseen. To the extent that the cost was not reasonably foreseeable by an experienced contractor, taking account of the information available to tenders, the instruction constitutes a Variation and Article 13 applies.

4.7 Setting Out

Setting-out is a initial step in the project construction field, according to the FIDIC contract conditions, this step requires the Contractor to do the Works according to the data provided by the Owner, which has a crucial influence to carry out the subsequent construction for the Contractor. If the Setting-out is not ready, the design of the Construction Drawings will also be restricted, affecting the subsequent construction progress, therefore. The degree of setting-out affects the construction progress of the project. In the 1999 edition of the FIDIC Red Book contract conditions, detailed provisions on the Setting-out are given, but the 2017 edition of the FIDIC Red Book adds more specific contents.

Different from the 1999 FIDIC Red Book, the 2017 FIDIC Red Book divides the Setting-out into three parts in details, and each part explains a specific content respectively. Such a clearer idea is convenient for the guidance of the Contractors and Supervision Engineers in practice. As with the 1999 FIDIC Red Book, the 2017 FIDIC Red Book specifies in detail in Sub-Clause 4.7.1 what contractual procedures the Contractor should follow. However, the 2017 FIDIC Red Book is more specific. The main contents include checking the accuracy of the data before use, reporting the checking results to the Supervision Engineer, correcting the errors in the project elevation, dimension and linearity, as well as correct positioning of all parts of the project.

This clause specifies not only the content of the work for which the Contractor is responsible, but also the procedure of the work, which is not found in the 1999 edition of the FIDIC Red Book. If the reader has the experience of working on the construction site, it can be found that the content and procedures of the 2017 FIDIC are basically the same as the actual work process, which is where it is novel and makes the Contract Provisions in line with the actual situation. If the Contractor finds any error in the data, he shall notify the Engineer within the time specified in the Contract or as soon as possible after receipt of the data. It specifies what the Contractor should do if the error is found, which is the Contractor's obligation to fulfill his contract. If such errors result in delays or costs to the Contractor, the Contractor shall be entitled to recover the time period and costs.

After the Contractor notifies the Supervison Engineer, what should the supervisor do? In accordance with Sub-Clause 4.7.3, the Engineer shall, upon receipt of the Contractor's notice, agree or determine whether there is an error in accordance with Sub-Clause 3.7 [Agreement or Determination]. Whether, as an experienced contractor, the error could have been detected prior to the submission of tenders, or whether the Contractor's notice exceeded the requirements of Sub-Clause 4.7.2. and what action (if any) the Contractor should be required to take to correct the error. At the same time, the Works carried out by the Supervision Engineer in accordance with the Contract shall be completed within the time specified in Sub-Clause 3.7.3 [Time limits].

If the Engineer decides that, as an experienced Contractor, the error cannot be detected, then Sub-Clause 13.3.1 [Variation by Instruction] applies to the action (if any) required of the Contractor to be taken in response to the error. And if the Contractor incurs delay (and) or cost as a result of such error, the Contractor shall be entitled to a claim under Sub-Clause 20.2 for time delay and cost plus profit. It is stipulated here that the Supervision Engineer shall, upon receipt of the Contractor's notice, complete the abovementioned things that the Supervision Engineer shall do within the time limit specified in the Contract. That is to say, the Contract not only stipulates what the Contractor should do within the specified time, but also stipulates what the Supervision Engineer should do within the specified time. Such provisions are not only requirements for the Contractor, but also requirements for the Supervision Engineer, which is a practical procedure.

In the contract of Setting-out, 2017 FIDIC Red Book contract conditions has made the corresponding provisions from three aspects respectively to the behavior of the Supervision Engineer and the Contractor, among them, the first two aspects are aimed at the requirements of the Contractor, that is, the Contractor should fulfill the contractual obligations in the construction process of setting-out under a contract, in a nutshell, "audit" and "notice". The Contractor must first review the relevant data, if there is any error, notify the Supervision Engineer within the specified period of time. The last aspect is about obligation of the Supervision Engineer, namely "decision", the Supervision Engineer must first decide whether there are mistakes, whether for experienced contractor they cannot find mistakes, then decide what to take measures to correct, and finally entitle contractor to their rights.

The 2017 FIDIC Red Book provides a clear process on the construction Setting-out, as well as the rights and obligations of the Contractor and the Supervision Engineer in this process. In the actual implementation process, it can not only ensure that the Contractor Works in accordance with the provisions of the Contract, but also ensure that the rights and interests of the Contractor are not harmed.

4. 8 Health and Safety Obligations

This Sub-Clause is to propose the health and safety procedure in construction to the Contractor from the view point of humanism and protection of the benefits of the public.

In fact, to the Contractor, the work of safety procedure relatively not only to his social image, but also to cause him a great many problems concerning management on the Site. For example, for the work conducted in mid-air, after the happening of an accident, the work efficiency rate and attendance rate may drop dramatically.

What's more, some prequalification documents about project tendering contain the item of accident rate, requiring the Contract to complete the report about the finished work. This works as one of the criteria examine the Contractor's pre-qualification.

---

4. 9 Quality Management and Compliance Verification Systems

Sub-Clause 4. 9 of the FIDIC Red Book 2017 specifies a set of quality management and verification system to guide the implementation of the project. According to the provisions of this Article, this system involves the rights and obligations of the Supervision Engineer and the Contractor in this system. Firstly, let's talk about the role of the Contractor who is responsible for preparing and implementing the Quality Management System (hereafter referred to as the "QM System") in accordance with the Specification, which shall include the relevant procedures as set out in Sub-Clause 4. 9. 1 of the FIDIC Red Book 2017 to demonstrate the Contractor's compliance with the Contract requirements. Within 28 days after the commencement date, the Contractor shall submit the QM System to the Supervison Engineer, and after the submission, the Contractor shall immediately submit the QM System to the Supervison Engineer if the quality management system is updated or modified according to the implementation of the project. The Contractor shall also conduct an internal audit of its QM System on a semi-annual basis and report the results to the Supervision Engineer within 7 days after completion of the audit. If the Contractor's quality assurance certificate is required to comply with the external audit, the Contractor shall immediately notify the Supervision Engineer of any problems arising from the internal audit.

Secondly, the role of the Supervision Engineer. After receiving the QM System submitted by the Contractor, the Supervision Engineer can review the system. If the system does not comply with the Contract, the Contractor shall be notified to modify the system. If, within 21 days after receiving the QM System, the Supervision Engineer fails to give notice that the system is not in conformity with the Contract, he shall be deemed to have no objection to the system. In addition, if the Contractor fails to implement the QM System correctly, the Supervison Engineer may at any time send a notice to the Contractor, upon receipt of which the Contractor shall make corrections immediately. Both the Contractor and the Supervision Engineer should act in strict accordance with the Contract Provisions, especially the time stipulated in the Contract, which is the joint efforts of both sides to ensure the quality of the project, but also the implementation of the Contract Provisions.

Finally, there is a verification system which the Contractor is responsible for preparing and implementing to demonstrate that the design (if any), materials supplied by the Owner (if any), plant, engineering and workmanship comply with the Contract. This verification system shall be established in accordance with the specified details (if any) and shall include the methods and reports of the Contractor's conduct of tests and inspections. If any inspection or test finds any non-conformance to the Contract, this shall be carried out in accordance with Sub-Clause 7. 5. The Contractor shall also prepare and submit to the Supervision Engineer a set of verification documents for the item or paragraph, which shall be prepared and prepared in accordance with the requirements of the Code or in a manner acceptable to the Supervision Engineer. In the implementation of overseas projects, we have already adopted such a system. The 2017 FIDIC contract conditions are determined in the form of words based on the actual situation, which has a certain guiding role.

As for the reasons for the addition of a quality management and verification system in the 2017 FIDIC Red Book, it can be found through the above analysis that the quality and verification system proposed in the 2017 FIDIC Red Book not only specifies what the Contractor should do, but also specifies the role of the Supervision Engineer in this system. Through this procedural regulation, it not only can ensure that the Contractor will strictly control the quality of the project in accordance with the Contract Provisions, but also ensure that the Contractor is protected by the Contract. At the same time, in practice, the Contractor shall be aware that compliance with the QM System and verification system shall not relieve the Contractor of any of his duties, obligations or responsibilities under the Contract. That is to say, even if the contractor complies with the relevant provisions of the QM System and verification system, some quality problems still occur during the implementation of the project or after the completion of the construction. The Contractor and the Supervision Engineer shall investigate the problem. If the Contractor is responsible, the Contractor shall be responsible. If not, it shall be dealt with in accordance with the Contract.

4.10　Use of Site Data

Site data generally included hydrological, geological and environmental conditions. Due to the reason that it's almost completely impossible for the Contractor, nor does the Employer to obtain all the data relevant to the Site conditions before the commencement of the Works, the "uncertainties" of the Site condition become an underlying risk factor in the execution of the Works. Thus how to fairly divide the risks between the Employer and the Contractor becomes the hot issue that all Contractors concern about.

For the Employer, he hall make available to the Contractor data which came or come into his possession either before or after the Base Date. Failure in this respect may have significant consequences. In some countries, negligent or intentional withhold of data may entitle the Contractor to termination, and consequential personal injury may result in private or criminal liability.

The Contractor is responsible for interpretation of the Site data, and for obtaining other information, so far as was practicable. The practicability of obtaining information will already depend upon the time allowed for the preparation of the tender.

Cautious attitude is necessary to deal with this kind of site conditions issues, please refer to the suggestions as follows:

(1)To study carefully the site data provided by the Employer, especially those that can be interpreted in different ways.

(2)To conduct a site survey.

(3) To ask the Employer to clarify the Discussions in case ambiguity occurs, by taking chance of the meeting before tendering.

(4)To study under what conditions will the Contractor be entitled to claim.

(5)To study how to create advantageous but reasonable conditions for claim before tendering or in the executing of the Works.

◆**Discussion:**

What's the result after the interpretation and valuation of the Contractor on the Site data?

To such an extent the site conditions will affect the project expenditures that if the site risks are overvalued, the Contractor's offer will inevitably become less competitive. In the contrary, if the Contractor gives a much lower appraisal to the risks, the happening of which will cause a great loss to the Contractor.

4.11   Sufficiency of the Accepted Contract Amount

In order to prevent that the Contractor asserts the tendering price has not covered all contract contents due to the omission of certain items, and further raise the claim against the Employer, the contracts of the international projects specify that offer is apt to cover the Contractor's entire obligation under the Contract.

4.12   Unforeseeable Physical Conditions

Sub-Clause 4.12 of the 2017 FIDIC Red Book explains the physical conditions, that is, the natural physical conditions and man-made or natural physical obstacles encountered by the Contractor in the course of the execution of the project, including subsurface conditions and hydrological conditions, excluding climatic conditions and their effects. Unforeseeable is for the Contractor, with a time limit, and if the Contractor considers that the physical condition could not have been foreseen at the base date and that the physical condition caused delays and additional costs to the Contractor, the following procedure applies. However, if the Contractor could foresee such a situation on the base date, he shall take full account of such a situation in his tender offer and make adequate preparations.

The Contractor shall notify the Supervision Engineer of any unforeseen physical condition as soon as possible and at a good time so that the Supervision Engineer may have the opportunity to conduct an inspection and investigation immediately before the physical condition is disturbed. The Contractor's notice to the Supervision Engineer shall include a description of the physical conditions, a description of the reasons for the physical conditions which the Contractor considers to be unforeseen and a description of the negative impact of such physical conditions on the project schedule (and) or additional costs to the construction. Upon receipt of the notice, the Supervision Engineer shall, within 7 days or such longer period as the Contractor agrees, carry out an inspection and investigation of the physical condition. At the same time, the Contractor shall carry out the Works in a manner appropriate and reasonable to the physical conditions so that the Supervision Engineer can inspect and investigate them.

The Contractor shall comply with any instructions given by the Supervision Engineer to deal with the physical conditions, and if such instructions constitute a change, Sub-Clause 13.3.1 shall be used. The Contractor shall be entitled under Sub-Clause 20.2 to the delay (and) of the time limit and the costs if such physical conditions cause the Contractor to incur delays (and) or additional costs in compliance with Sub-Clause 4.12.1 to Sub-Clause 4.12.3. In the 4.12.4 terms according to the decisions made by the 20.2.5 Sub-Clause or agreement, you need to consider whether the physical condition is unforeseen and unpredictable, the Supervision Engineer can also review the similar engineering part of the other physical conditions (if any), whether can expect more favorable and the base date. And to some extent, in the event of a more favorable physical condition, the Supervision Engineer may consider deducting from the additional charges to be determined in accordance with Sub-Clause 4.12.5 the cost arising from a more favorable physical condition. However, the net increase or decrease under Sub-Clause 4.12.5 shall not result in a net decrease in the contract addition.

4.13　Rights of Way and Facilities

During the execution of the Works, both of the equipment and personnel of the Contractor's need to be transported to and from the Site. And the public roads will be at the disposal of the Contractor and his personnel of they're along the Site. In the contrary, the Contractor may need to obtain some special or temporary ways if the Site locates at the remote place.

◆ **Discussion:**

Who shall be responsible for obtaining the rights of way?

This Sub-Clause specifies that the responsibility of obtaining the special or temporary rights of way will be of the Contractor's. This means the Contractor need to carry on a detailed research when conducting the Site survey about the roads or routs that need to be used in the execution of the Works, as well as whether some private roads are passable, or some temporary and specific roads need to be constructed, etc. All these factors need to be presented to the Contractor before he makes an offer.

4. 14　Avoidance of Interference

Construction work may bring an adverse effect to the surrounding environment such as noise, pollution and traffic jams, etc. This Sub-Clause is specified to constrain the Contractor to interfere with the public as little as practicable. In international projects, such restrictions are not only stated in the Contract but also in the applicable laws of different states.

For instance, when excavating the ground at the center of cities with high population density, it will be advisable to also sprinkle on the dusty roads.

In another example, in China, it's proclaimed in many cities that all the construction work which will produce noise must pause during the period when the university entrance examinations take place.

4. 15　Access Rout

A great deal of equipment will need to be transported to and from the Site during the execution of the Works, especially some heavy-duty equipment. Thus it's important to ensure that there will be access to the Site.

The word "route" indicates something which can be represented as a line on a map, typically overland without implying that a road to the site exists. It is only assumed that there is a route by which access would be physically practicable. The Contractor is entitled to make use of the route without negotiation with its Owners, but his entitlement does not indicate that the route is suitable for transport. The wording of the Sub-Clause does not preclude the possibility that he might to construct a road along the route.

If the Site is totally surrounded by land owned by the third party, the Contractor should clarify:

(1) the alignment of the route through the third Parties' lands, along with the Employer will be granting the right of access;

(2) how the Contractor can gain access, for example, whether access will be hindered by third Parties' control measures.

Two decisions of the courts demonstrate the principles involved in apportioning responsibility for providing access to site.

In the case of Penvidic Contracting Co Ltd v International Nickel Co. of Canada Ltd, the contract involved the laying of track and top ballasting on a railroad. Penvidic was the contractor and work to properly grade and sub-ballast was constantly delayed by the failure of other Contractors the right of way in front of its machinery. In addition the International Nickel Co failed to obtain the necessary way leaves and permissions to cross various hydro lines and highways.

It was held that the extent of possession or access provided by an Employer would vary with the nature of the work and the circumstances. In the case of a new project the main contractor would normally be entitled to exclusive possession of the entire site in the absence of express terms to the contrary. Term would normally be implied that the site would be handed over within a reasonable time and, in most cases, with a sufficient uninterrupted possession to allow the contractor to carry out his obligations by the method of his choice. It was held that International Nickel Co had failed to do so and that this was a breach of contract entitling Penvidic to damages.

In LRE Engineering Services Ltd v Otto Simon Carves Ltd, Simon Carves was the contractor for building works at steelworks at Port Talbot. LRE were subcontractors and had completed a very substantial proportion of the works when a steel strike broke out. The activities of pickets at the site prevented LRE from completing the work until some considerable time later, causing them to incur considerable additional costs. LRE maintained that Simon Carves was in breach of contract in that it had an absolute obligation to see that there was available entry to the site at all times. This was not accepted. It was held instead that the term "access" had more than one meaning in the relevant Clause. In one part of the clause it meant "physical means of access" since that part also referred to the condition of the access. Another part placed an obligation on Simon Carves to "afford access" to LRE. On this interpretation it was held that there was no breach of contract. Simon Carves had provided LRE with the opportunity of entering the site by the required means of access. The fact that they were prevented from doing so was not a breach of contract.

4.16 Transport of Good

This Sub-Clause specifies that the Contractor has to take full responsibility for the transportation of any Plant or a major item of other Goods, he is required to give notice of the intended arrival of the objects and to indemnify the Employer in respect of claims arising from their transport. And Goods must be insured when they are within the country.

4.17 Contractor's Equipment

Contractor's equipment, which included Subcontractor's equipment, is deemed to be intended for the execution of the Works, and not for use elsewhere.

◆ **Discussion**:

Is there any extra use of the Contractor's equipment?

Some of the Equipment are quite expensive, when such equipment are retained in the Site of the Works, they are considered to act as a special role of "guarantee". Literally, there's no strict definition on this sort of "guarantee", while in practice, when disputes arise between the Contractor and the Employer, especially when the project faces with the possibility if suspension which is caused by the Contractor, the Employer will distrain upon these equipment as a method of protection of their benefits.

Consent is required before major items leave the Site, especially for transport vehicles, which come forth and back through the Site daily.

4.18　Protection of Environment

The protection of environment has been the focus among global issues and attracted more attention from different countries. Because the construction tends to cause pollutions to environment, there have been more strict requirements imposed on construction procedure which are stated in the international construction contracts in recent years.

In some countries, the protection of environment arouses great interest of people especially in countries relying on the tourism as the main source of national income. Such countries also have very stern environment protection laws.

A Contractor who has been well equipped with the techniques of modern management should be equally taught how to handle the problem of protection of environment in construction. For this issue not only relatively to their obligation under the Contract or law, but also to the build-up of social image of the company.

The Contractor is required by this Sub-Clause to take all reasonable steps to protect the environment and is required to limit emission to specified value. If he fails to do so, the Contractor would be liable.

(1) *Compulsory cease of work during the national entrance examination to university;*

(2) *Government compulsory limit on night work in urban area;*

(3) *Compulsory expert demonstration on excavation engineering scheme;*

(4) *Compulsory protection on surrounding architecture.*

4.19　Temporary Utilities

On the construction Site, electricity, water and gas are necessities for the staff to live on, usually solved by the Contractor himself, which doesn't exclude the possibilities that these can be provided to the Contractor under charge, if only at the convenience of the Employer. The first sentence of the Sub-Clause excluded the Employer's responsibility, except to the extent (if any) to which he has undertaken to make specified services available.

If the Employer is to make any of these services available, details and prices must be given in CON's Specification. If the Contractor will need to rely upon the continued availability of a service, the Contractor should indicate who bears the cost of a failure in the supply. IT may be reasonable for the Employer to be responsible for services which he controls, and for other specifies services to be at the risk of the Contractor.

4.20　Progress Reports

The Employer and the Engineer learn the progress of the construction work and manage the Contractor through Progress Reports, which are important management documents.

In practice, before the submission of the first report, the Contractor will negotiate with the Engineer and determine the format of monthly report, on which the monthly reports will be based.

With the growing popularity of the use of computer, especially after the applied software have been used for the purpose of construction management, it has become much easier and more convenient to work on a report and submit it subsequently.

In addition to the items listed from (a) to (h), there are more that are required to be included into the reports like the number of the monthly accidents about quality and according remedying measures. For example, the notice issued by the Employer or the Engineer when quality defects of the Contractor have been discovered, which is called Non-performance Report. If the reports have not been submitted in time, the Engineer is entitled to reject the application of the Interim Payment Certificate by the Contractor.

Progress Report includes:

(a) progress chart and illustrations;

(b) site photos;

(c) examination certificate of equipment and materials;

(d) provide specific personnel numbers and equipment items;

(e) relevant documents on material quality guarantee;

(f) filing of claim documents;

(g) safety items;

(h) progress comparison.

4.21 Security of the Site

This Sub-Clause states that the Contractor is responsible for the security works. In practice, the Contracts may specify that the Contractor has to recruit security guards from specialist security companies to ensure the safety of the Site and protects the Site against theft and sabotage.

For some particular Plant, for example, the warehouse for storage of dynamite, which is used for explosive work, may requires the local troops to be on guard. During the execution of the Works, the events with adverse effect may happen one after another, for instance, staff member is shot or kidnapped, etc. and these will hamper the normal progress of the Works. Facing with such projects with high risks, the Contractor has to not only give risk evaluation in tendering but also take certain precautions in the construction period.

4.22 Contractor's Operation on Site

The Contactor should carry out their works on the Site in compliance with certain rules, for example, do not cause inconvenience to the occupier of the adjacent land, properly arrange the activities on the Site, etc.

The Contractor is required to confine his operations to the Site and any additional areas, which do not become parts of the Site.

These agreed areas are obtained by the Contractor, the Engineer is not responsible for them, Plant and Materials are not required to be delivered thereto, and Permanent Works are not executed thereon.

The equipment or materials shall be put at the place to which they are appointed rather than being willfully disposed of, which may cause accidents.

For instance, once in a project, a driver placed a bulldozer on the ground to be backfilled before he was off the duty. That night, the heavy rain caused the collapse of the ground and the bulldozer slid into a deep ditch. As the result, the Contractor suffered a great loss.

This lesson proves that a clear site will contribute to high efficient work.

4.23 Archaeological and Geological Findings

Many countries, especially those highly civilized ancient countries, owns laws of relic protections. And there're also chapters with similar title in construction contract. In this Sub-Clause, fossils and other antiquities are the property and also the liability of the Employer.

The Contractor is required to give notice upon discovering of the finding and await instructions for dealing with it.

◆Discussion:

Will there be any practical problems arising from this?

This Clause doesn't set restrictions on the Contractor concerning the right of claims, but encourages the Contractor to make efforts to protect the findings and specifies that it's one of his obligations.

※**Vocabulary**

1. adequacy *n.* 适当;恰当
2. consumable *adj.* 消耗性的
3. as-built 竣工;完工
4. coordination *n.* 协调
5. dismantle *v.* 拆卸;拆开;拆除
6. reassemble *v.* 重组;重新整合;重新装配
7. enforceabe *adj.* 可执行的;可强制执行的
8. revoke *v.* 取消,废除,撤销(许可、法律、协议等)
9. possession *n.* 占有;拥有
10. rectify *v.* 纠正;修正;矫正
11. alignment *n.* 结盟;联合
12. dimension *n.* 方面;部分
13. be subject to 受支配;从属于;可以……的;常遭受……

14. institute *v.* 建立(体系等);制定(规章等);开始;开创

15. contingency *n.* 可能发生的事;不测之事;突发事件

16. hydrological *adj.* 水文学的

17. indemnify *v.* 保证赔偿

18. exclusively *adv.* 排他地;独占地;专有地;完全地

19. nuisance *n.* 讨厌的人;麻烦的事情

20. hazardous *adj.* (尤指对健康或安全)有危险的,有危害的

21. surplus *n.* 过剩;剩余;过剩量;剩余额

22. fossil *n.* 化石

23. archaeological *n.* 考古学

24. authentication *v.* 鉴别;鉴定

25. strive for 奋斗,争取;谋求;讲求

5 Subcontracting

5.1 Subcontractors

This Clause sets out the conditions under which subcontracting is not permitted and where the Contractor is not required to obtain the consent of the Engineer and the Contractor is required to notify the Engineer within a specified period of time prior to the commencement of the work of the Subcontractor.

5.2 Nominated Subcontractor

5.2.1 Definition of Nominated Subcontractor

In accordance with the second sentence of Sub-Clause 4.4, "the Contractor shall be responsible for the acts or default of any Subcontractor (including nominated Subcontractor)". The Employer and the Engineer should not deal directly with a nominated Subcontractor (or with any Subcontractor) but should only deal with the Contractor (unless he agrees otherwise).

Subcontractor is preferred by the Contractor in some large-scale projects, with the agreement obtained from the Engineer. While the Employer may wish to subcontract some work about he key parts or Plant to specialist companies with rich experience, which they're also keen on and trusted, to ensure the work quality and that their particular needs will be met.

In the Contract, "nominated Subcontractor" means a Subcontractor:

(1) who is stated in the Contract as being a nominated Subcontractor; or

(2) whom the Engineer, under Article 13, instructs the Contractor to employ as a nominated Subcontractor.

After reading this provision, we get to know that nominated Subcontractor shall be determined before the Contract is signed, otherwise the instruction issued by the Engineer to employ a

Subcontractor constitutes Variation under Article 13.

But there're apparent advantages of instructing the employment of a nominated Subcontractor because the Employer or the Engineer can:

(1) choose the Specialist company;

(2) participate the choice of plant;

(3) avoid participation in co-ordination of the interface between the nominated Subcontractor and the Contractor's Works.

Here're also some advices on those who wish to become Subcontractors:

Unless they can be certain of the profitability of the subcontracted projects, they're advised not enter into a Subcontract in a haste, because normally the Contractor is harsh to the Subcontractor.

The first choice they may consider is to join the Contractor to constitute a join-venture, consortium or other unincorporated grouping of two or more person, under which they will take the joint and several responsibility to the Employer and gain more chances in negotiation.

5.2.2　Objection to Nomination

◆ **Discussion:**

Is the Contractor obliged to accept the nominated Subcontractor who is chosen by the Employer?

If the Contractor wishes to object to the nomination, he must do so promptly, describing all the grounds on which his objections are based. This Sub-Clause has listed the most likely grounds for objection under CONS Contract, though the grounds need not to be restricted to those described in the subparagraphs. Because the Contractor has to take the whole responsibility for the quality and working period of the Works, thus it may diverge from FIDIC's intention by enforcing the Contractor to employ any Subcontractor when he's unwilling to do so.

Objection reasons are as follows:

(1) Sufficient proofs to show that this Subcontractor is incapable, insufficient in resources or incompetent in financial background.

(2) No clear statement that if the Subcontractor defaults on his duties, the Contractor will not be not exempted from losses.

(3) No guarantee that if any problems occur to the Subcontractor's work, the Subcontractor himself will take full responsibilities and subsequent result.

◆ **Discussion:**

How can the Employer react to such an objection?

The Sub-Clause provides the Employer with a possible resolution of the objection, namely indemnification. That is to say, if only the Contractor raise reasonable objection, the Employer can't insist on employing any Subcontractor unless he can indemnify and hold the Contractor against and from the consequences of all the matters.

5.2.3 Payment to Nominated Subcontractor

Structure analysis of this Sub-Clause:

(1)The Contractor shall be paid the amounts which he pays to the nominated Subcontractor, and the Engineer is required to certify such actual amounts.

(2)"Other charges" here means the Overheads and Profits the Contractor he has collected from the Employer for the Works he has carried out to manage the Subcontractors. It is usually a percentage of the Subcontract Price and is specified in the Appendix to Tender or the Schedules.

(3)Provisional sum shall be used when Plant, Materials or services are to be purchased by the Contractor from a nominated Subcontractor, as stated in 13.5.9 provisional sum.

5.2.4 Evidence of Payment

The Engineer is entitled to request the Contractor to supply reasonable evidenced of previous payment, though normally he would not do so unless he has reason to believe that the Contractor is in default under the Sub-Clause.

The snag in construing this provision is that we can hardly understand why shall the Engineer pay directly to the Subcontractor and subsequently claim it back from the Contractor?

◆**Discussion:**

Shall the Contractor be liable to the Employer for the default of the Subcontractor?

Normally, the Contractor shall be liable to the Employer, especially when problems occur to the working processes or provided materials, except the Employer insists on employing the Subcontractor irrespective of the reasonable objection from the Contractor and indemnify the Contractor against all possible losses.

In such a case, if the delay of the work of the Subcontractor affects the Contractor, the Contractor will be entitled to claim for extension of time. And the failure of completing the work in time will incur costs to the Employer. Because the Contractor has been exempted from the liability to the Employer, the Employer can't claim for compensation from the Contractor, neither will the Contractor pass on the liability to the Subcontractor. The Subcontractor can almost succeed in defaulting on his obligations.

In order to solve this sort of problem, in practice, the Employer is apt to sign an agreement with the nominated Subcontractor, stipulating the nominated Subcontractor has to perform his obligations under the agreement. Correspondingly, the Employer will undertake to the Subcontractor that if the Contractor fails to pay the due amount, the Employer will pay directly to the nominated Subcontractor (Figure 6.10).

An construction project of office building for rent. The construction period is 18 months. Management fees are 12.5% of the total contract price. While the handover of the construction period is postponed, and the Contractor claimed for damages. One of the reason is that the nominated

Contractor breached the contract. And the failure of completing the work in time will incur costs to the Employer. In order to solve this sort of problem, in practice, the Employer is apt to sign an agreement with the nominated Subcontractor, stipulating the nominated Subcontractor has to perform his obligations under the agreement.

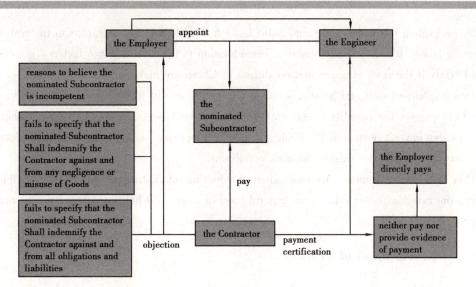

Figure 6.10

※ **Vocabulary**

1. exempt *adj.* 被免除的；被豁免的
2. discharge *v.* 清偿（债务）
3. breach *v.* 违反，破坏（条约、法律或承诺）
4. postpone *v.* 推迟；使延期；延缓

6　Staff and Labor

6.1　Engagement of Staff and Labor

This Sub-Clause removes any implication of obligation on the part of the Employer to provide personnel, except to the extent (if any) that the Employer has undertaken to do so.

The arrangement of the staff and labour depends on specific circumstances. For those the Contractor has brought with him along from their home country, the Contractor has to provide them with housing by building up new houses near the Site or inside, or rent the local houses for them. For the local staff, if the construction site is not far from the local community, the Contractor will provide means of transportations. He is in no way under the obligations of providing housing nor feeding, but he has to ensure the drinking water on the Site is available.

Whatever the Contractor like to do, he must verify the labor contract and make sure it will be in compliance with the local labour law.

6.2　Rates of Wages and Conditions of Labour

By integrating this Sub-Clause into Sub-Clause 6.4 will they two constitute an integral clause concerning labor. It's specifically stated in consideration to the following two factors:

(1) Only if the rates of wages and conditions of labour are higher than the general level, can they recruit qualified staff and labour, so as to ensure the quality and progress of the work.

(2) To protect the benefits of the workers in case the labour laws of the country where the project locates haven't been well established, and the Employer can also avoid getting involved in unnecessary disputes about wages and work conditions.

This Sub-Clause reminds us that when conducting marketing census in the Employer's country, the investigation into the local general level of wages will help to improve the accuracy of tendering price.

6.3　Recruitment of Persons

This Sub-Clause tends to protect the benefits of the Employer. It is also reasonable to allow the Contractor to undermine the Employer's activities, either on project or elsewhere, by encouraging the Employer's Personnel to transfer their employment to the Contractor. Without such prohibition, the confidential particulars of the Contractor may get released. Without such prohibition, the confidential particulars of the Contractor may get released.

6.4　Labour Laws

Labour law in different countries may be different to each other but all cover the same issues:

(1) Recruitment procedure and discharge procedure;

(2) Lowest rates of wages;

(3) Welfare conditions, such as the labour safety utensils;

(4) Social insurance or Employer liability insurance;

(5) Sickness leave and vacation with pay;

(6) Working time and over-time pay, etc.

6.5　Working Hours

The Employer may wish to specify the working hours, besides, the Employer's Personnel may also wish to know the Contractor's working hours in advance, in order to plan and manage their activities.

Under CONS, if the Engineer wishes to specify working hours, they should be stated in the Appendix to Tender. If the Employer's Personnel wish to know the Contractor's intentions, the item in the Appendix to Tender may be left blank in the tender documents, to be completed by each tenderer.

◆ **Discussion** :

Is the Contractor allowed to work over-time in holidays?

The viewpoint of the Employer may diverge from that of the Contractor due to this reason. If the Contractor wants to work on the locally recognized days of rest, then the Employer or Engineer may need to correspondingly arrange overtime work too in order to ensure the Contractor's work will be in accordance with the Specifications, and such a decision will require the Employer to give extra overwork pay to their personnel. But on the whole, the Employer and the Contractor agree on the same target to complete the Works as soon as possible, thus normally the application for overwork form the Contractor will be approved.

6.6　Facilities to Staff and Labour

The Sub-Clause removes any implication of obligation on the part of the Employer to arrange facilities for the Contractor's personnel.

The requirement of providing necessary facilities by the Contractor is also included in the "service range" of the Contractor or the "requirements of the Employer" of which the facilities included: the on-site offices of the Employer, office facilities such as computers, telephones, fax-machine, and transportation vehicles, etc. The content and amount of the providing must be clarified before tendering, for example, whether the Contractor is also required to afford the relevant costs such as fuel charges and telephone fees.

But it may be difficult to establish what accommodation and facilities are "necessary" until the effects of their inadequacy have become apparent.

6.7　Health and Safety of Personnel

There're many factors threatening health and safety of the personnel during the execution of the Works and accidents often happen unexpectedly.

As an experienced administrator, the Contractor should be discreet in dealing with these matters. He's supposed to maintain the balance between he construction progress and safety, appoint qualified engineer to deal with safety issues, provide adequate training about safety to project staff, make complete and feasible safety rules and specific measures to implement these rules. Stipulations of this Sub-Clause coincide with the No. 167 Convention of the International Labour Organization.

6.8　Contractor's Superintendence

In order to guarantee the smooth operation and safety of the Works, it's required that the Contractors has to provide all necessary services and undertakes that he will perform the obligations under the Contract.

It may be difficult to establish what is "necessary" and how many are "sufficient" under this Sub-Clause, and these relate the quantity and quality requirements of the superintendence. Specifically, superintendence includes the following aspects:

(1) scope management;

(2) time management;

(3) cost management;

(4) human resource management;

(5) risk management;

(6) quality management;

(7) communication management.

Highlights: Normal management staff should be a specialist in at least one aspect and an excellent superintendent should be both a specialist in one aspect and a generalist in all the above aspects.

6.9   Contractor's Personnel

High level of management and achievement depends upon use of high quality management staff and technicians. This Sub-Clause shows the demands on the Contractor's Personnel quality, which comprise technical and professional ethics.

The Engineer is entitled to remove any person employed on the Site or Works, including the Contractor's Representative, so that the overall quality of the personnel can be ensured. Typically, the Contractor may readily be persuaded to remove the person, and such removal by agreement is preferable to enforcement under this Sub-Clause.

Meanwhile, in order to prevent the Engineer misusing such entitlement, restrictive conditions of (a), (b) and (c) are specified:

(a) persists in any misconduct or lack of care;

(b) carries out duties incompetently or negligently;

(c) fails to conform with any provisions of the Contract; or

(d) persists in any conduct which is prejudicial to safety, health, or the protection of the environment.

And if the Contractor demonstrates that the opinion of the Engineer was unreasonable and unfounded, the Contractor may be entitled to compensation under applicable law.

6.10   Contractor's Records

In order to facilitate the evaluation of claims and variations, it is necessary to establish basic record-keeping from the commencement of a contract. The providing of the data and details will be greatly helpful for the Employer to know about the project progress.

In practice, the records also provide a good source for both parties to trace up and support their claims if disputes arise. For instance, the Employer may accuse the Contractor of their fault which is proved by such records showing the Contractor's insufficient input of personnel and equipment. The Contractor's claims (for extension of working period) may be rejected on grounds of this.

The data required to be submitted must be included in each of the Contractor's reports, in accordance with Sub-Clause 4.21 (d).

6.11 Disorderly Conduct

The happening of riots during the execution of the Works may add to the complication of project management.

In international projects, it happens frequently for workers to go on strike and the interests of the local staff conflict with that of the foreign staff.

This Sub-Clause specifies that the Contractor has to take responsibility for these events in order to reduce the happening of such riot and preserve the peace near or on the site afterwards.

6.12 Key Personnel

※Vocabulary

1. engagement *n.* 约会;约定
2. feeding *v.* 养;喂;饲养
3. unavoidable *adj.* 不可避免的;无法阻止的
4. precaution *n.* 预防措施;防备
5. epidemics *n.* (疾病的)流行,传播
6. superintendence *n.* 指挥,主管,监督
7. prejudicial *adj.* 有害的;不利的
8. replacement *n.* 替代;替换;取代
9. outstanding *adj.* (款项)未支付的,未结清的
10. riotous *adj.* (行为或事件)狂欢的,喧闹的,放纵的

7 Plant, Materials and Workmanship

7.1 Manner of Execution

This Sub-Clause specifies general requirements in respect of the manner in which the Works are to be executed. More detailed requirements will be derived from other provisions in the Contract.

3 rules are specified to be followed when executing the Works for the Contract:

(1) the first rule requires the Contractor just to follow what's specified in the Contract;

(2) the second is additional to the first one, the recognized good practice will become the standard when no exact construction methods are specified;

(3) the third raises the requirements on the construction manner from the views of safety of the facilities and materials.

The Sub-Paragraph prohibits the use of hazardous materials. In this context, there're different hazardous situations:

Many manufacturing processes are hazardous but do not result in hazardous "Materials" ① Materials must not require the use of hazardous Site procedures. ② Materials must nor be hazardous thereafter, during their working life or during any subsequent procedures for their demolition and disposal.

Under CONS, the Engineer is not empowered to relax this provision of the Contract. If he consents to the use of Materials which are subsequently found to be hazardous, the Contractor will have to replace the Materials.

7.2　Samples

This Sub-Clause specifies that the Contractor has to submit to the Engineer samples of Materials prior to using the materials in the Works (Figure 6.11).

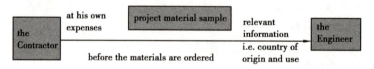

Figure 6.11

7.3　Inspection

Inspection is one of the ways of quality control. And the Contract specifies the Contractor is obliged to give the Employer's Personnel full opportunity to inspect and tests (Figure 6.12).

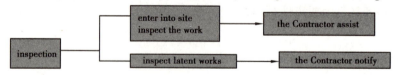

Figure 6.12

This Sub-Clause comprises two parts: the first part specifies that the Employer's Personnel are to be given all reasonable access to inspect and test materials and workmanship and the Contractor is obliged to assist the Employer's Personnel to carry out these inspection and test. The second part lists the procedure to examine the Works, including the procedure of packaging, storage and check-up before transportation.

This Sub-Clause states that "the Engineer shall then either carry out the examination, inspection, measurement or testing without unreasonable delay", but no specific time limits are specifies. It should be considered to give a specific time limit to redefine an "unreasonable delay" in the Particular Condition.

In practice, when large bulk of cement is required, the Contractor will claim on relevant data of the cement directly from the manufacturer according to the Specification and design requirements.

After acquiring the technical data, the Contractor will submit them to the Engineer asking for their consent before he gives the order to the manufacturer, so as to avoid the dilemma that the Engineer refuses to use the purchased Materials.

Some Contracts specify that certain Plant requires the permits of the Employer before orders are given and can only be purchased from the suppliers who are on the list approved by the Employer.

7.4　Testing by the Contractor

Testing can be classified into 3 types:

(1) testing carries during the execution of the Works;

(2) tests on Completion; and

(3) tests after Completion.

Under CONS, there're only the first two sorts of Tests. Additional tests would be instructed as Variations under Article 13.

7.5　Defects and Rejection

◆ **Discussion:**

How if the testing result doesn't comply with the Contract provisions and the Materials or Workmanship are found to be defective?

The first paragraph applies if, following any of the activities described in Sub-Clause 7.3 or Sub-Clause 7.4, something is found to be defective. The Contractor is then required to remedy the defects and make the thing comply with the Contract.

There're typically two reasons if the Engineer rejects the Works of the Contractor. The first due to the defects of the work itself, for example, cracks are found on the concrete which is made by casting. The other is the failure of keeping in compliance with the Contract though no flaws can be found in the product itself, for instance, the Contract specifies that the origin of the UPS applying to the works shall be France, while the Contractor purchase the UPS from Singapore manufacturer.

In practice, it's possible that the two Parties do not agree with each other as to the testing result because of lack of explicit statement of testing standard. In order to prevent the Engineer from misusing his right, this Sub-Clause requires him to give the reasons when he rejects the works of the Contractor.

Claim clause: Since retesting double the work amount of the Employer and cause him to double pay his personnel, this Sub-Clause specifies that the Employer is entitled to claims for incurred costs. This is a fair decision because retesting is caused by the fault of the Contractor.

7.6　Remedial Work

◆Discussion：

After the Material, the Plant and the workmanship have been tested and approved, shall the Engineer withdraw from further issuing any instruction?

This Sub-Clause consists of two parts：Firstly, the Engineer is empowered to issue instructions. Secondly, which Party shall pay the costs.

Regardless of the previous approval to the completed work of the Contractor, if the Engineer finds the approval work fails to comply with the contract subsequently, he is allowed to issue instructions, requiring the Contractor to replace any Plant or Materials or re-execute the Works. It's a typical provision that the approval of the Engineer won't relieve the Contractor from any obligations under the Contract, which ultimately are to provide to the Employer Works in compliance with the Contract.

◆Discussion：

Does the Supervision Engineer have the right to direct the Contractor to perform remedial work at any time? Or is there no time limit for the Supervision Engineer's instructions?

At any time prior to the issuance of the project handover certificate, except for any prior inspection, inspection, metering or testing, or test certificate, or notice of no objection from the Supervising Engineer, the Supervision Engineer can order the Contractor to repair or remedy (if need be, on site), or removed from the scene and replace any not meet the requirements of the contract equipment or materials and return to the project, as well as the implementation of any of the project safety emergency repair work whether it was due to an accident, unforeseen event, or other circumstances. The terms of this Contract give the Supervision Engineer the right to issue instructions and also stipulate that he may issue the project handover certificate at any time prior to the issuance. However, whether caused by the Contractor or not, the Contractor shall act in accordance with the provisions of the Contract.

The Contractor shall, upon receipt of the instructions of the Supervision Engineer, complete the relevant work as soon as possible and no later than the time (if any) specified in the instructions or, in the case of urgent remedial work to the safety of the Works. The Contractor shall comply with the instructions of the Supervision Engineer without delay. All repairs required under this clause shall be at the expense of the Contractor, if caused by the Contractor himself. The Contractor shall be entitled to an extension of the time limit (and) or payment of costs plus profit if the execution of the Works is caused by the act of the Owner or the Owner's personnel and causes delay (and) or costs to be incurred by the Contractor. If it is due to abnormal events, in such cases the provisions concerning abnormal events shall be followed.

In general, the Contractor shall comply with the above instructions of the Supervision Engineer, and if the Contractor fails to comply with the Supervision Engineer's instructions, the Owner may, in his sole discretion, hire and pay others to carry out the Works. Unless the work is not caused by the Contractor, the Contractor shall be entitled to payment from the Owner under this Clause. Otherwise, the Owner shall be entitled to receive payment from the Contractor for any additional expenses incurred by the Contractor under the Contract as a result of the Contractor's fault, without prejudice to any other rights the Owner may have under the Contract or elsewhere. That is to say, the payment hereunder shall not affect the acquisition of any other right to which the Employer is entitled under the Contract.

Therefore, in the case of similar problems, the Contractor should consult the relevant contract documents, and at the same time understand the specific reasons for the occurrence of the incident, and then make a correct judgment according to the relevant provisions of the Contract. During the implementation of the project, as long as the handover certificate has not been issued, the Supervision Engineer has the right to instruct the Contractor to carry out the remedial work at any time. This is the right granted to the Supervision Engineer by the Contract and the obligation of the Contractor as stipulated in the Contract. The Contract also sets out the rights of the Owner in the event that the Contractor fails to fulfil his contractual obligations. That is, the Supervision Engineer may, at any time prior to the issuance of the handover certificate, instruct the Contractor to carry out remedial work.

The FIDIC Red Book 2017 edition gives a clear explanation of the instructions of the Supervision Engineer. According to the understanding of the conditions of the Contract, the Supervision Engineer may issue instructions to the Contractor at any time when necessary for the implementation of the project. The only limitation here is that the execution of remedial work is also necessary for the execution of the Works, so the Supervision Engineer may issue instructions to the Contractor at any time, including the Defect Liability Period, in accordance with the Contract. That is to say, there is no time limit for the Supervision Engineer's instruction before the performance certificate is issued.

7.7 Ownership of Plant and Materials

Typically, it's specified that before the Plant and Materials are installed or consumed in the Works, their ownership belongs to the Employer. The change in ownership occurs as soon as the Contractor is entitled to payment and not when he subsequently receives payment.

Under Sub-paragraph (b), the change in ownership occurs as soon as the Contractor is entitled to payment and not when he subsequently receives payment. While when the change of ownership occurs, the Contractor most probably hasn't been entitled with payment in full and the promised payment might not have been realized. This may be against the applicable law in some countries, thus it's specified that the precondition is "to the extent consistent with the laws of the Country".

7.8　Royalties

The Contractor is typically entitled to use the earth, rock and other natural materials for any earthwork which may be required on the Site, without paying the Employer for these Materials. But if the Contractor needs to obtain Materials outside the Site, he has to negotiate with the owner of the origin place and pay for what he wants.

Sewage treatment station is often built-up inside the Site, and thoughtful treatment methods have been specified in the Contract provisions as to the disposal of materials from demolitions and excavations and of other surplus material, for example, some rubbish must be burnt and some other must be buried. If it's unallowable to dispose the rubbish on the Site, then the Contractor has to dump the rubbish outside, all at his own cost.

※Vocabulary

1. recognized *adj.* 公认的，经过验证的；认可的；普遍接受的
2. apparatus *n.* 器械；器具；仪器；设备
3. additional *adj.* 额外的；附加的；添加的
4. promptly *adv.* 立即；马上；及时
5. workmanship *n.* 工艺；手艺
6. rejection *n.* 拒绝；摒弃；剔除物
7. encumbrance *n.* 拖累；障碍；累赘
8. disposal *n.* （废物等的）丢掉，清理，销毁，处理

8　Commencement, Delay and Suspension

Progress management is a main part of the project management. Time, costs and quality are the criteria to judge whether a project a successful or not. In view of the project progress, factors that are in connection with time management included commencement of work, progress, completion of work, defect notification period and extension of working period. The Sub-Clause 8-11 are all about time management.

8.1　Commencement of Works

The Engineer shall give the Contractor not less than 7 days' notice of the Commencement Date. Commencement of work is an important milestone in the execution of the Works. The Contractor concerns the most about when to commence the work after receiving the Letter of Acceptance.

The notice should be given soon after the Contract becomes legally effective and need only state:

"We hereby give notice, in the term of Sub-Clause 8.1 of the Conditions of Contract, that the commencement Date shall be⋯"

The Contractor will commence the preparation of the Works after he receives the Letter of Acceptance, but will be prevented from making appropriate arrangement if the notification is purposely withheld by the Employer. The idle equipment and personnel will incur costs to the Contractor, thus limitation is set to be "within 42 days after the Contractor receives the Letter of Acceptance".

8.2　Time for Completion

Time for completion means a period of time, which is more often called "working period" in China. The Contractor has to complete all the Works within this period of time, and enable the Works to be able to stand up to the valuation stipulated in the Sub-Clause 10.1 [Taking over of the Works and Sections], and make the Works to be ready for being taken-over by the Employer, unless the Contractor has successfully claimed for extension. If different parts of the Works are required to be completed within different Times for Completion, these parts should be defined as Sections: in the Appendix to Tender under CONS. Precise geographical definitions are advisable, in order to minimize ambiguity regarding each party's responsibility when the Employer take over a Section.

8.3　Programme

Time limits in connection with program are specified (Figure 6.13):

(1) the Contractor shall submit time programme to the Engineer within 28 days after receiving the notice;

(2) the Engineer shall within 21 days after receiving a programme gives notice to the Contractor stating the extent to which it does not comply with the Contract.

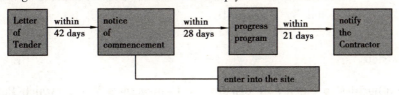

Figure 6.13

Contractor should revise the program whenever the previous program is inconsistent with:

(1) actual progress;

(2) the Contractor's obligation;

(3) his intention.

◆ **Discussion:**

Is any difference between program and contract documents?

No. Program is drafted and submitted by the Contractor to the Engineer after the Contract is signed. And program is more of reference document, the provision of which will be invoked by the

Contractor in execution of Works. It doesn't alter the role of either Party, nor relieve either Party from their responsibility under the Contract.

If the specific date of hand-over of Site is neglected in the Appendix to Tender, then the program provides a reference time schedule for the Employer to make arrangement until the hand-over of the Site to the Contractor.

Besides, it may also work as criteria for the Works of the Engineer, whether to issue instructions or drawings.

◆Discussion:

How if the Contractor fails to submit the program in time?

This Sub-Clause doesn't provide a solution if the Contractor fails to submit it in time. On the whole, the delay of submission of program won't cause a big problem to the Employer. While in order to simulate the Contractor to act properly in submitting program, it's advisable to add one more condition for payment which is that the Employer needn't pay the Contractor before the Contractor submit the program.

8.4　Advance Warning

The three Parties can notify each other of warnings about what may happen in the list.

8.5　Extension of Time for Completion

This Sub-Clause does not include a description list of all events which can give rise to an extension but gives examples (a) to (e).

These events comprise two types:

(1) the delay of time for completion caused by the failure of the Employer;

(2) delays caused by external impediment.

8.6　Delays caused by Authorities

◆Discussion:

If the authorities' act delay or disrupt the Contractor's Work, which Party shall be blamed for?

The disruption of the authority enable the Contractor to claim for extension of time only if the Contractor's claim can be substantiated by his proofs that these requirements listed in this Sub-Clause as (a), (b), (c) are perfectly met.

The execution of the Works is often affected by the public policies and regulations such as the construction noise control in special times imposed by the Department of Environmental. Protection and the pipeline projects control in the free trade districts, etc.

8.7　Rate of Progress

Based on this Sub-Clause the Engineer can control the rate of progress of the Contractor. It's mainly about that under two circumstances the Engineer can require the Contractor to increase the work hours and the number of Contractor's Personnel and Goods at the risk and cost of the Contractor's and pay the Employer his incurred additional costs for the increase of work amount.

Two problems may arise in practice:

(1) How if the Contractor refuses to obey the Engineer's instruction?

It seems that only Sub-Clause 15.2 [Termination for Contractor's Default] will apply to this situation, which may be inapplicable in practice unless the Contractor's progress has fallen far behind the programme and the Employer is unconfident that Contractor can complete the Works in time.

(2) Assume that the Contractor did as the Engineer required, and also raised the Claims for extension of working time but failed to get the approval from the Engineer. If the Contractor finally accomplishes his tasks in time, and succeeds in getting extension of time from the arbitrator, will the Contractor be entitled to claim for reimbursement for the increase of his work amount?

Two solutions: Firstly, the notice from the Engineer can be regarded as a constructive change order, which has altered the original working period, thus claims for compensation can be entitled under the Article 13 [Variations and Adjustments]. Secondly, the final result of time grants proves the Engineer has unreasonably withheld the determinations to grant the Contractor extension of time, which is against the stipulations in Sub-Clause 1.3 and hereby constitutes a breach of Contract. The Employer is deemed to be liable for this.

8.8　Delay Damage

The concept of "Delay damages" is widely accepted in international projects and regarded as reasonable and effective binding mechanism.

They may require the sum to have been calculated as:

(1) a reasonable estimate of the Employer's losses or foregone benefits, which may be equivalent to financing charges for the Contract Price per day; plus

(2) the daily cost of the Employer's Personnel involved in supervising the execution of the Works during the period of prolongation.

For the limit of the delay damage, if it is to be stated, the usual percentage in international contracts generally varies between 5% and 15%.

Damages vary from penalty as stipulated in laws, the amount of the former is equal to the loss the Employer suffers for the default of the Contractor, and the later is means of punishment whose amount is usually mush higher than the real loss. The standard of "delay damages" is determined by the Employer before the Contract is signed as reasonable estimation to the damages, thus may be inconsistent with the actual loss.

If the Employer considers himself to be entitled t be paid delay damages, he is required to give particulars in accordance with Sub-Clause 2.5. Sub-Clause 2.5 concludes by stating that the Employer is not entitled to withhold the amount from payments due to the Contractor, unless and until the procedures described in Sub-Clause 2.5 has been followed.

8.9　Employer's Suspension

It is obvious that certain works must be suspended, for example, because of a flood season. In these obvious cases, it is the Contractor who is at risk if he persists in executing work which should obviously be suspended.

If and to the extent that the Cause is notified and is the responsibility of the Contractor, the following Sub-Clause 8.9—Sub-Clause 8.11 shall not apply, otherwise, you can find the entitlement of the Contractor to be compensated in these three Sub-Clauses.

8.10　Consequences of Employer's Suspension

(1)The procedure to deal with a suspension

Firstly, he gives notice under CONS. Although no time limit prescribed for him to give the notice, he should do so as soon as possible after he receives the instruction to suspend. The Contractor's entitlement for claims have been clarified and what remains is to determine the costs incurred during the suspension period, due to the idle equipment and personnel and on site overheads.

(2)The way of calculating the incurred costs during the suspension period

The Employer normally won't agree to pay full working rates because both of the equipment and personnel are just stand-by. For example, in a negotiation both parties finally agreed on a rate which is 70% of the Unit Contract Price.

8.11　Payment for Plant and Materials in Event of Suspension

If the Works is under normal progress, the only entitlement of payment of Plant and Materials would be under the Article 14 and the payment would follow the normal procedures stated therein. But the suspension of work may affect the procurement of Plant and Materials. For a suspension which is not due to the Contractor's shortcomings, he becomes entitled to payment for the suspended Plant and Materials after 28 days, if he takes the necessary actions for them to become the Employer's property.

8.12　Prolonged Suspension

◆Discussion：

In case the Contractor is unwilling to wait, will he be entitled to take further actions?

This Sub-Clause tends to protect the benefits of the Contractor because though entitlement of Claims is granted, excessive delay may foil the plan of the company and cause him some problems. So the Contractor can make choice from the options provided in this Sub-Clause by either omitting the affected part of the Works or terminating the whole Works.

8.13　Resumption of Work

If the Contractor didn't choose to omit part of the work nor terminate the whole Works, then the resumption of work has to follow the procedures specified in this Sub-Clause.

This Sub-Clause requires a joint examination on the Works before the resumption of works starts and the Contractor has to make good any deterioration or defect in or loss of the Works.

※Vocabulary

1. commencement *n.* 开始
2. take-over 接管,接收
3. inconsistent *adj.* 不能始终如一的;时好时坏的
4. anticipate *v.* 预期;预料;预计
5. proposal *n.* 提议;建议;提案
6. disruption *n.* 中断;扰乱;混乱
7. fall behind 落后;下降;退后;逾期(付款等)
8. faulty *adj.* (设备等)有问题的,有毛病的,出故障的
9. suspension *n.* 暂停;延缓
10. jointly *adv.* 共同地,联合地,连带地
11. deterioration *n.* 恶化;变坏;退化;堕落

9　Tests on Completion

Article 9 is intended to be applicable to any type of tests which the Contractor is required to carry out at completion, before the Taking-Over procedures described in Article 10.

9.1　Contractor's Obligations

This Sub-Clause specifies the Contractor's obligations when carrying out tests on completion, the preconditions of tests, the particular circumstances he needs to make allowance for, etc (Figure 6.14).

The tests on Completion are the tests which are required by the Employer in order to determine whether the Works (or a section, if any) have reached the stage at which the Employer should take over the Works or Section. Tests on Completion must be specified in detail in CONS' Specification.

It's specified at the beginning of this Sub-Clause that the Contractor needs to provide the documents in accordance with Sub-Paragraph (d) of Sub-Clause 4.1 [Contractor's General Obligations].

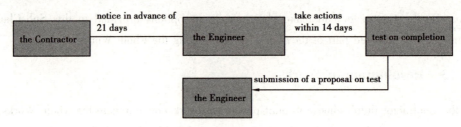

Figure 6. 14

◆ **Discussion**：

What kind of the documents are these？

They're the Contractor's Documents. Please refer to the definition of 1. 1. 6. 1. "Contractor's Documents" means the calculations, computer programs and other software, drawings, manuals, models and other documents of a technical nature (if any) supplied by the Contractor under the Contract.

9. 2 Delayed Tests

This provision deals with two situations separately：Firstly, it's the default of the Employer；the other, default of the Contractor.

(1) If the Tests on Completion are delayed by the Employer, the immediate effect is the applicability of Sub-Clause 7. 4 (the fifth paragraph, the Contractor can claim according to Sub-Clause 20. 1).

(2) If the delay is excessive, Sub-Clause 10. 3 becomes applicable, which entitles the Contractor to compensations for carrying out Tests on Completion during the Defects Notification Period.

(3) If the Tests on Completion is delayed by the Contractor, The Employer's Personnel can make their own arrangements to carry out the tests at the risk and cost of the Contractor. The Contractor should first be given the opportunity to rectify his default. If Tests are thereafter carried out by the Employer's Personnel, the Contractor is required to accept the results of the Tests, although he is not entitled to receive a report.

9. 3 Retesting

If the Engineer requires this Plant, Materials or workmanship to be retested, the tests shall be repeated under the same terms and conditions. If the rejection and retesting cause the Employer to incur additional costs, the Contractor shall subject to Sub-Clause 2. 5 Employer's Claims pay these costs to the Employer.

If tests are repeated after the cause of previous failures has been remedies, and it seems likely that other related work may have been affected by the remedied work, that other work may therefore need to be retested.

9.4　Failure to Pass Tests on Completion

This Sub-Clause provides three solutions if the Works or a Section fails to pass the Tests on Completion repeated under Sub-Clause 9.3, the Engineer shall be entitled to:

(a) order further repetition of Tests on Completion under Sub-Clause 9.3;

(b) if the failure deprives the Employer of substantially the whole benefit of the Works or Section, reject the Works or Section (as the case may be), in which event the Employer shall have the same remedies as are provided in sub-paragraph (c) of Sub-Clause 11.4 [Failure to Remedy Defects]; or

(c) issue a Taking-Over Certificate, if the Employer so requests.

There's no limit on the number of repetition which may be ordered. And if the Contractor cannot carry out the remedial Works, the Employer may apply Article 15 or seek agreement to a reduction in the Contract Price. Typically, he might first indicate the reduction he would require, and seek the Contractor's agreement prior to the issue of a Taking-over Certificate. If the agreement cannot be reached prior to the issue of the Taking-Over Certificate under Sub-Paragraph (c), then Sub-Clause (a) or (b) could be applied (Figure 6.15).

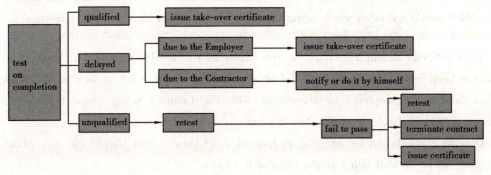

Figure 6.15

※**Vocabulary**

1. allowance *n.* (定期发给的)津贴,补助

2. repetition *n.* (常指令人不快的事件的)反复发生,重复出现,重演

10　Employer's Taking Over

10.1　Taking Over the Works and Sections

Except as stated in Sub-Clause 9.4 [Failure to Pass Tests on Completion], the Works shall be taken over by the Employer when (Figure 6.16):

(1) the Works have been completed inaccordance with the Contract, including the matters described in Sub-Clause 8.2 [Time for Completion] and except as allowed in Sub-Paragraph (a)

below; and

(2) a Taking-Over Certificate for the Works has been issued, or is deemed to have been issued in accordance with this Sub-Clause.

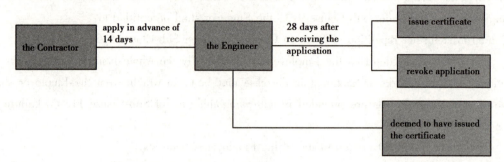

Figure 6.16

Sample form of Taking-over Certificate for the Works

Having received your notice under Sub-clause 10.1 of the Conditions of Contract, we hereby certify that the Works were completed in accordance with the Contract on _____ (date), except for minor outstanding work and defects (which include those listed in the attached Snagging List and) which should not substantially affect the use of the Works for their intended purpose.

The Contractor should learn from the Sub-Clause that he needn't wait until all the outstanding works has been finished to apply for a Taking-Over Certificate, but act as soon as the Works or Section have been completed in accordance with the Contract being aware that the minor outstanding work and defects won't affect the use of the Works or Section.

Drawing a conclusion by referring to both of the Clause 9 and Clause 10, the whole test procedure can be divided into 8 stages (Figure 6.17):

(1) Preparation for Tests on Completion;

(2) Applying for Tests on Completion;

(3) Submitting documents;

(4) Tests on Completion;

(5) Tests on Completion completed;

(6) Applying for Taking-over Certificate;

(7) Issuing of Taking-over Certificate;

(8) Taking-over by the Employer.

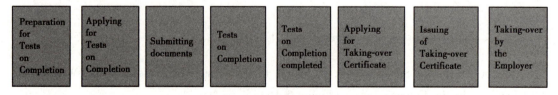

Figure 6.17

10.2　Taking Over Parts

This Sub-Clause grants the Employer's right of taking over any part once it has been completed. Because most of these decisions of taking-over are made without notifying the Contractor at advance, the Contractor's arrangements of work may be affected. Under this circumstance, the Contractor is entitled to payment of any such Cost plus reasonable profit.

It's possible that the Employer may use any part of the Works before the Taking-Over Certificate is issued. It's specified that the part which is used shall be deemed to have been taken over by the Employer, and the Engineer shall grant the Contractor opportunity to carry out the tests on completion on this part, and the tests shall be done within the Defects Notification Period.

10.3　Interference with Tests on Completion

Typically, the Tests on Completion are the events which immediately precede completion and taking over. It is therefore reasonable that if such tests are prevented by the Employer, he becomes responsible for the relevant Works or Section instead of just the part.

When the first sentence mentions 14 days, it doesn't indicate which day is the beginning of the 14 days period. But as shown in the context, it should be the 14days following the date when the Contractor is fully prepared to carry out tests. For example, if the Contractor gives the notice that he will be ready for tests after the 1st of August, then the test on completion should be carried out before the 15th of August. The specific date or dates should be included in the instructions given by the Engineer, otherwise the Contractor will be entitled to extension of time or costs plus profit.

10.4　Surface Requiring Reinstatement

This Sub-Clause specifies that a certificate shall not be deemed to certify completing of any ground or other surfaces requiring reinstatement, but depend upon whether it has been stated in the Taking-Over Certificate. If not, this work shall be regarded as part of the outstanding work to be completed by the Contractor during the Defects Notification Period.

While this Sub-Clause covers only a Section or part of the Works, which may lead to misunderstanding that if the certificate is about the whole Works, then it shall be deemed to certify the completion of the grounds or surfaces requiring reinstatement even if they're not stated in the Taking-Over Certificate. Which is obviously not the truth. Thus it's advisable to modify the relevant sentence and change it into "a certificate for a Section or part of the Works or the whole Works".

※Vocabulary

1. deem *v.* 认为;视为;相信

2. substantially *adv.* 非常地；巨大地

3. cease *v.* 停止；终止

4. remainder *n.* 剩余部分；剩余物；余下的人（或物）

5. interference *n.* 干涉；干预；介入

6. reinstatement *n.* （法律、做法等的）恢复；（设施等的）修复

11　Defects after Taking Over

11.1　Completion of Outstanding Work and Remedying Defects

◆Discussion：

Which day is the beginning of the defects notification period?

Please refer to the definition 1.1.27 of the Defects Notification Period and see which day is the commencement date of this period. It's the period specified in the Contract for notifying defects, calculated from the date which the Works (or, possibly, a Section) are completed and taken over.

◆Discussion：

Does the Works to be implemented during the defects notification period refer only to defects remedying?

Under Sub-Clause 10.1, the Contractor is entitled to a Taking-Over Certificate notwithstanding that some works, namely outstanding works, may still be incomplete. This Sub-Clause stipulates that except for the responsibility to remedy defects or damage before the expiry date of the Defects Notification Period, the Contractor also has to complete the works which is outstanding within such reasonable time.

As to the scope of the "outstanding works" and to what extent shall the defects be remedied, they shall be subjected to the conditions required by the Contractor It is desirable for there to be a joint inspection of the Works or Section, which should be conducted a few days before the expiry of the Defects Notification Period and should be attended by representatives of the Parties and the Engineer.

The Employer is also obliged to notify the Contractor if a defect appears or damage occurs but not remedy by himself, unless he has demonstrable grounds for believing that the Contractor would fail to carry out the Works with the necessary skill and care.

11.2　Cost of Remedying Defects

The defects of the Works can either be caused by the Contractor or some other reasons. If it is attributable to the Contractor, he will have to pay the costs and take corresponding risks, otherwise, it's the Employer who shall take the responsibilities.

◆**Discussion**:

Have you found any problems with this statement?

As stated in the text, it's the Employer who shall notify the Contractor if it's found to be of other reasons, and the Employer may justifiably refuse to give the notice if such an action will incur costs to himself.

11.3   Extension of Defects Notification Period

The circumstances stated in the first paragraph may have occurred before or after taking-over, and may have been due to the Contractor's shortcomings. If the Contractor is not responsible for the defect or demands, the remedial work would constitute a Variation and entitle the Contractor to additional payment, including compensation for the extension of the Defects Notification Period. If it's not due to the Contractor's shortcomings, the Employer will be entitled to extend the Defects Notification Period but no more than 2 years.

And if a defect prevents the Works, Section or a major item of Plant being operated for a certain number of days, the Employer is entitled to require the Defects Notification Period to be extended by that number of days.

11.4   Failure to Remedy Defects

Before the Employer takes use any of the three suggested measures, he must make sure:

(1) give an advance notice to the Contractor about the date on or by which the defect or damage is to be remedied and the date should be prescribed to be within a reasonable period of time.

(2) the defects are due to the Contractor's shortcoming.

What constitutes "reasonable" must depend on such factors such as the proximity of the Site to the Contractor's equipment and personnel, the delivery period for replacement Plant and the operational status of the Works.

11.5   Remedying of Defective Work off Site

Some defects may not be suitable to be remedied on site or will incur high costs, for example, the defects in some large equipment. Under such circumstance, it's recommended for the equipment to be demolished and sent to the manufacturer to be fixed—the remedial work is necessary to be carried out off the Site.

The Employer can't withhold the consent unreasonably but may impose reasonable conditions, for instance, requiring the Contractor either to increase the amount of the Performance Security or to provide another form of security. The requirements may do the Employer good, but will unavoidably incur costs to the Contractor. Therefore, the Contractor can benefit from his reputation, a reflection of "credit value" in commercial society.

11.6　Further Tests after Remedying Defects

If repetition of tests is instructed by the Engineer, the Contractor must carry out such work. If the Contractor refuses to carry out the tests, the Employer can refer to Sub-Clause 9.2 [Delayed Tests] to protect his own benefits.

And if the Contractor considers none of the Sub-Paragraph of Sub-Clause 11.2 applies and that he is therefore entitled to be paid for repeating a test, he should promptly respond to the instruction by giving notice and detailed particulars of his claims in accordance with the procedure specified in Sub-Clause 20.1. And the Employer can extend the Defects Notification Period by referring to the Sub-Clause 11.3 [Extension of Defects Notification Period] in such case in order to protect himself.

11.7　Right of Access after Taking Over

The Contractor needs to obtain the right access in order to remedy defects or carry out necessary examination work during the Defects Notification Period.

This Sub-Clause is a comprehensive provision, taking into consideration both of the needs for the Contractor to carry out the remedial work and the needs of security of the Employer since some projects are of high confidentiality.

The 2017 FIDIC Red Book also acknowledges that the Contractor may enter the Right of Way within the Defector Notification Period. However, if the Contractor plans to enter, the Contractor shall notify the Owner in advance, stating the part of the entry, the reason for the entry, and the date of the entry, taking into account the relevant circumstances and the Owner's safety requirements. After the Contractor gives notice, does it mean that the right of way can be entered on the planned date? The answer is no. It shall wait for the consent of the Owner. According to the provisions of the Contract, the Owner shall notify the Contractor within 7 days upon receipt of the Contractor's notice and agree to the Contractor's request. Or suggest other reasonable dates and give reasons. If the Owner fails to give the Contractor such notice within 7 days, he shall be deemed to have agreed to the Contractor's access to the right of way on the date planned by the Owner. That is to say, after the project is handed over to the Owner, the Contractor enters the right of way again and needs to obtain the consent of the Owner.

Obviously, according to the FIDIC Red Book 2017, the Contractor may enter the Right of Way within the Defects Notification Period, but only with the consent of the Owner. The reader may ask that the project is not finally transferred to the Owner, I can enter the right of way whenever I want, that is my right, why do I need the consent of the Owner. Here, the reader should be aware of the fact that after the project is transferred to the Owner, the custodianship of the project is also transferred to the Owner, that is, the Contractor is no longer responsible for the custodianship of the project. This is in line with the legal provisions, the project is the property of the Owner, the Owner can not let you go in and out of his property scope. Such provisions of the

Contract are actually in the protection of the Contractor, if the Contractors enter into the scope of the right of way, a part of the project appears damaged. It's convenient according to the Contract provisions to judge the attribution of responsibility.

With respect to this additional claim point in the 2017 FIDIC Red Book, the Contractor has requested access to the right of way and has incurred additional costs due to the delay of the Owner, and the Contractor may make a cost plus profit claim pursuant to Sub-Clause 20.2. This is a new claim point, since it is a claim point, the Contractor should deal with it in accordance with the Contract. In such case, the same as the general claim procedure, the notice of claim should be issued, and the corresponding record should be made, and the detailed claim report should be submitted according to the Contract. I think this is one of the reasons why the Contract requires notice to be sent to the Owner.

In addition, part of the construction of the project is with timeliness. If the Contractor can deal with it in time, it may not only benefit the Owner, but also reduce the investment of the Contractor. If this advantage is lost due to the reason of the Owner, the Contractor will incur additional costs, which should be borne by the Owner.

11.8 Contractor to Search

Because the Contractor is the executant of the Works, if any thing wrong occurs to the Works, the Employer may wish the Contractor to conduct the research for the cause.

Since the result of search relates to the liability of both Parties, thus it's required that the Contractor has to conduct the research under the guidance of the Engineer, so as to ensure the objectiveness of the research.

Unless the defect is to be remedied at the cost of the Contractor under Sub-Clause 11.2 [Cost of Remedying Defects], the Cost of the search plus reasonable profit shall be agreed or determined by the Engineer in accordance with Sub-Clause 3.5 [Engineer's Instructions] and shall be included in the Contract Price.

The remedying work are divided into two types under Sub-Clause 11.2 [Cost of Remedying Defects], if and to the extent that the work is attributable to:

(1) any design for which the Contractor is responsible;

(2) Plant, Materials or workmanship not being in accordance with the Contract; or

(3) failure by the Contractor to comply with any other obligation.

They shall be executed at the risk and cost of the Contractor, otherwise, they shall be borne by the Employer.

11.9 Performance Certificate

The Performance Certificate provides written confirmation that the Engineer:

(1) considers that the Contractor has completed his performance of obligations under the Contract; and

(2)accepts the Works.

The Performance Certificate should be issued within 28 days after the latest of the expiry of the Defects Notification Periods, unless the Contractor is then known to have outstanding obligations. For example, these obligations include further Contractor's Documents to be supplied, tests to be passed, searched to be completed, and defects to be remedied. In this case, the Performance Certificate should be issued as soon thereafter as the Contractor has supplied all the Contractor's Documents and completed and tested all the Works. It may be difficult to establish how soon is "as soon as", but normally it won't exceed the limit of 28 days after the Contractor has completed all the outstanding Works.

For example, these obligations include further Contractor's Documents to be supplied, tests to be passed, searched to be completed, and defects to be remedied.

◆ **Discussion**:

How if the Performance Certificate is delayed or withheld by the Engineer after the Contractor has completed all of his obligations?

Because issue of Performance Certificate is associated with the refund of retention money and return of Performance Security, if it's delayed or withheld, the Contractor's interests may be damaged. In such a case, the Contractor is advised to invoke Sub-Clause 1.3 [Notices and Other Communications] "certificates, consents and determinations shall not be unreasonably withheld or delayed".

11.10 Unfulfilled Obligations

It's most probably that when the Performance Certificate is issued, both Parties still have unfulfilled obligations such as:

(1)the Employer still have not made all the payments due under the Contract;

(2)the Employer still have not released all the Performance Security;

(3)the Works do not comply with the Contract (e.g. because of latent defects);

(4)the Contractor applies for the Final Payment Certificate;

(5)the Engineer issues the Final Payment Certificate;

(6)disputes get to be solved;

(7)the site needs to be cleared.

11.11 Clearance of Site

The Contractor may retain on the Site reasonable amount of Plant and Materials in order to complete the outstanding obligation and remedy defects during the Defects Notification Period. But upon receiving the Performance Certificate, the Contractor has to remove any remaining Contractor's Equipment, surplus materials, wreckage, rubbish and Temporary Works from the

Site.

This Sub-Clause specifies that the Contractor has to clear the Site within 28 days after receiving the Performance Certificate in prevent of the Contractor's long term take-up of the Site, otherwise the Employer is entitled to dispose of any remaining items.

※Vocabulary

1. removal *n.* 消除；去除
2. attributable *adj.* 可归因于……的，可归结于……的
3. suspension *n.* 暂停；延缓
4. expire *v.* 到期；期满；失效
5. dispose *v.* 处理，处置；安排
6. restore *v.* 使恢复；使康复；使复原

12 Measurement and Valuation

Article 12 is based upon the principle that the Works are to be valued by measuring the quantity of each item of work under Sub-Clause 12.2 and applying the appropriate rate per unit or the appropriate lump-sum price under Sub-Clause 12.3.

12.1 Works to be Measured

This Sub-Clause provides two sorts of measurements. The first is to conduct on-site measurements which are supposed to be done by a join activity by the representative of the Contractor and the Engineer. The second is to measure the items from records. It's the Engineer who should prepare the records.

FIDIC Contract is unit price contract, which emphasizes on the separation of quantity and price, so to speak, the quantity can vary but the unit price remains unchanged. As specified in the "Notice to Tender", the unit price weights against other factors.

If the unit price in B. Q. contradicts with the total price, it's the unit price should be subjected to. If unit price figures contradict with description, description words should be subjected to.

From this Sub-Clause we can see that all the payments are actually calculated based on the measured quantity of work. Thus the Contract under such a calculation mode can be called "unit price contract after remeasurement".

The "Schedules" are defined as including a "Bill of Quantities", which is also called Price Sheet in tendering documents. It's the base on which the tendering prices are calculated.

B. Q generally consists of several items and sub-items for users to look up. For instance, in real estate project, these items are grouped according to processes, including clearance of Site, excavation, concrete process, brickwork process, bitumen process, carpenter process, join pointing process, steel structure, drainage pipe, plaster process, water and electricity, painting, internal decoration and fence, etc.

A capable contractor can often find the gaps between the B. Q. and actual work, and eventually gain more than what has been stated in the Contract. While under such particular circumstances when the offered price is even lower than the cost, the work will remain no longer profitable, because the more you do, the more you lose.

12.2　Method of Measurement

The method of measurement may comprise:

(1) three basic methods including unit price, lump-sum, cost-plus;

(2) a publication which specifies principles of measurement and which is incorporated into the Bill of Quantities; or

(3) for a contract which does not contain many or complex items of work, principles included in each of the item description in the Bill of Quantity.

12.3　Evaluation of the Works

This Sub-Clause is comprised by three parts: Firstly, under normal circumstances, Contract Price is agreed or determined by evaluating each item of work, applying the measurement agreed or determined in accordance with the above Sub-Clause 12. 1 and Sub-Clause 12. 2 and the appropriate rate or price for the item. Secondly, if the measured quantity has changed too much comparing with the quantity stated in the B. Q, the rate or price need to be adjusted. Thirdly, if the Works is instructed under Article 13, a new rate or price should also be considered.

Sub-paragraph (a) specifies four criteria which are applicable without reference to Article 13, and a new rate shall only be appropriate if all four criteria are satisfied. The first two criteria relate to change in quantity, the third criterion relates to its effect on Cost, and the fourth criterion allows adjustment of some items to be precluded.

One of four criteria is that the Cost actually incurred divided by the measured quantity must be less than 99% or more than 101% of the what the Cost would have been divided by the quantity stated in the B. Q. , while in practice, the Contractor and the Engineer's opinions may diverge as to the calculation of the Cost per unit quantity. What is advisable is that the Contractor shall present the reasons why he think the rate should be increased, and the Engineer shall give out proofs confirming why he think the rate should be reduced and put them on table to discuss. Before two Parties come to an agreement, the Engineer shall determine a provisional rate or price for the purpose of Interim Payment Certificate. What if we don't agree with the unit price decided by the Supervision Engineer? Then, within 28 days after receiving the decision of the Supervision Engineer, either Party can send a notice of dissatisfaction according to the terms of the Contract, and submit the issue to DAAB for adjudication, or even arbitration.

12.4　Omissions

The Contractor is entitled to compensation for the costs reasonably incurred in the expectation of carrying out work subsequently omitted under the Variation.

Case 1: If the Contractor has ordered formwork for work which was subsequently omitted by Variation, the Accepted Contract Amount would typically have included direct cost plus profit in respect of this formwork. The Contractor would then be entitled to recover cost and profit.

Case 2: When some work has been omitted, relevant payment will subsequently be deducted from the Contract, while the overheads occurred in the headquarters office or during on-site work won't diminish, and this will incur cost to the Contractor. So the Contractor shall be able to claim back the sum of money by invoking this Sub-Clause.

※Vocabulary

1. assert *v.* 坚称;断言;坚决表明
2. derive *v.* 获得;取得;得到
3. omission *n.* 省略的东西;删节的东西;遗漏的东西
4. measurement *n.* (质量、价值或影响的)衡量,评估,估量

13　Variations and Adjustments

Variations can be initiated in any of three ways:

(1)The Variation may be instructed without prior agreement as to feasibility or price, which may be appropriate for urgent work.

(2)The Contractor may initiate his own proposals, which may be approved as a Variation, or he may be given other instructions which constitute a Variation.

(3)A proposal may be requested, in an endeavor to reach prior agreement on its effect and thereby minimize dispute.

13.1　Right to Vary

Variations may be initiated by the Engineer at any time prior to issuing the Taking-Over Certificate for the Works, either by an instruction or by a request for the Contractor to submit a proposal.

However, under the following circumstances, the Contractor may refuse to implement the variation order issued by the Supervision Engineer, that is, the scope and nature of the change Works are different from the Works under construction and the Contractor cannot foresee it; the goods required for the implementation of the Variation Order are not immediately available to the Contractor; Variation orders that adversely affect the Contractor's health, safety and environmental obligations. In case of the above, the Contractor shall immediately notify the Supervision Engineer and explain in detail the reasons why the change order cannot be carried out. Therefore, not all variations are required to be implemented by the Contractor. Upon receipt of the relevant notice from the Contractor, the Supervision Engineer shall immediately confirm, cancel or change the variation order, which means that the variation order issued can be canceled or changed.

This Sub-Clause states that "The Contactor shall execute and be bound by each Variation, unless the Contractor promptly gives notice to the Engineer stating the reason with supporting particulars. Upon receiving the notice, the Engineer shall cancel, confirm or vary the instruction. " And we can further derive that if the Engineer insists on the instruction to Variation under this circumstance, the notice and particulars given by the Contractor will provide reliable proofs for him to claim for compensation or extension subsequently, showing that to carry out the Variation is rather difficult due to the reason stated above. Thus the Engineer shall take into allowance in his determinations of the "degree of difficulties" of the Works.

As for the content of the variation order issued by the Supervision Engineer, we can also refer to Sub-Clause 13. 1. After reading, we can find that the Supervision Engineer cannot issue a variation order, delete part of the Contract Works, and then ask the Owner to carry out the change order by himself or give it to others. On this point, if the Supervision Engineer deletes part of the project in the Contract, then, the Supervision Engineer's behavior already belongs to the modification of the Contract, which is not allowed in the Contract, and the Supervision engineer has no such right. The Contract seriously states that the Supervision Engineer shall not modify the Contract unless agreed by the Owner and the Contractor. In other words, if the Owner and the Contractor agree to delete a part of the Contract, the Supervision Engineer can issue a variation order with mutual approval.

Finally, although the Contract does not give the Contractor the right to change the Contract, the Contract does give the Contractor the right to provide the proposal. If the Contractor considers that any part of the Works can be optimized, the Contractor may, at his own expense, prepare the relevant proposals and then submit them to the Supervision Engineer. After receiving the scheme, the supervision project shall review the Contractor's scheme in accordance with the contract procedure, during which the Contractor shall not delay the progress of the project implementation. If the Supervision Engineer agrees to the proposal provided by the Contractor, he shall issue a variation order to the Contractor in accordance with the Contract and shall also consider sharing the costs, benefits, (and) or delays between the Contractor and the Owner in accordance with the Contract. If the Supervision Engineer does not agree, the related expenses shall be borne by the Contractor. Obviously, the Contractor can submit the proposal and make the change, and at the same time, the Contractor gets paid for it.

13. 2　Value Engineering

"Value Engineering" is a new concept in engineering economics, with its focus on how to optimize the function per unit of costs, thus to maximize the output of capital, this Sub-Clause introduces the use of this term. Since engineering projects involve large amount of capital, optimized design and execution schemes will result in huge profits. This Clause is often invoked in the new-edition engineering contracts in recent years in order to stimulate the Contractor to propose improved methods that will benefit both Parties.

Because the Contractor is the executant of the project and familiar with the actual situation of the project, he will often propose ideas to accelerate completion or reduce costs based on his rich experience. The Contractor may wish to propose changes in the following situations:

(1) The proposal may appear to be of benefit to the Contractor, in which case he may offer a reduction in the Contract Price in order to encourage the Employer's acceptance.

(2) The proposal may appear to be of benefit to the Employer, by improving the quality of the Works (by reducing the cost of maintenance or operation, or improving productivity or efficiency). This might involve an increase in the Cost, and thus in the Contract Price.

CONS 13.2 concludes with Sub-Paragraphs covering the possibility that the value engineering proposal may involve a change in the Employer's (or Engineer's) design of the Permanent Works. Problems may sometimes arise in these situations usually because the Parties failed to agree aspects such as design liability. They are entitled to agree what they wish, but the Sub-Paragraphs define the position if they fail to reach and record their agreement.

13.3 Variation Procedure

The variations are issued by the Supervision Engineer according to the Contract. In summary, there are two types of variations, namely the variation order directly issued by the Supervision Engineer and the variations proposed by the Contractor. Firstly, let's talk about the variation order issued by the Supervision Engineer. During the implementation of the project, the Supervision Engineer may issue the variation order to the Contractor in accordance with Sub-Clause 3.5. Unless it cannot be implemented according to the Contract, the Contractor shall submit a detailed explanation to the Supervision Engineer within 28 days after receiving the Supervision Engineer's instruction. The content of this description includes the resources and construction plan to implement the variation Works; to implement the construction plan of the alteration Works; and the Contractor's plan for the implementation period and cost of the alteration Works. In the event that the Contractor and the Owner agree to delete any part of the Contract Works to be carried out by another person, the Contractor's plan shall also include loss of profits, other losses and damages to the Contractor as a result thereof.

After receiving the above information from the Contractor, the Supervision Engineer shall make a decision to adjust the construction period and contract price according to the Contract, and the decision shall be completed within the time specified in the Contract. The Contractor shall have the right to adjust the time limit and contract price after the supervision of the Works has issued a change order, and this right shall not be exercised according to the terms of the Claim. After the project starts, the Contractor shall submit to the Supervision Engineer overall construction plan of the project, including related resources input, and the plan does not include implementation of variation order. So, after change by the Supervision Engineer, the Contractor needs to arrange the construction resources, the construction methods and construction plan. This will affect the overall implementation of the project and investment, so the Contractor needs extra time and cost.

The second is the proposal of the Contractor. Although the Contractor has no right to make any changes, the Supervision Engineer can ask the Contractor to submit a plan for reference before issuing the variation order. If the Supervision Engineer has such requirements, the Contractor can submit relevant information to the Supervision Engineer according to the above content. If the Contractor is unable to implement the variation order, the Contractor shall provide the Supervisor with a detailed explanation of why the variation order cannot be implemented, and the Supervision Engineer shall consider canceling or altering the variation order.

It states that "The Engineer shall, as soon as practicable after receiving such proposal, respond with approval, disapproval or comments." Hereby three sorts of consequences after the Engineer review the proposal may happen:

(1) The Engineer comments on the proposal of the Contractor as being unreasonable and requires the Contractor to modify it.

(2) The Engineer thinks the proposal is reasonable but still shows disapproval due to unaffordable costs.

(3) The Engineer thinks the proposal is reasonable and incurred costs are acceptable, thus he shows approval and instructs it as a Variation to the Contractor. In this situation, the Engineer will grant the Contractor reimbursement of costs and extension time based in the proposal.

◆ **Discussion**:

This Sub-Clause states that he Engineer can show reject the proposal, so can the Contractor claim for reimbursement costs for drafting the proposal?

In this new edition, it's clearly stated that the Contractor can be entitled for such Cost subject to Sub-Clause 20.2.

◆ **Discussion**:

What should we do if the construction period and cost determined by the Supervision Engineer differ greatly from the Contractor's plan?

We can first negotiate with the Owner according to Article 3.7 of the Contract, if no agreement can be reached, the notice of dissatisfaction should be given within the specified time and then referred to the DAAB for adjudication.

13.4 Provisional Sums

Provisional Sums are determined in different ways: they can be either prescribed in the tendering documents by the Employer and then added into the tendering price by the Contractor; or to be filled by the Contractor before they constitute part of the Contract Price. This depends upon decision strategy. Considering the percentage they account for, they won't exert much influence on the Contract Price.

At their sole judgment, the Contractor can decide on the amount of the Provisional Sums, higher when they make allowance for the likelihood of the happening of the work relates to the provisional sums, and lower when they consider the relevant work are less likely to happen, since this will help to reduce the tendering price and make it more competent.

Under CONS, Provisional Sums are often included in the Bill of Quantities for parts of the Works which are not required to be priced at the risk of the Contractor. For example, Provisional Sums may be appropriate for any Materials which the Engineer is to select, or for any uncertain parts of the Works. Such arrangements provide considerable flexibility, because the Works may be executed by a nominated Subcontractor or by the Contractor and valued under Article 12 or on a cost-plus basis.

What should the Contractor do after receiving the Supervision Engineer's instruction? In this regard, there are also clear provisions in the FIDIC 2017 Red Book. In the case of the Works to be carried out, the Subcontractor carrying out the Works shall be asked for a quotation. In the case of the supply of equipment, materials, engineering or services, the supplier should be asked for a quote. On offer, the Contractor shall provide detailed written requirements to the Subcontractor or Supplier in accordance with the provisions of the Contract. Upon receipt of the quotation, the Contractor shall submit it to the Supervision Engineer who shall give notice instructing the Contractor to accept one of the quotations or reject all of them. However, the Contractor shall have the right to choose any of the quotations if the Supervision Engineer does not reply within 7 days.

Why do Provisional Sums do through so many procedures? We know from the name of the provisional payment that the so-called provisional payment is only a temporary amount stipulated by the Owner, which may or may not be used. Since it is the property of the Owner, if the Owner is a government department, the use of any amount should be implemented in accordance with the provisions of the state, otherwise it is illegal. Even if the Owner is a private business, he or she wants to use his or her assets in the right way, to do the same thing for the least amount of money. In addition, this procedure stipulated in the Contract can ensure that the use of the provisional funds is transparent and open, so as to protect the interests of the proprietor and the interests of the Contractor.

An invoice, payment voucher and account or receipt should be attached to the bill each time the provisional amount is used to confirm the use of the provisional amount. Therefore, through the careful analysis of the contract terms, we know under what circumstances the temporary payment can be used, how the Contractor and Supervision Engineer should deal with such a situation, and finally, what information should be used to confirm the amount of the temporary payment in the bill measurement.

13.5 Daywork

Daywork, which is sometimes called "time-work", is typically necessary for minor or contingent work paid at cost-plus basis.

The Daywork schedule to be priced by tenderers and included in the Contract should define:

(a) a time charge rate for each person or category (e. g. money per person per hour);

(b) a time charge rate for each category of Contractor's Equipment (e. g. money per hour per unit); and

(c) the payment due for each category of Materials. This is usually on a basis similar to that described in Sub-Clause 13. 5 (b). However, for some Materials (e. g. natural Materials and Materials manufactured on the Site), it may be appropriate to provide items for pricing on a money per unit quantity basis.

However, FIDIC contract conditions are not applicable in all circumstances, and usually need some other widely recognized documents as technical support. Especially when it relates to the Daywork covered by Provisional Sums, FIDIC will refer to the "Schedules of Dayworks carried out Incidental to Contract work" edited by the Civil Engineering Contractors Association.

According to the schedules, the Contractor will charge extra overheads of 12. 5% to 148% on the Works and Materials that regarded as Daywork, which may include insurances, tool charges and transportation fees, etc. Of which, a rate of 12. 5% can be charged on staff transportation and 88% can charged on Daywork done by the nominated Subcontractor. This percentage also provides reference for the Contractor to choose Subcontractors when filling in the Appendix of Tender, allowing some adjustment to be made considering the extent of their influence on the tendering price.

When appropriate dealt with, Daywork can turn out to be an opportunity to make extra income. For instance, in an oversea highway renovation project, $230,000 is set aside as Provisional Sums to repair the highway, while FIDIC Contact also states that Daywork is to be calculated on the basis of FCEC Schedules of Dayworks which results in as much as $700,000 of Daywork payment. This happens after the Engineer has tried their best to cut back the costs. Finally the Employer agrees to give the payment in prevent that disruption of the construction may cause the collapse of transportation to and from the capital.

13. 6 Adjustments for Changes in Laws

If after the base date, project legal changes in host countries, for example, the project host countries raise the proportion of workers' social security, increase the import tariff rates of construction materials, equipment and accessories, adjust the way the Contractor's equipment depreciation, adjusted the VAT rate and so on, these will increase the cost of the Contractor, at the same time, also increased the Owner of the project investment, These effects could not be predicted or considered at the tender stage. In addition, in order to promote the development of infrastructure, the host country of the project may also reduce the tariff rate of imported construction materials, equipment and accessories, reduce the tax rate of value-added tax, etc. , thus reducing the cost of the Contractor and the investment of the Owner. The host country may also issue new laws that will not affect the implementation of the project.

In accordance with the conditions of contract in the FIDIC 2017 Red Book, any of the following changes after the Base Date which affect the performance of the Contractor's obligations under the Contract in the country of the Project shall be deemed to be a change in law. These include: changes in national laws, the enactment of new laws, as well as the repeal or amendment of existing laws; the judicial or governmental branch interprets or enforces the change in the law; Variations to any permits, permits, licenses or approvals obtained by the Owner or the Contractor pursuant to the Contract; or changes to any permits, permits, licenses (and) or approvals required by the Contractor pursuant to the Contract.

The above changes in law may affect the Contractor and the Owner, and both the Contractor and the Owner shall take appropriate measures in accordance with the provisions of this Contract. For the Contractor, if any change in law causes delay (and) or additional costs to the Contractor, the Contractor shall, in accordance with Sub-Clause 20.2 of the Contract, give notice of claim and submit detailed claim report to the Supervision Engineer within the specified period of time, and the Contractor shall have the right to claim for time limit and cost. However, legal changes may also have an impact on the Owner. If the legal changes reduce the relevant expenses, the Owner shall also, in accordance with Sub-Clause 20.2 of the Contract, send a notice of claim to the Supervision Engineer within the prescribed time and submit a detailed claim report. The Owner has the right to reduce the Contract Price.

If a change in law results in an adjustment in the execution of the Works, the Contractor shall immediately notify the Supervision Engineer with detailed instructions; Or the supervision of the project shall immediately notify the Contractor, and shall also attach a detailed explanation. Then, the Supervision Engineer shall issue a change order to the Contractor in accordance with the Contract, or issue a change order to the Contractor in accordance with the Contract to submit the plan.

Subject to the provisions of this Clause, both the Contractor and the Owner shall respond in accordance with Sub-Clause 20.2 of the Contract during the implementation of the project, for example, after the base date and after the occurrence of any legal change. If notice is not given to the Supervision Engineer within the time specified in the Contract, he will lose his right to claim. The Supervision Engineer shall also, in accordance with the provisions of the Contract, make a fair determination of the Owner's and Contractor's claims, or issue a variation order and take further contractual measures in accordance with the terms of the Contract.

For example, in the Xiao langdi hydro-project, the modification of Chinese Labour law, that the working days of 5 and half were reduced to 5 days, entitled the Contractor to claim for enormous sum of money.

13.7 Adjustments for Changes in Cost

Applying the payment formulae is a comparatively easy and more acceptable way to make profits, being of a more utilitarian role than making claims. The earnings are realized before the signing of contract instead of after that, thus can be applied to all the due payment after valuation. It has to be mentioned that the formula only applies to long working period project, which is normally more than 1 year.

Fluctuation Adjustment Formula:

$$P_n = a + b \cdot L_n/L_0 + c \cdot M_n/M_0 + d \cdot E_n/E_0 + \cdots$$

Of which, the adjustment multiplier "P_n" is "to be applied to the estimated contract value". Note that P_n will usually exceed "1" reflecting the escalation costs due to inflation and also possible be smaller than "1" reflecting the reduction of costs due to deflation.

Typically, the Employer will have defined the fixed (non-adjustable) coefficient "a" before the tender documents are issued to tenders, but may prefer each tenderer to define the other coefficient and all the sources of the cost indices in the table for each currency, so that they can fairly reflect:

(1) the proportion of Cost (e. g. different tenderers may anticipate different percentage for labour and equipment); and

(2) the sources of the cost indices (each of which should relate to the currency of Cost, which may also differ between tenderers).

A project contract allows for the price adjustment and adopts the Adjustment Formula. After the analysis and calculation on the quotation, the proportions of different adjustment items accounting for the Contract Price are determined. Please refer to the table below about the reference price on the day that is 28 day prior to the latest date for submission of the Tender. The accomplished project amount in the 1st month is $2,300,000.

Table 6.2

Adjustment items	Proportion of the Contract Price(I)	Reference price on the day that is 28 day prior to the latest date for submission of the Tender(T_0)	Published reference price in I month(T_i)	T_i/T_0	$I \cdot (T_i/T_0)$
Unadjustable	0.30	N/A	N/A	1	0.30
Wage (dollar/day)	0.25	3	3.6	1.2	0.30
Steel (dollar/t)	0.12	520	580	1.115	0.134
Cement (dollar/t)	0.06	80	82	1.025	0.062
Fuel (dollar/litre)	0.08	0.4	0.48	1.2	0.096
Wood (dollar/cubic meter)	0.1	420	480	1.143	0.114
Other materials (according to price index)	0.09	100	120	1.2	0.108
In total	1				1.114

So, the adjusted project amount in first i month is:

$$P_i = P_0 \times I \times (T_i / T_0) = 2.3 \times 1.114 = 2.5622 \text{ (million dollars)}$$

Of which, the adjusted amount caused by price index is:

$$P_i - P_0 = 2.5622 - 2.30 = 0.2622 \text{ (million dollars)}$$

For instance, in a railway renovation project with loans from the World Bank, the Contract Price was 5.34 million US dollars, the working period was 32 months and later extended to be 38 months by the Employer. During the period when the project was executed, the Congress proclaimed to improve the lowest wage standard and 17,500 in local currency per month was increased to 30,000 in local currency per month. This largely contributed to the increase of labor coefficient, which almost doubled and also led to the escalation of labor costs. As a result, the adjusted amount reached as much as 1.4 million US dollars and was in excess of 26% of what had been stated in the Contract Price.

◆**Discussion**:

Learning form the case above, what will you suggest to the Employer as measures of self-protection?

Adjustment formulae is an important way to protect the Contractor from being affected by the price fluctuation. It's advisable that the Employer shall be entitled to set limit to adjustment, for example, to state in Contract that 10% of changes are allowable, and the excessive part shall be the risk of the Contractor. Whilst no such stipulations had been specified in this Contract, thus correspondingly the adjusted value increased with the escalation of costs indices, free from any limitation.

※**Vocabulary**

1. borehole *n.* (尤指为了寻找石油或水而在地上凿的)钻孔,井眼

2. exploratory *adj.* (行动)探究的,探测的,探索性的

3. accelerate *v.* (使)加快;(使)增速

4. await *v.* 等候;等待

5. proportion *n.* 比例

6. overheads *n.* (企业等的)日常管理费用;杂项开支;一般经费(overhead 的复数)

7. quotation *n.* 报价;开价

8. voucher *n.* 代金券;票券

9. substantiation *n.* 实体化;证实,证明;使实体化

10. adjustable *adj.* (位置或大小)可调整的

11. indicative *adj.* 指示的;象征的;暗示的

12. tabulated *v.* 将……制成表格;以表格形式排列

13. render *v.* 致使;造成

14. unbalance *v.* 使失衡;使紊乱;使失常

14　Contract Price and Payment

14.1　The Contract Price

◆**Discussion**：

What is the difference between the Accepted Contract Amount and the Contract Price？

The former is a provisional price which is submitted by the Contractor as quotation and determined after tendering evaluation and negotiations. And the latter is the total due payment paid to the Contractor. This shows the evolution in description wording on payment of the Works and avoids the uncertainties in using the word of "Contract Price" and the ambiguity of the concept which occur in previous editions.

14.2　Advance Payment

This Sub-Clause specifies that total advance payment must be included in the Appendix to Tender and sets out the procedures to be followed in repaying the advances.

Whenever the Contractor is required to be paid prior to the Employer having received anything in return, the Employer will probably require some security for his outlay. This security is to be in the form of a guarantee, which is to be issued by an entity approved by the Employer. It is required to be in the form annexed to the Particular Conditions, or in another form approved by the Employer. The Particular Condition should therefore include details of the Employer's requirement regarding the entity, and the details of the specified form.

◆**Discussion**：

What is the definition of the advance payment？

The Employer shall pay the Contractor a sum of money called advance payment when the Contractor submit bank guarantee of advance payment according to this Sub-Clause. It may be regarded as interest free loan for the Contractor to launch his work. The amount of advance payment, times of installments, payment schedule (when there's more than one payment), applicable currency and its proportion shall comply with what has been specified in the Appendix to Tender.

◆**Discussion**：

Will repayment of advance paymentaffect extension of the guarantee？

The guarantee is required to be valid until the advance payment has been repaid. And this Sub-Clause requires the guarantee to be extended if, 28 days before its expiry date, the advance has not been repaid in full. If the advance has not been repaid by the date 28 days before the guarantee expires, and the Contractor fails to extend it, this Sub-Clause entitled the Employer to call the guarantee. The period of 28 days is specified so as to allow the Employer a reasonable period within which to make the necessary arrangements for the call.

◆ **Discussion**:

How does the payment progress affect the use of the advance payment?

The repayment program needs careful consideration when put into work, since being haste or too much procrastination will both adversely affect the use of the advance payment. The specifications in this Sub-Clause are rather thoughtful and reasonable.

Here is a formula to calculate the repayment of advances:

$$R = \frac{A(C-aS)}{(b-a)S}$$

Of which: R represents the accumulated repaid advances deducted from Interim Payment Certificates; A represents total advance payment; S represents the Accepted Contract Amount; C represents the accumulated due payment shown in interim payment certificates, it's value depends upon the detailed specifications in the Contract, for example, is it before the deduction of retention money or after that (generally excludes retention money)? Is it before the adjustment or after that (generally before adjustments)? And the scope of C is: $aS < C < bS$. a represents the percentage of the interim payments in all interim payments when their accumulated value has begun to exceed the 15% of the Accepted Contract Amount less Provisional Sums and deductions commence. b represents the percentage of the accumulated interim payments accounting for the Accepted Contract Amount, when all the advance payments have been repaid.

14.3 Application of Interim Certificate

This Sub-Clause consists of three parts:

(1) time to submit Monthly Statement;

(2) supporting documents submitted together with the Statement;

(3) items included in the Statement.

It's only specified that the after the end of each month shall a Statement be submitted rather than to impose strict time limit on the submission of Statement. Because the Contractor will try their best to submit the Statement as early as possible even without being urged, and the earlier they take action, the earlier they will receive the payment.

It's stated that the Statement form needs to be approved by the Engineer. In practice, in order to avoid the form being rejected by the Engineer, the Contractor can choose the negotiate with the Engineer in advance and determine the form before it's submitted. When considering what form to approve, the Engineer should take account of the need to facilitate his rapid checking of the various amounts, and take account of the financial provisions in the Contract on which the amounts are to be based. He should allow the Contractor to utilize any computerized system with which the Contractor's staff are familiar, provided it produced clear and comprehensible Statement.

The "Contract Value" is value of the Works in accordance with the Contract, namely the applicable part of the Contract Price, in accordance with Sub-Clause 14.1(a). Under CONS, the calculation of Contract Value is based on the measurement of the quantities of the Works executed up to the end of a month, in accordance with Sub-Clause 12.3.

Each Statement must be accompanied by supporting documents and these documents are required to include the progress report specified in Sub-Clause 4.21 for the relevant period.

14.4　Schedule of Payments

Interim payments typically are based upon monthly measurements of quantities of Works, applying the rates and prices from a Bill of Quantities. However, a schedule of payments may sometimes be considered appropriate for a contract under CONS. If project progresses steadily, it's convenient to apply Schedule of Payment, while in fact, real work progress does not always keep pace with the plan (no matter it falls behind or goes ahead), thus the Schedule of Payment may not be as effective as they are expected to be.

It's specified that the Engineer may revise installments if actual progress is found to be less than that on which this schedule of payment was based, but does not mention the other situation when the actual progress if more than that of the plan. It's understandable that in the opinion of the Employer, it's good enough for the execution of Works to comply with the original plan, and speeding-up of work pace is not encouraged due to its possible adverse effect on project quality.

Except for in a privately-financed commercial project, such as BOT project, and quality of the work being ensured, the Employer won't press for completion of the Works in advance. Based on experiences, this payment mode is not advised to apply on unit price contracts after remeasurement, but is acceptable for contracts on lump-sum basis.

A project needs a large amount of investment, and the Employer needs time to make budget and prepare for giving payment, the Schedule of Payment is the one to help them plan installments. And if there is no such Schedule of Payments, the last paragraph requires the Contractor to submit non-binding estimates every three months, which is actually the Contractor's quarterly cash flow plan.

14.5　Plant and Materials Intended for the Works

For civil engineering projects, Materials and Plant account for a large percent of the Contract Price value, hereby forcing the Contractor to raise enough money to procure these Goods. In international trade, credit card is typically required for procurement of goods, and the Contractor needs to present bank credit card with equal amount to procurement contracts value when issuing orders. Sufficient deposit in bank account is required in order to prepare a credit card. In one word, the Contractor needs large amount of cash to procure Materials and Plant. Hence it's customary to pay for the Materials and Plan in advance. This Sub-Clause specifies the payment mechanism for Materials and Plant under CONS.

We learn that there're two types of Materials and Plant listed in the Appendix to Tender and the listed Materials and Plant can acquire advance payment equal to 80% of their costs before they are installed or used in the Works. When their contact value has been included as part of the Permanent Works, the payment paid at advance will be deduced. This shows that the Materials and Plant are actually paid by two installments under CONS.

◆ **Discussion**:

Pros and cons of the advance payment

It's specified that the Contractor needs to open a bank guarantee in order to get advance payment, the bank guarantee is to be provided under sub-paragraph (b) by an entity, and in a form, approved by the Employer. This may be helpful to ensure the safety of the Employer's money, while on the whole it's more disadvantageous because it increases the "business costs". The Contractor needs to pay bank services fees and keep a large amount of money in his account, and rationally, all tenderers will include this in their tendering price, thus increase the cost of the Works. Submission of guarantee is mainly to prevent the Contractor to take advantage of goods procurement to do the Employer out of project payment. While in practice, it doesn't make sense at all.

14.6 Issue of Interim Payment Certificate

Under CONS, the Contractor received a copy of an Interim Payment Certificate which notifies him of the payment to which he is entitled, as fairly determined by the Engineer. This procedure may require less time than the 28 days mentioned in the first paragraph.

This Sub-Clause stipulates the procedure and conditions for issuing of Interim Payment Certificate:

(1) time limit for the Engineer to issue Interim Payment Certificate;

(2) minimum amount of Interim Payment Certificate;

(3) conditions to distain certain payment;

(4) rights of the Engineer to revise the payment.

This Sub-Clause concluded with a sentence confirming that certification or payment is not to be taken as indicating "acceptance, approval, consent or satisfaction". This sentence is required so as to discourage:

(1) the Employer from withholding an interim payment if he feels entitled to withhold acceptance, approval, consent or satisfaction; and

(2) the Contractor from relying upon certificates or payment as evidence of acceptance, approval, consent or satisfaction in respect of paid work.

It's specified that if only the Contractor's work doesn't comply with the Contract or he does not perform his obligations in accordance with the Contract, the Engineer is entitled to withhold the costs or value of the work. For example, when quality problems occur to the concreting, the Engineer as stated is to be entitled to withhold the progress payment. Such a statement does not mean that payment certificate shall be withheld but just the relevant amount of payment instead.

14.7　Payment

This Sub-Clause specifies the payment time.

◆**Discussion**：

Time management technics：two 28-day verse one 56-day

In previous edition, payment of the amount certified in each Interim Payment Certificate is phased into two periods and each period is as long as 28 days. Within the first 28 days, the Engineer will issue Payment Certificate, and the Employer is required to pay the Contractor within the following 28 days after receiving the Payment Certificate. The new specification in new edition provides more flexibility for the Employer, since no matter how soon the Engineer issue the payment certificate upon receiving the Statement, the Employer can wait until the 56th date to make payments.

In effect, the Employer usually prolong the waiting time in Particular Conditions, the extent of which depends upon the Contractor's financial strength. If the Contractor can't maintain the work at his own cost, thus cause the slow-down or even suspension of the Works, this may entitle the Employer to claim for extension of working period.

14.8　Delayed Payment

Project capital running out will lead to project suspension or even termination. As stated, financing charges commuunded monthly are to be calculated at the annual rate of three percentage pointes above the discount rate of the central bank in the country of the currency of payment. This is more of a punishment. If this rate is considered inappropriate when tendering documents are being prepared, a new rate may be defined in the Particular Conditions. The Contractor is entitled to these financing charges without being required to give notice and without a Payment Certificate under CONS. However, it may be preferable for financing charges to be included in Payment Certificates under CONS for accounting purpose.

In practice, the Contractor should know that in the Contract, in addition to specify the obligation of the Employer to pay extra interest charges for delayed payment, the Contractor shall be also entitled with the right to suspend work or terminate contract. Because though the Employer can pay for fined interest, the failure of raising procurement money will affect the procurement of Plant and Materials and prolong the working period, consequences of which shall be at the risk of the Contractor.

14.9   Release of Retention Money

◆ Discussion：

What is Retention Money?

The accumulated moneys (if specified in the Contract) which are deducted and retained by the Employer from the payment otherwise due to the Contractor and which are only paid after completion

◆ Discussion：

How about regulation on retain and release of the retention money?

Retention money is retained under Sub-Clause 14.3 (c) and is release in installments based upon the Taking-Over Certificates issued under Article 10. It's specified in Sub-Clause 14.3 that any amount to be deducted for retention, calculated by applying the percentage of retention stated in the Appendix to Tender to the total of the estimated contract value of the Works executed, the percentage is normally around 10%, until the amount so retained by the Employer reaches the limit of stated in the Appendix to Tender, which is about 5%.

In international projects, retention money is an important issue deserving special attention. For example, 5% may be reasonable profit of a project, and as stated the percentage of retention money is also about 5% of the contract price, therefore the Contractor's revenue may be fully counterfeited if he fails to claim back the retention money.

Retention money is used to compensate the costs during the period of project maintenance which incur if the Works doesn't comply with the specifications but the Contractor refuse or unable to rectify the shortcomings. It's held by the Employer as kind of economic guarantee.

Whether the retention money can be claimed back and how much can be claimed back depend on quality of the Works, attitude of the Employer, the persons who dun for debts, and the district or country where the project locates. For example, in such a place like Hong Kong which has complete legislation system and standardized operation specifications, it's less likely to become a big headache for the Employer.

14.10   Statement of Completion

This Sub-Clause specifies the basic procedure for the Employer to pay what remains due to the Contractor when the Works has been completed. In order to notify the Employer the due payment, the Statement not only include the value of all works done in accordance with the Contractor up to the date, but also include any further sums which the Contractor considers to be due and an estimate of any other amounts which the Contractor considers will become due to him under the Contract, enabling the Employer to make according arrangements (Figure 6.18).

The Statement at completion is the basis of the cessation of liability and encourages the early settlement of financial aspects.

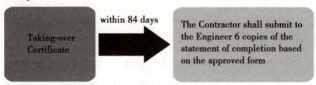

Figure 6.18

14.11   Final Statement

14.12   Discharge

When submitting the "Final Statement", after agreement or after resolution of all disputes under Sub-Clause 20.4 or Sub-Clause 20.5, the Contractor confirms his agreement in this written discharge (Figure 6.19).

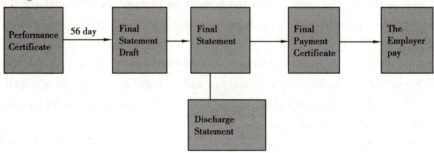

Figure 6.19

Sample Form of Discharge

We ——_____ hereby confirm, in the terms of Sub-Clause 14.12 of the Conditions of Contractor, that the total of the attached Final Statement, namely —— _____ represents the full and final settlement of all moneys sue to us under or in connection with the Contract. This discharge shall only become effective when we have received the Performance Security and the outstanding balance of this total of the attached Final Statement.

◆Discussion:

Which day shall be the effective day of the discharge certificate?

The last sentence is questioned in a book to construe FIIDC contract conditions, " This discharge may state that is becomes effective when the Contractor has received the Performance Security and the out-standing balance of this total in which event the discharge will be effective on such date. " Literally, such a date should be the date when the Contractor has received the Performance Security and the out-standing balance. In effect, such a date should be the date when the Contractor receives the out-standing balance. We all know that the Employer shall return to the Contractor Performance Security within 21 days after he receives a copy of the Performance Certificate from the Engineer. While the out-standing balance is required to be paid within (56+ 28+56) days after the Performance Certificate is issued and may be further delayed if any disputes arise. Thus typically, return of the Performance Security will happen earlier than paying of out-standing balance. Ambiguity occurs when it's so stated.

14.13 Issue of Final Payment Certificate

After the Contractor has submitted the Final Statement and discharge, the Engineer then issues the Final Payment Certificate. The last paragraph provides for the possibility that the Contractor fails to apply for a Final Payment Certificate within the prescribed period, 56 days as stated in Sub-Clause 14.11. At the first thought, this shall not happen since it's presumed that every Contractor wishes to receive the due payment as early as possible.

This possibility may be defined by the sentence in this Sub-Clause that there's balance due from the Contractor to the Employer, as the case may be, before the issue of the Final Payment Certificate. The Contractor will justifiably decline to apply for the Certificate when he realizes the situation.

In this event, the Engineer should request the Contractor to submit his application within 28 days. Unless it is received within 28 days, the Engineer is required to issue the Final Payment Certificate without further delay. Under Sub-Clause 1.3, Certificates shall not be unreasonably withheld or delayed.

14.14 Cessation of Employer's Liability

◆**Discussion**:

Contrasting to that the Contractor's contractual obligations are fulfilled by being awarded performance certificate, how to acknowledge the fulfillment of the Employer's contractual obligations?

This Sub-Clause implies the conclusions as follows:

(1) If the Engineer and the Contractor have agreed on the payment in the Final Statement, after the Employer pay the due payment to the Contractor stated in the Final Payment Certificate issued by the Engineer, the Employer's payment liability is deemed to be ceased.

(2) If two Parties fail on agree on the payment in the Final Statement, after the Employer has paid the agreed part stated in the Engineer's provisional decision, and the payment confirmed after arbitration, the Employer's payment liability is deemed to be ceased.

Noted that the Contractor is required to submit:

(1) the notice in respect of each claim, within four weeks after he should have become aware of the relevant event or circumstance giving rise to the claim;

(2) the Statement at completion, stating the actual or estimated amount of each claim, within

twelve weeks after the Taking-Over Certificate for the Works; and

(3) particulars of each claim, within periods proposed and approved in accordance with the procedures described in Sub-Clause 20.1.

14.15 Currencies of Payment

FIDIC contract sometimes will require the Contractor to include in tendering documents with analysis on estimates of foreign currencies demand, tenderers is allowed to choose foreign currencies but no more than 3. Of which, analysis and explanation are required to be made on use of foreign currencies in quotation, such as:

(1) payment for employing foreign staff;

(2) imported materials, including both of Permanent Works and temporary Works;

(3) mechanical equipment of the Contractor;

(4) transportation fees in foreign countries, insurance fees and insurance service fees;

(5) incurred costs including overheads, contingencies, and profits in foreign countries.

By summarizing the above items, can we estimate proportions of foreign currencies.

※Vocabulary

1. breakdown *n.* (关系的)破裂;(计划、讨论等的)失败,结束

2. mobilization *n.* 动员

3. installment *n.* 部分;分期付款

4. indicated *adj.* 表明的;指示的

5. amortization *n.* 分期偿还;(会计)摊销

6. deterioration *n.* 恶化;变坏;退化;堕落

7. expiry *n.* (合同、最终期限、签证等的)期满,到期

8. settlement *n.* (争议双方的)正式协议,和解

9. verify *n.* 证实;证明

10. discharge *v.* 清偿(债务)

11. be liable to 该受(罚);应遵守……;有……的倾向;易于……

12. expressly *adj.* (命令)明白表示的,明确的

13. reckless *adj.* 轻率的;不计后果的;鲁莽的;无所顾忌的

14. misconduct *n.* (尤指专业人员的)渎职,不端行为,不当行为

15 Termination by Employer

According to the situation of owner termination, the 1999 edition enumerates 6 situations, while the 2017 edition enumerates 8 situations. The two additional paragraphs are respectively divided into two items (1) and (3) in the 1999 edition, which are stipulated respectively. Most of them are one-to-one correspondence, but in some cases they are expanded. For example, in paragraph (1) of the 2017 edition, there are two more cases of "correction notice, binding agreement or final binding decision, DAAB decision" than in the 1999 edition. Item (3) of the 2017 edition further extended the description of the performance defects in terms of the construction period, which not only stated in the 1999 edition that "failure to comply with the provisions of Article 8 may result in termination of the contract", but also exceeded the maximum value of the compensation for delay, which may lead to the termination of the Contract proposed by the Owner. A more detailed explanation of possible procedures relating to Contractor insolvency is provided in sub-paragraph (7) of the 2017 edition. In Item (8) of the 2017 edition, bribery was amended from the 1999 edition to corruption, fraud, coercion and malicious collusion.

15.1　Notice to Correct

Before the Employer believes that the Contractor's failure is sufficiently serious to merit termination under Sub-Clause 15.2, the Employer should consider whether termination appears to be the most appropriate course of action, and take legal advice, and issue a notice to require the Contractor to make good the failure and to remedy it within a specified reasonable time.

If the Employer intends to reply on a notice under this Sub-Clause the notice should:

(1) state that it is given under this Sub-Clause;

(2) describe the nature of the Contractor's failure; and

(3) specify a reasonable time within which the Contractor is to remedy the failure.

15.2　Termination for Contractor's Default

Clause 15.2 provides that the Owner shall be entitled to give notice of his intention to terminate the Contract in case the Contractor:

(1) fails to comply with a corrective action notice, a binding agreement or a final binding decision (Sub-Clause 3.7 [Agreement or Determination]) or a DAAB decision (Sub-Clause 21.4 [Obtaining DAAB's Decision]) and constitutes a material breach of obligation;

(2) abandons the project, or clearly show a tendency to continue to perform obligations under the Contract;

(3) fails without reasonable excuse to carry out the Works in accordance with Article 8 [Commencement, Delays and Suspension], or if the Contract provides for a maximum amount of damages for delay and the Contractor fails to comply with Sub-Clause 8.2 [Time for Completion], the damages for delay exceed the prescribed limit;

(4) fails, without reasonable excuse, to comply with the notification requirements within 28 days of receipt of a rejection notice from the Engineer (Sub-Clause 7.5 [Defects and Rejections]) or an instruction from the Engineer (Sub-Clause 7.6 [Remedial Work]);

(5) fails to comply with Sub-Clause 4.2 [Performance Security];

(6) subcontracts the Works in whole or in part in contravention of Sub-Clause 4.4 [Contractor's Documents] or assigning the Contract to another person without the necessary permission (Sub-Clause 1.7 [Assignment]);

（7）becomes bankrupt or insolvent, goes into liquidation of business, administration, reorganization, winding-up or dissolution; At the direction of a liquidator, receiver, manager or trustee, enter into contracts or agreements with creditors of the Contractor or have any event which has a similar effect to the foregoing; Or if the Contractor is a joint venture and one of the members of the joint venture does not immediately confirm to the Employer that the contractual obligations of the member in question will continue to be fulfilled under Sub-Clause 1. 14 （a）；

（8）at any time in connection with the Works or the Contracts it is found, based on reasonable evidence, to have engaged in corruption, fraud, malicious collusion or duress.

In the event of such occurrence, the Engineer may give notice of correction to the Contractor. If the Contractor fails to remedy such non-performance within 14 days of receipt of such notice, the Owner may terminate the Contract by giving a second notice. In the event of any of the above non-performance conditions under Items （6）, （7）, （8） （illegal subcontracting or subcontracting, bankruptcy, bribery）, the Owner may terminate the Contract immediately by giving notice to the Contractor without the need for 14 days notice.

Subject to the relevant provisions of the FIDIC 2017 Red Book, the Contractor shall carry out the relevant activities accordingly, including the transfer of any subcontract on the Project to the Employer in compliance with any reasonable instructions given by the Employer in the notice of termination to protect the life, property or safety of the Works. The Contractor shall be careful to comply with the Owner's reasonable instructions. If the Contractor considers the Owner's instructions to be unreasonable, he may make reasonable and detailed suggestions and take other measures. The Contractor shall hand over to the Supervision Engineer any Goods, Contractor's documents and design documents for which the Contractor is responsible as required by the Owner. However, during the handover process, proper records must be kept and the Contractor shall be entitled to receive the appropriate payment from the owner. The Contractor shall also leave the Project Site, if not, the Owner shall have the right to evict the Contractor from the Site.

After the termination of the Project Contract, the Contractor shall comply with the Owner's requirements in the termination notice, but the Contractor shall also keep relevant records as evidence of subsequent settlement with the Owner. These records including implementation of completed project, measurement data, construction records of completed unmetered works, correspondence and other written records in the process of project implementation, Survey design work carried out by the contractor, records of equipment and facilities provided by the Contractor to the Supervision Engineer, as well as information on the construction of the Contractor's own campsite and related costs, etc. The more detailed the information, the better. If necessary, it can be signed and confirmed jointly with the Supervision Engineer, and the Contractor shall keep one copy and formally submit one copy to the Supervision Engineer. This is the most appropriate way to ensure the protection of its own interests in the upcoming settlement of contract termination.

In terms of termination procedures, the 2017 version gives a clearer picture of two phases. In the case of Owner termination, the first stage is to give notice of intention to terminate and the second stage is to give notice of termination. In the case of the Contractor, in addition to the prior suspension procedure, an early warning mechanism of the first notice has been added, giving the

Contractor the right to issue a formal notice of termination if the Owner fails to correct the situation within a specified period of time after the notice is given. In the case of the 2017 version, this amounts to adding an early warning mechanism to help buffer the rules of the Contract to be somewhat "flexible".

15.3 Valuation after Termination for Contractor's Default

From the point of view of the procedures after termination, after the termination proposed by the Owner, the Contractor should protect the project and site according to the instructions of the Owner, assist the Owner to sign the Subcontract, and leave the site after delivering the relevant documents produced by the Contractor and items required by the Owner to the Engineer. Few changes have been made in this section since the 1999 edition.

This Sub-Clause requires the Engineer to determine the value of work completed by the Contractor, including first of all, the value of the Works completed by the Contractor, and the Permanent Works, Materials, Plant and other Temporary Works purchased by the Contractor for execution of the Works, as well as files and design documents the Contractor made for the Works, etc.

15.4 Payment after Termination for Contractor's Default

After termination, the Employer would probably have had to make other arrangements for the completion of the Works, including the rectification of any defects.

Interruption of the execution of Contract will lead to the exceeding of the real costs than the tendering price submitted by the first Contractor and prolong the construction period of the new Contractor than he planned, thus incur costs to the Employer. So the Employer may recover his losses, damages and extra costs incurred by termination of the Contract from the first Contractor.

◆ **Discussion:**

How can the Employer recover his losses incurred by the termination of the Contract from the first Contractor?
(1) the Performance Security;
(2) the retention money retained;
(3) the construction equipment on-site;
(4) retained Contract Payment.

15.5 Termination for Employer's Convenience

According to the FIDIC 2017 Red Book, the Owner has the right to terminate the Contract at any time, provided that the Owner gives the Contractor a clear notice in accordance with the provisions of the Contract. Upon receipt of this notice by the Contractor, the Contract is not terminated immediately, but there is a requirement for a period of time, namely 28 days. There are two factors that determine the effective date of the termination of the Contract, namely the termination notice and the Performance Security. If the Owner gives notice of termination and then returns the Performance Security to the Contractor, the effective date of termination shall be 28 days after the Contractor receives the Performance Security. Otherwise, the effective date of termination shall be 28 days from the date of receipt of the Contractor's notice.

Upon the effectiveness of such termination, the Contractor shall perform its obligations in accordance with the Contract and cease to carry out further works, except such works as may be directed by the Supervison Engineer to protect the life, property or safety of the Project. In the event that the Supervisor's instructions incur additional costs to the Contractor, the Contractor shall have the right to receive such costs and profits and to transfer to the Supervisor all Contractor's documents, equipment, materials and other work for which the Owner has paid. It is the contractual obligation of the Contractor at the site to remove all goods other than those necessary for safety from the site and evacuate the site.

15.6　Valuation after Termination for Employer's Convenience

15.7　Payment after Termination for Employer's Convenience

However, in Article 15, in the event of termination by the owner at his own convenience, the 2017 edition has amended the relevant provisions on valuation and payment in such case. This may happen because the Owner has a sudden financial crisis, or thinks the project is unfeasible, so the Owner can not continue the project, or the project will bring more losses. In 1999, according to Sub-Clause 15.5 [Termination for Employer's Convenience] the Owner shall in accordance with Sub-Clause 19.6 [Optional Termination, Payment and Release] pay to the Contractor. Article 19 of the 1999 edition is in the event of Force Majeure, which means that in the event of Sub-Clause 15.5 [Termination for Employer's Convenience], the Contractor is not compensated for loss of profits.

However, this has been changed in the 2017 edition. Clause 15.6 [Valuation after Termination for Employer's Convenience] states that in the event of termination of the Contract by the Employer for his own benefit, the Contractor shall be entitled to receive compensation for loss of profits in addition to payment for the completed part of the Works. In this case, the change of Contractor's payment reflects the change of risk sharing. The provisions of 1999 version are more favorable to the Owner, but the termination of the Contract by the Owner out of his own interests is completely caused by the Owner and cannot be attributed to the Contractor or force majeure. Therefore, the change made in 2017 version is reasonable. It is also consistent with the payment to the Contractor under Clause 16 as a result of the Owner's default.

Upon withdrawal from the Site, the Contractor shall be entitled to payment from the Owner accordingly by providing to the Supervision Engineer a detailed description of supporting documents demonstrating the amount of the Works completed, including the value of the Works executed and the equipment and materials ordered by the Contractor for the Project, which have been paid by the Owner. The Contractor shall put these equipment and material in the location specified by the Owner, if the Contractor can be expected to finish the project, in this case, the reasonable costs or liabilities incurred by the Contractor, the costs of removing the Contractor's temporary facilities and equipment from the Site and returning them to the Contractor's country of origin, and the remaining amount of the costs of removing the Contractor's staff and Labour for the Project shall be by reference to additions or subtractions to the terms of the Final Payment Certificate. And the loss of profits or other losses and damages to the Contractor as a result of the termination of the Contract shall be taken into consideration.

After the termination of the Contract, the Contractor shall retain the relevant documents and materials to the maximum extent possible, in particular those documents and materials which are closely related to the Contractor's interests in order to maximize the protection of his own interests. If conditions permit, after the Contractor prepares the relevant documents and materials, it is better to sign and confirm with the Supervision Engineer, submit a formal copy to the Supervision Engineering in the form of a letter, and copy to the Owner. This will not only facilitate the Supervision Engineer's reference in subsequent decisions, but also reduce unnecessary contract disputes, while ensuring the interests of the Contractor.

Upon receipt of the Certificate of Payment from the Supervison Engineer, the Owner shall pay to the Contractor such amount as is due to him and shall not carry out or arrange for the execution of the Works or any part thereof until such payment has been made to the Contractor. In addition, upon notice of termination given by the Owner to the Contractor, he shall immediately lose his right to use the Contractor's Documents and shall return them to the Contractor, except for those documents which have been paid by the Owner or which are due to the Contractor in the Payment Certificate. The Owner also immediately loses the use of Contractor's Equipment, temporary facilities, access or other facilities of the Contractor. The Owner shall immediately return the Contractor's Performance Security.

※ Vocabulary

1. trustee *n.* (财产)受托人,托管人
2. liquidation *n.* 清偿;结算;清算;清除
3. insolvent *adj.* 无清偿能力的;资不抵债的;破产的
4. bribe *n.* 贿赂
        v. 向……行贿
5. gratuity *n.* 小费;赏钱
6. inducement *n.* 诱惑;引诱物

16　Suspension and Termination by Contractor

For the case of contractor termination, the 1999 edition enumerates 7 cases, while the 2017 edition lists 10 cases, in which items (4), (6) and (7) have no corresponding items in the 1999 edition. Other minor changes include: the amount payable in item (3) of the 2017 edition is based on "any Payment Certificate", as opposed to "Interim Payment Certificate" of the 1999 edition. The suspension in Sub-Clause (8) covers not only Sub-Clause 8. 11 of the 1999 version, but also the time to wait for a Payment Certificate in Sub-Clause (2) of this Clause.

16. 1 Suspension by Contractor

In the case of termination by the Contractor, the 2017 edition of the Conditions of Contract sets up a prefixed "Suspension" Sub-Clause in Clause 16. 1 [Suspension by Contracto], which specifies the circumstances under which the Contractor is entitled to suspend the execution of the Works. This provision is reasonable because "contract termination" is a very serious event. If the Owner gives the Contractor the right to terminate the Contract as soon as he breaches the Contract, it would be too abrupt and not conducive to the overall interests of both Parties. However, if the Owner does not correct after suspension and warning from the Contractor, the Contractor shall be entitled to give notice of termination of the Contract.

Sub-Clause 16. 1 [Suspension by Contractor] provides that the Contractor shall be entitled to suspend the Works under the following circumstances:

(1) The engineer fails to issue the payment certificate as required;

(2) Where the Contractor requests proof of project financing from the Employer under Sub-Clause 2. 4 [Employer's Financial Arrangements], the Owner fails to provide in time;

(3) The Employer fails to pay the project payment in time as stipulated in the Contract;

(4) The Owner has failed to comply with. the binding agreement, final agreement under Sub-Clause 3. 7 [Agreement or Determination], or a DAAB decision in Sub-Clause 21. 4 [Obtaining DAAB's Decision]. And the above circumstances constitute the Owner of a serious breach of contractual obligations.

16. 2 Termination by Contractor

Sub-Clause 16. 2 provides that the Contractor shall be entitled to issue a notice of termination if:

(1) the Contractor fails to comply with Sub-Clause 2. 4 [Employer's Financial Arrangements] under Sub-Clause 16. 1 [Suspension by Contractor]. No reasonable evidence is received within 42 days after the notice of the matter stipulated in the fund arrangement;

(2) the Engineer fails to issue the relevant payment certificate within 56 days of receipt of the statement and supporting documents;

(3) within 42 days after the due date of payment provided for in Sub-Clause 14. 7 [Payment], the Contractor has not received payment under any the amount due on the Payment Certificate;

(4) the Employer fails to comply with a binding agreement, final and binding decision or a DAAB decision under Sub-Clause 3. 7 [Agreement or Determination] or Sub-Clause 21. 4 [Obtaining DAAB's decision] and constitutes a material breach;

(5) the Owner materially fails to perform its obligations under the Contract and constitutes a material breach;

(6) the Contractor does not receive notification of the commencement date under Sub-Clause 8.1 [Commencement of Works] 84 days after receipt of the Letter of Acceptance;

(7) the Owner fails to comply with Sub-Clause 1.6 [Contract Agreement] or fails to comply with Sub-Clause 1.7 [Assignment] to assign the interest under the Contract;

(8) continued shutdown under Sub-Clause 8.12 [Prolonged Suspension] affects the whole of the Works;

(9) bankruptcy or insolvency, liquidation, receivership, reorganization, winding up or dissolution; to follow the instructions of the liquidator, receiver, administrator or trustee, to enter into contracts or agreements with creditors of the Owner, or to have any event which has a similar effect to the foregoing;

(10) at any time in connection with the Works or the Contracts, is found on reasonable evidence to be involved in corruption, fraud, malicious collusion or coercion.

In the event of such occurrence, the Contractor shall have the right to terminate the Contract by giving 14 days notice to the Owner, if any.

In the event of Items (7)—(10) (Transfer, Work Suspension, Bankruptcy, Bribery), the Contractor may terminate immediately.

16.3 Contractor's Obligations After Termination

Upon termination of the Project Contract, the Contractor shall immediately cease further execution of the project except for those Works which are required by the Supervision Engineer to be necessary for the life, property and safety of the project. In other words, the Contractor's obligation to continue the execution of the Project ends with the termination of the Contract and the Owner loses the right to continue to require the Contractor to perform the Project.

Upon termination of the Project Contract, the Contractor shall, in accordance with the Contract, transfer to the Engineer the Contractor's Documents, Equipment, Materials and other work for which payment has been received, if paid by the Owner. During the execution of the Project, the Contractor's Documents, Equipment, Materials and other work shall be the property of the Contractor, and the Contractor shall transfer such property to the Owner if the Owner has performed all obligations payable to the Contractor. This is the Contractor's obligation. In addition, the Contractor shall remove all his goods and property from the site and return the project site to the Owner, which is also the obligation of the Contractor.

16.4 Payment after Termination by Contractor

The Contractor is entitled to receive the Performance Security, and to payment of an amount to be determined as described in Sub-Clause 18.5 and of the amount of any loss or damage which he suffered.

Sub-Clause 14.2 requires the Contractor to repay the advance payment immediately upon termination. The advance payment guarantee should be returned to the Contractor as soon as the advance payment has been repaid in full. If the Contractor fails to repay the advance payment, the Employer may call the advance payment guarantee.

※ Vocabulary

1. suspend *v.* 暂缓;推迟;暂停
2. prolong *v.* 延长;拉长;拖长
3. cease *v.* 停止;终止;结束

    　　　 n. 停止
4. sustain *v.* 使持续;保持

17　Care of the Works and Indemnities

17.1　Responsibility for Care of the Works

◆ Discussion:

Should the Contractor bear all the responsibility?

As we all know, in the process of project implementation, there may be incidents that the Contractor is responsible for, incidents that the Owner is responsible for, incidents that both Parties are responsible for, and incidents that neither Party is responsible for. It is clear that the events for which the Contractor is responsible are generally caused by the Contractor and that the Contractor shall be liable for loss or damage even if a handover certificate is issued. In addition, although the handover certificate has been issued, the Contractor shall be liable for loss or damage if the incident occurred prior to the issuance of the handover certificate and the Contractor is responsible.

17.2　Liability for Care of the Works

◆ Discussion:

Under what circumstances is the Contractor not liable for any loss or damage to the Works, the Goods or the Contractor's Documents?

The FIDIC 2017 Red Book can help us answer questions and doubts. It has been analyzed and understood that there are many of these circumstances, and that the execution of the Works, as required by the Contract, will inevitably affect the right of way, lighting, air, water or other easement, whether permanent or temporary, and not due to the Contractor's method of construction. In this case, the Contractor is not liable.

Except as expressly specified in the Contract, the Employer shall use or occupy any part of the Permanent Works, and after the use or occupation of such part by the Employer, the responsibility for the care of the Works shall then pass to the Employer and the Contractor shall be responsible only for the outstanding Works. Any defect, error, defect or omission in the design of any Works to be provided by the Employer or in the specifications and drawings. And as an experienced Contractor, it is impossible to find out when checking the site, drawings and specifications before submitting the tender, in addition, such as defects, errors, defects or omissions are not part of the Contractor's design under the Contract. The Contractor is not responsible for this.

Except for those natural events for which the Contractor is liable as specified in the Contract, the operation of any force of nature which, as an experienced contractor, could not foresee, reasonably anticipate and take adequate precautions against, and the events or circumstances listed in the Unusual Events Clause, these events are not the responsibility of the Contractor and do not require the Contractor to be held liable. Finally, the Owner is responsible for events caused by the Owner and his personnel, whether before or after the issuance of the handover certificate, the Owner shall assume the corresponding responsibility.

According to the FIDIC 2017 Red Book, none of the foregoing events is the Contractor's responsibility unless the Works, Goods or Contractor's Documents have been rejected by the Supervision Engineer prior to the occurrence of the foregoing events. That is to say, if the Works, Goods or Contractor's Documents are not in conformity with the Contract or for other reasons rejected by the Supervision Engineer prior to the occurrence of the above mentioned events, the Contractor shall be responsible for the loss or damage resulting there from. The Contractor shall not be responsible for any loss or damage resulting there from if the Works, Goods or Contractor's Documents comply with the Contract and have been approved by the Supervision Engineer.

In the process of project implementation, the Contractor shall fulfill his obligations according to the Contract and comply with the law, neither violating the Contract nor violating the law, that is, to avoid the loss or damage caused by his own factors as far as possible. After the occurrence of any event for which the Owner is responsible or for which the Contractor is not required to be responsible according to the Contract, the Contractor shall act in accordance with the Contract, notify the Supervision Engineer, and then safeguard his own rights and interests according to the Contract.

17.3　Intellectual and Industrial Property Rights

This Sub-Clause provides appropriate protection to each Party in respect of any breaches of copying or of other intellectual or industrial property right. If a third party make a claim in respect of any of the matters mentioned in this Sub-Clause, the Parties should each consider taking advice from a lawyer familiar with the applicable intellectual.

The third Party mentioned in this Sub-Clause is the Party other than Employer and Contractor who raise the claims alleging infringement. If the Contractor is directly responsible for the infringement event, claimers may claim against Contractor; if it's the Employer who should be responsible for the event, then the Employer should go to conduct negotiations in lieu of the Contractor and ask the Contractor to assist. If the Employer refuses to conduct negotiation in lieu of the Contractor, the Contractor can accept the claims against him but at the cost of the Employer.

17.4　Indemnities by Contractor

In general, the Contract Documents of the project have clearly defined the event for which each Party is responsible for compensation. Upon commencement of the Project, the Contractor shall be responsible for indemnifying third Parties for claims, damage, losses and expenses, including attorney's fees, and shall indemnify the Owner, the Owner's personnel and their agents from injury in the event of such occurrence.

These events include any personal injury, illness, infection or death occurring in or during the execution of the Project by the Contractor or arising out of the execution of the Project by the Contractor, except as a result of negligence, malicious act or default by the Owner, the Owner's Personnel, or any of the Owner's agents.

It is very clear here that the Contractor shall be liable for any personal injury or death to a third Party caused by the Contractor, unless caused by the Owner or his agent. Any damage or loss to the property, immovable property or personal property of a third Party, other than the Works, these are caused by or in connection with the execution of the Works by the Contractor and by the negligence, bad faith or default of the Contractor, the Contractor's Personnel and their agents, or persons directly or indirectly employed by them.

From this, we can know that the damage or loss of the property of a third Party caused only by the Contractor shall be compensated by the Contractor.

In addition, if the Contractor is required by the Contract to be responsible for the design of any part of the Permanent Works and any other design to be carried out under the Contract. The Contractor shall indemnify the Contractor and shall keep the Owner harmless from injury in the event of any act, error or omission of the Contractor in carrying out his design duties which, at the completion of the works, does not fulfil his intended purpose.

In addition to the aforesaid compensation for persons and property, the Contractor shall also be liable for the Works which he is responsible for designing and shall be liable if the Works do not conform to the intended purpose of the Contract. In other words, the Contractor shall correct the work in accordance with the Contract at his own cost.

17.5　Indemnities by Employer

In the same way, the Owner shall be liable for any claims, damages, losses and expenses, including attorney's fees, from third Parties, and shall hold the Contractor, Contractor's Personnel and their agents harmless after such an event occurs. These include personal injury, illness, infection or death, or loss or damage to any property other than the Works, resulting from negligence, malice or breach of the Contract by the Owner, the Owner's Personnel or any of his agents. This Paragraph is obvious, as long as they're caused by the personal and property incidents caused by Employer's Personnel, they all belong to the Owner's compensation.

In addition, the Employer shall be liable for any damage or loss to any property, immovable property or personal property resulting from the occurrence of any of the events specified in Sub-Clause 17. 2 of this Contract, then such damages shall also be the Employer's compensation. In accordance with the Contract, all the events listed in Sub-Clause 17. 2 are Owner's Risk Events and the Owner shall be liable to indemnify a third Party after the occurrence of such Events. However, if the Contractor also incurs delays or additional costs as a result of these events, the Contractor may also claim against the Owner for the duration and costs of the project in accordance with the Contract.

17. 6　Shared Indemnities

The Contractor's compensation to the Owner under Sub-Clause 17. 3 and Sub-Clause 17. 4 shall be reduced in accordance with the provisions of the Contract if such damage, loss or injury occurs as a result of an event specified in Sub-Clause 17. 2. Similarly, in the event of such damage, loss or injury as a result of the events specified in Sub-Clause 17. 1 and Sub-Clause 17. 3, the Employer's compensation to the Contractor under Sub-Clause 17. 5 shall be reduced accordingly. In other words, in the event of damage, loss or injury resulting from an event for which both the Contractor and the Owner are responsible, the Parties shall be jointly liable and shall reduce their liability to each other.

※Vocabulary

1. injury *n.* 伤害,损害;受伤处;伤害的行为
2. respective *adj.* 分别的;各自的
3. willful *adj.* 故意的;有意的;成心的(尤指意在造成伤害)
4. attributable *adj.* 可归因于……的;可归结于……的
5. negligence *n.* 疏忽;失误;失职
6. hostility *n.* 敌意;对抗;敌对行为
7. rebellion *n.* 谋反;叛乱;反叛
8. insurrection *n.* 起义;造反;叛乱
9. usurped *v.* 夺取;篡夺;侵占
10. riot *n.* 暴乱;骚动;暴动
11. commotion *n.* 喧闹;混乱;骚动
12. munitions *n.* 军需品;(尤指)军火
13. ionizing *v.* (使)电离;(使)成离子(ionize 的现在分词)
14. sonic *adj.* 声的;声音的
15. infringement *n.* (对他人权利等的)侵犯;侵害
16. allege *v.* (未提出证据而)断言;指称;声称

18　Exceptional Events

18.1　Exceptional Events

In FIDIC 2017 edition, "Exceptional Events" is defined by the Contract terms, the definition of full choreography in Article 18 the first Paragraph 18.1 the first paragraph, the Exceptional Events here refers to some kind of event or situation, and at the same time satisfy the following four conditions:

(1) Party can't control;

(2) the Party fails to make reasonable preparations for the Contract before signing it;

(3) after the occurrence, the Party can not be reasonably avoided or overcome;

(4) can not be attributed mainly to other Parties.

As for the definition of the scope of force majeure itself, that is, whether it is an "event" or a "circumstance" that impedes the performance of the Contract, the wording varies in various judicial fields. For example, in some judicial fields, the law stipulates force majeure as an "event", but does not include the "circumstance" in the provisions of force majeure. In view of this, FIDIC 2017 defines Force Majeure as an "event" or a "circumstance", which largely covers the definition of Force Majeure itself and matters that may be encountered in practice in various jurisdictions.

On the basis of the qualitative interpretation in paragraph 1 of Sub-Clause 18.1, paragraph 2 of Sub-Clause 18.1 further lists, in a non-restrictive manner, specific events or circumstances that might constitute exceptional events. In general, subparagraphs (a) to (e) refer to "man-made disasters", such as war, insurrection, insurrection, strikes, etc.. Subparagraph (f) refers to "natural disasters", such as earthquakes, tsunamis, volcanic activity, hurricanes or typhoons. Different from FIDIC 1999 edition, the circumstances of strikes or lockouts covered in the original (iii) are listed separately as sub-item (d) of the new edition, and the tsunami has been added in the sub-item (f) of natural disasters. This slight difference should be adjusted according to the actual situation of the international project.

18.2　Notice of Exceptional Events

Sub-Clause 18.2 of FIDIC 2017 edition set out the procedural requirement for the affected Party after the occurrence of an exceptional event or circumstance—to give the other Party a notice within 14 days of the occurrence of the Exceptional Event and to indicate that the performance of the obligation has been or will be hindered. Notification of an Exceptional Event shall not be a direct claim against the construction period or cost, but rather requires the affected Party to describe the Exceptional Event and circumstances in order to enable the other party to take appropriate action in a timely manner and is the basis of the necessary claims procedure in Sub-Clause 18.4 [Consequences of an Exceptional Events].

Unlike FIDIC 1999, it is provided that if the affected Party gives notice of an Exceptional Event after 14 days, the extent to which the affected Party is exempt from performance is limited to that portion of the obligation from the date on which the notice is received by the other Party. If the affected Party delays in giving notice of the Exceptional Event, it shall not be entitled to claim a waiver of liability based on the Exceptional Event for part of the delay period.

It is important to note that Sub-Clause 20.2 the first period of 28 days of notice of claim have limitation on demand, combined with the Clause 18.4 of the references to the provisions of Clause 20.2, the contractor must also satisfy the first two Sub-Clause 18.2 and Sub-Clause 20.2 in notice limitation requirement, can only be lodged a complete effective claim on impact of Exceptional Events.

18.3 Duty to Minimize Delay

The first paragraph of Sub-Clause 18.3 [Duty to Minimize Delay] of FIDIC 2017 Edition is basically in line with the spirit of the "Loss Mitigation Rules" under common law and civil law systems.

However, the derogation obligations of the Parties in this Article focus on the "delay" of the project period and do not further provide the consequences of the violation of this provision. Therefore, it should be noted that, even if the Contract terms are not clear, in practice, based on the universally applicable "loss mitigation rules" in various judicial fields, in the event of an Exceptional Event, the Parties shall consciously take reasonable measures to reduce any loss that may be caused by the Exceptional Event.

Good contract conditions shall impose constrain on the speculation act of either Party, especially under the current environment. This Sub-Clause is purposed to impose constraint on such speculation acts. In practice, more often that one Party under contract may dispose with an event passively with certain intention, aiming to make illegal profits, hence result in an undue loss.

18.4 Consequences of an Exceptional Event

As to whether or not the Contractor is entitled to a claim for costs arising out of a force majeure event, under the arrangements of this Sub-Clause, no claim for costs shall be brought under subparagraph (f) of the category of natural disasters in the matter set out in Sub-Clause 18.1.

The remaining matters set out in Sub-Clause 18.1, for example, those set out in subparagraphs (b) to (e), shall be those which occurred in the country in which the Works are to be carried out. Other items not listed, which constitute Exceptional Events as defined in Sub-Clause 18.1, are not entitled to a claim for costs, but are entitled to a claim for construction period. Therefore, the foregoing claims arrangement means that whether and in which category the items of Exceptional Events are explicitly listed is critical to whether or not the Contractor is able to claim his interest in the costs.

18.5　Optional Termination

Paragraph 1 of Sub-Clause 18.5 of FIDIC 2017 also gives the Owner and Contractor the right to terminate the Contract in Exceptional Events, effective 7 days after notice of termination is given. Specifically, it can be divided into two situations:

(1) the implementation of virtually all the progress of the project was hindered for 84 consecutive days due to the Exceptional Events in the notice (this situation requires substantial consideration of the hindered continuity, and is not limited to a single Exceptional Event, that is, the continuous obstruction for 84 days due to a variety of Exceptional Events at the same time);

(2) for an interruption of the Exceptional Event in the same Notice for a total of 140 days (which is limited to the Exceptional Event in the same Notice).

18.6　Release from Performance under the Law

Finally, in accordance with Sub-Clause 18.6 of FIDIC 2017, two extreme circumstances beyond the control of either Party, whether or not they constitute Exceptional Events, may directly result in the release of a contractual obligation:

(1) Such circumstances render a Party unable or unable to legally perform its contractual obligations;

(2) Each Party shall have the right to rescind further performance of this Contract in accordance with applicable law.

These two cases are extreme and need to be discussed in detail according to the applicable legal rules, such as the force majeure rule under the civil law system, the change of circumstances rule or the Contract defeat rule under the common law system. This Clause is difficult to apply in practice, so we should resort to legal analysis according to the specific situation.

※ Vocabulary

1. hostilities *n.* 战争行动
2. invasion *n.* 武装入侵;侵略
3. catastrophe *n.* 重大灾难;灾祸;横祸
4. procrastinate *v.* 拖延;耽搁;延迟
5. contamination *n.* 污染;弄脏;毒害;玷污
6. volcanic *adj.* 火山的;由火山引发的
7. relief *n.* 宽慰;安心;欣慰;解脱
8. continuous *adj.* 连续不断的;持续的;不中断的

19   Insurance

19.1   General Requirements

1) General requirements

Sub-Clause 19.1 provides that the Contractor shall take out such insurance and keep it in force.

Sub-Clause 19.2 states that the Contractor shall cover the Works, Goods, Professional Liability (design for which the Contractor is responsible), Personal and Property Damage, Employee Injury and other insurance as required by law and regulations. The 2017 edition of FIDIC general contract conditions only stipulate the content that should be insured by the Contractor. It is also reasonable for the Contractor to insure the risk accidents occurring during the implementation of the project. The communication between the insurer and the Contractor enables the insurer to understand the implementation of the project more directly, and the claim settlement of the accident is more timely and efficient.

In the project, the Owner can also choose to insure part of the insurance by the Owner according to the specific situation of the project, for example, the project all risks insurance, third Party liability insurance, Employer's liability insurance, etc. Project insurance by the Owner during the implementation period can enhance the owner's initiative in the risk control of the whole project. Meanwhile, unified package insurance by the Owner can also help to reduce the premium. If there are some risks to be covered by the Owner, the Owner should seek professional advice in the draft tender documents, modify the relevant provisions in the contract conditions, and shall list in detail the Owner purchase conditions, compensation limits, deductibles and exclusions. It is desirable to provide a format of the Owner's insurance policy so that tenderers can determine which insurance is to be covered by themselves and thus estimate the corresponding premium. For projects that use loans, lending banks and financial institutions often have mandatory requirements for insurance during the implementation and operation of the project.

2) Communication in insurance Parties

Sub-Clause 19.1 states that the insurance company and the terms of the policy shall be subject to the consent of the Employer and shall be in accordance with the terms of insurance agreed upon by the Parties prior to the issue of the Letter of Acceptance. The Contractor shall, when requested by the Owner, provide the insurance policy specified in the Contract. Immediately after payment of the premium, the Contractor shall provide the Employer with the Payment Certificate or the Insurance Company's Certificate confirming that the premium has been paid.

When insured, the insured shall fully inform the insurer (insurance company) of the important facts concerning the insurance. After the insurance is effected, the insured (the

Contractor in this Contract) shall notify the insurer of any material change in the nature, extent and progress of the Works during the execution of the Works.

If there is a material change in the policy risk, or if an event has occurred that has caused or is likely to cause a claim under the policy, the insured shall notify the underwriters and take timely preventive action to stop the loss. Only if the insurer agrees to change the risk scope of the policy (and possibly the amount of the premium), will the insurer pay for the additional risk of the project.

3) Deductibles

Sub-Clause 19.1 states that the amount of deductible specified in the policy shall not exceed the amount specified in the Contract Data Sheet (if not specified in the Contract Data Sheet, the amount agreed by the Owner shall prevail).

The deductible is the amount that the insurer is exempt from indemnifying against the loss of each risk incident. A policy may have a single or set of deductibles for different items of loss, and the deductibles and limits of claims together define the insurer's coverage.

Typically, the lower the deductible, the higher the premium rate. Considering the different risks at different stages of the project, deductibles should be differentiated and adjusted accordingly.

4) Compliance with the terms of this Contract and Policy

If the Contractor does not take out insurance in accordance with Sub-Clause 19.2 [Insurance to be provided by the Contractor] and keep the insurance in force, which the Owner may take out and keep in force and for which the premium paid shall be reimbursed from the Contractor, compensation may be obtained by deducting from any amount due to the Contractor or may be claimed separately from the Contractor.

In the event that neither the Contractor nor the Owner comply with the terms of the insurance insured under the provisions of the Contract, the Party in breach of the terms of insurance shall indemnify the other Party for all direct losses (including legal costs) resulting therefrom.

It also states that Article 20 [Employer's and Contractor's Claims] does not apply to a situation where, in the event that a Party fails to comply with the provisions of this Contract and Policy, the aggrieved Party may directly claim against the other Party without having to go through the claims procedure provided for in the General Conditions of Contract.

5) Shared responsibilities

Sub-Clause 19.1 provides that, if the Contract provides for joint liability, the Parties to the Contract shall be liable for a loss not recoverable by the insurer in proportion to their share of the liability provided that such loss is not attributable to the contractor or the Owner's default. If such part of the loss is caused by the breach of Contract of either Party, the breaching Party shall be liable for such loss.

The Contract may also provide for joint liability for losses caused by exceptional events that will not be covered by insurance. At the same time, the insurance will not reduce the contractual obligations and responsibilities of both Parties to the Contract.

19.2 Insurance to be provided by the Contractor

19.2.1 The Works

The work process is subject to the Sub-Clause 19. 2. 1. This Sub-Clause requires the Contractor to insure the Works, Contractor's Documents, materials to be used in the work and manufacturing equipment for full replacement value in the name of both the Owner and the Contractor.

This Clause is the insurance requirement for all risks insurance of project and contains the following four meanings:

(1) The construction project and installation project account for different proportion in project, project all risks insurance correspond to project all risks insurance, installation project all risks insurance or construction installation project all risks insurance.

(2) For the purpose of insurable interest and avoidance of recourse, the insured shall include the Owner, Contractor and Subcontractors ("Subcontractors" herein include Subcontractors, designers, consultants, suppliers, other Parties providing goods or services in connection with the insured works and their Subcontractors at all levels).

In addition, lending banks and financial institutions that finance projects will also be required to be included in the insured list.

(3) This Clause requires that insurance cover the Works, Contractor's Documents, and Materials and Production Equipment intended to be used in the Works. The Master Policy covers the Works, materials intended to be used in the Works and Plant. Contractor's Documents are normally covered by the extension "Plan and Documents Clause".

This extension shall indemnify the Contractor only for the cost of redrawing, reproducing and not for the cost of redesigning the Contractor's Documents resulting from the loss of the Contractor's Documents as a result of the insured risks.

(4) The insurance amount of the Project all risks insurance should be the project (contain the Material that Plans to use at the Project and Production Equipment) of the replacement value, usually take the total price of the Project Contract as the insurance amount.

In the event that Materials and manufacturing Equipment intended to be used in the Project are supplied by the Employer, the amount of insurance shall also include the value of such Materials and Manufacturing Equipment provided by the Employer.

15% of the replacement value of the Works, Contractor's Documents, Materials intended for use in the Works and Production Equipment (or such other amount as may be specified in the Contract Data Sheet) shall be applied to any additional costs associated with the repair of damage, including professional fees and the removal of debris.

If the entire Project is lost and reconstruction work is required, it is usually necessary to clean up the site and the debris, as well as to examine and evaluate the damaged parts of the project before reconstruction. These costs are not included in the cost of the new Project. Therefore, the 2017 edition of FIDIC requires that additional costs associated with repair losses be taken into account in all engineering risks.

1) Duration of insurance against project all risks

The principal insurance coverage of the Project All Risks shall be from the Commencement Date to the date of issuance of the Works Taking-Over Certificate, but shall be extended to the Defects Notification Period.

Since the insurance period is calculated since commencement date, the Contractor is required to carry out insurance inquiry before winning the bid (some large engineering projects insurance companies also need to carry out insurance inquiry in the insurance market). The starting time of project all risks insurance shall be determined according to the actual situation. The uncertainty of the time and condition of project handover may lead to the change of insurance period.

The expiration date of the insurance period in the policy is the "date on which the Taking-Over Certificate of Works is issued" calculated by the Contractor according to the completion date specified in the Contract. If the actual date of handover of the Works is later than that date, the Contractor shall give prior notice to the Insurance Company and, with the consent of the Insurance Company and an appropriate increase in premium, extend the principal insurance period.

The insurance period shall be extended to the Defects Notification Period, during which the coverage shall be limited to engineering losses due to design errors, defects in raw materials and poor workmanship. This requirement can be satisfied by adding a Guarantee Period Clause to all risks of the Works. "Extended Maintenance Clause" can be added under the Project All Risks item. To protect the Contractor against losses of the works arising out of the maintenance carried out in accordance with the Contract of the Works and losses of the Works arising out of construction causes during the construction period prior to the issuance of the Handover certificate and during the Defects Notification Period.

2) Exclusion of liability against all risks of construction

The Contractor's exclusions against Project All Risks may include:

(1) The cost of repairing any defective or other parts of the Works (including defective Materials and Workmanship) which do not conform to the Contract, but does not exclude the cost of repairing the loss of any other part of the Works caused by such defects or discrepancies;

(2) Indirect losses, including the reduction of the contract price due to delay;

(3) Natural wear and tear, shortage and theft;

(4) Risks arising from exceptional events, unless otherwise specified in the Contract Data Sheet.

The exclusions of all risks usually include the above four and some other exclusions. Particular attention shall be given to Paragraph 1: All Risks shall cover losses and expenses for replacement, repair and correction of other parts of the Works arising out of accidents arising out of errors in the design of the Works, defects in raw materials or poor workmanship.

However, no compensation shall be made for the loss of the part of the project itself directly affected by design errors, defects in raw materials or poor workmanship.

Whether an Exceptional Event is insurable varies by insurance market and item type and therefore needs to be specifically specified in the Contract Data Sheet.

19.2.2 Goods

Sub-Clause 19.2.2 requires the Contractor to insure, in the name of the Owner and the Contractor, the Goods and other Articles arriving at the Site for the amount specified in the Contract Data Sheet or for the full replacement value for the period from the arrival of the Goods at the Site until they are no longer required for the Works.

Subject to Sub-Clause 1.1 [Definitions], the Goods shall include Contractor's Construction Equipment, Materials, Production Equipment and Temporary Works. Materials, Production Equipment and Temporary Works to be used on site.

Has been covered by project all risks, the Contractor's Construction Equipment shall be purchased separately for construction machines risks insurance. To buy insurance for Contractor's Construction Equipment there are two ways: the first is to expand "Construction/Erection Machinery Clause" under the project all risks; the second is to buy property insurance for Contractor's Construction Equipment alone. Either way, the insurance company is not liable for damage to construction equipment due to inherent mechanical or electrical faults, and for damage to vehicles, ships and aircraft licensed for public transport. The premiums of these two ways are collected beyond the project all risks premiums, and the premiums are calculated according to the annual rate, and the insurance period is calculated according to the year or the period during which the Contractor's construction equipment enters the site.

If the property insurance is purchased separately for the Contractor's Construction Equipment, it can be insured according to a single Project, or all the construction equipment can be packaged and purchased annually regardless of the Project, but it may not be able to meet the specific requirements of the Project owner for the construction equipment insurance.

The arrangement of project all risks insurance and cargo insurance in the 2017 edition of FIDIC contract conditions is worth discussing, and there are too many duplications with the relevant provisions of project all risks.

It is suggested that the insurance of Contractor's Construction Equipment should be included separately and that a general provision of cargo insurance should be added to the general or special terms of Contract where appropriate.

The Contractor usually takes out cargo transportation insurance for the Goods for which he is responsible. If the Goods (Contractor's Construction Equipment, Materials and Production Equipment) involve only inland transport, an extension of the inland transport clause may be added to the engineering all risks to cover the loss or loss of the Goods due to a risk incident in the course of transport.

If the carriage of Goods involves several modes of transport, such as water or air, the insurance shall be separately covered.

In project all risks and risk of carriage of Goods, usually 50/50 allocation clause will be added under these two terms for insurance, namely outer packing is good after the Goods are transported to the site , and if the damage is found when the box is opened after a period of time of storage in the site, but the time of the damage cannot be determined, the compensation for the loss shall be apportionment of 50% between project all risks and cargo transportation risks.

There is no mention in the FIDIC Conditions of Contract 2017 of insurance for the Goods and Construction Equipment provided by the Owner, but it is clear that the Owner shall have all relevant insurance for the transport of Goods and Construction Equipment provided by the Owner.

In the project, the project participants will usually apply for transport insurance for their own motor vehicles, ships, etc. , which have public transport driving licenses, as well as for transport as a result of risk accidents caused by its own losses and third Party liability insurance.

19.2.3 Liability for breach of professional duty

Sub-Clause 19. 2. 3 requires the Contractor to have professional liability insurance (also referred to as occupational indemnity insurance) for the design for which he is responsible, which covers the Contractor's liability for any act, error or omission arising in the performance of his design obligations.

This professional liability insurance shall also indemnify the Contractor against any act, error or omission in the performance of the Contractor's design responsibilities which causes the completed Works (or Section, Part or major Plant) to fail to meet the intended purpose, if specified in the Contract Data Sheet.

The insurance period is specified in the Contract Data Sheet. The liability scope of Contractor's professional liability insurance is the material loss of the project itself caused by the accident caused by the mistakes or negligence of the design, and the personal injury and death of a third Party or property loss.

In the event of an accident due to a design defect, this scope of liability is much greater than the scope of the Designer's Risk Extension clause attached to the Project All Risks. The latter only compensates for the damage of other non-defective parts of the project caused by accidents, and does not compensate for the damage of the part of the project with design defects, and does not bear the third Party liability. The Owner may also decide whether or not to extend the coverage of the professional liability insurance to a standard that meets the intended purpose and stipulates accordingly in the Contract Data Sheet.

In the 2017 edition of FIDIC Red Book, Silver Book and Yellow Book, due to the different design scope of responsibility of the Contractor, the scope of professional liability insurance is also different, and the Red Book generally does not cover this kind of insurance.

Generally speaking, professional liability insurance requires a strong underwriting ability of the insurance company, so the amount paid will not be too high, which is roughly the design cost. At the same time, there will be a deductible agreement.

Professional liability insurance is mainly aimed at the Contractor who is responsible for the design of the speculative behavior, once the accident happens, the Contractor will pay very high insurance premium in the future. The 2017 edition of FIDIC specifically adds requirements for professional liability insurance, indicating that more and more Owners in the international engineering market will require such insurance.

19. 2. 4　Injury to person and damage to property

The requirements of third Party liability insurance in relation to Sub-Clause 19. 2. 4 are as follows:

The Contractor shall, in the name of the Owner and the Contractor, insure against the death or injury of any person or loss or damage to any property (other than the Works) arising out of the performance of the Contract and occurring prior to the issuance of the Performance Certificate, except for losses arising out of exceptional events.

The third party liability insurance protects the third Party (the relevant Party other than the Owner and Contractor) who does not participate in the implementation of the project in the site or adjacent to the site, and causes the personal injury or property loss due to the occurrence of the project risk accident. In the laws of various countries, most of the third Party liability insurance are mandatory requirements. The main purpose is to protect the public rights and interests affected by the implementation of the project. In general, third Party liability insurance provides a minimum limit for each occurrence of such a risk event, but no limit on the number of times.

The third party liability insurance may be added to all project risk, and sometimes the Owner's property other than the work itself is also covered by the third Party liability insurance. Third Party liability is based on infringement. Whereas the infringed third Party may claim either directly from the Contractor or from the Owner or Subcontractors, the insured shall include the Owner, the Contractor and their Subcontractors in order to avoid damage to all Parties involved in the project.

In addition, legal costs, investigation and evidence costs caused by infringement, etc. may also get compensation under third Party liability insurance.

The warranty shall include a "cross liability clause". The "cross liability clause" is the most common extension of the third Party liability insurance. It refers to the cover of the policy under the third Party liability. The policy will apply to all insured persons named in the policy as if each insured person held a separate policy. This Clause makes it clear that in the case of mutual liability between multiple insured in a risk accident, the insurance company cannot recover the insured who is liable. This insurance shall be effected prior to the commencement of Site Work by the Contractor and shall remain in force until the issuance of the Performance Certificate and shall not be less than the amount specified in the Contract Data Sheet or the amount agreed to by the Employer. The period of the third Party liability insurance shall correspond to the site liability insurance. If work has not been carried out in the site, naturally risk accidents resulting will not occur in the site and neither the adjacent area of the third Party or property damage.

If the third Party liability insurance is to be covered together with the all project risks, it should be noted that the duration of the insurance for all project risks in Sub-Clause 19. 2. 1 is not consistent with the duration of the insurance for the third Party liability insurance. The third Party liability insurance is required herein to cover the Defects Notification Period up to the issue of the Performance Certificate, which is solely for the Contractor's liability for injury or loss to third Parties in and near the Site as a result of the Contractor's work on the Site in order to complete the mending work and the elimination of the Defect during the Defects Notification Period.

19.2.5　Injury to employees

Sub-Clause 19.2.5 requires the Contractor to insure against claims, losses and expenses (including legal costs) arising out of injury, illness, illness or death of any of the Contractor's Personnel arising out of the execution of the Works. The Owner and the Engineer shall also be covered under this policy, except for losses and claims arising from the acts or omissions of the Owner or his personnel. This insurance shall remain in force throughout the period during which the Contractor's Personnel are involved in the execution of the Works. The Subcontractor's Personnel may be insured by the Subcontractor, but the Contractor shall be responsible for the Subcontractor's compliance with this Sub-Clause. This Sub-Clause requires the Contractor and his Subcontractors to insure against the Employer's liability for illness or death of his personnel arising out of an accident at work in the course of engineering work. Since the Employer and the Engineer are also participants in the Works, the Employer and the Engineer shall also be covered by the Employer's liability insurance.

19.2.6　Other insurance required by Laws and by local practice

Sub-Clause 19.1 [General Requirements] states that the Contractor is required in the Contract to cover only the minimum requirements of the Employer and may, at the Contractor's own expense, take out additional insurance if necessary. In addition, Sub-Clause 19.2.6 also requires the Contractor to take out insurance at his own expense in accordance with the law and local custom of the country in which the Works is to be performed. This Sub-Clause provides that the Employer will generally specify in the Contract Data Table the types and requirements to be covered if the Contractor is required to take out other special insurance in accordance with the local law or custom of the country in which the Works are to be performed. The Contractor shall be aware of such special requirements of the country in which the Works is to be performed and shall at his sole discretion determine whether adequate coverage is required for coverage not requested by the Employer.

※Vocabulary

1. Hostilities *n.* 战争行动
2. third party liability insurance 第三者责任保险
3. all risks insurance 综合险保险；全保险
4. desirable *adj.* 令人向往的，值得拥有的；可取的；性感的
　　　　　　n. 称心合意的人（或物），好的品质
5. insurance policy 保险单，保单

6. the insured 被保险人

7. preventive action［管理］预防措施

8. underwriters *n.* 承保人,保险商(尤指船只);核保人(对投保项目进行风险评估并决定保险费率)

9. deductible *adj.* 可扣除的,可减免的

        n. <美>免赔额

10. insurance in force 有效保险

11. breach of contract 违约;违反合同

12. joint liability 连带责任

13. replacement value 重置价值

14. insurance cover 保险金额;［保险］保险范围;安排必要的保险

15. master policy［保险］总保险单

16. exclusion of liability 责任免除

17. defective materials 有缺陷的材料

18. cargo insurance 货物保险

19. apportionment *n.* 分摊;分配;分派

20. professional liability insurance［保险］职业责任保险

21. occupational *adj.* 职业的,由职业引起的;占领的

22. negligence *n.* 疏忽,大意;<法律>玩忽职守

23. underwriting *n.* 保险业;［金融］证券包销

        v. 认购(underwrite 的现在分词);写在……下面;经营保险业

24. elimination *n.* 消除,排除;淘汰;消灭,铲除;排泄

25. sole discretion 全权处理

20　Employer's and Contactor's Claims

20.1　Claims

Because the Contractor's project implementation is disturbed by many factors, it is necessary to arrange relevant personnel to deal with these things, namely the Contract Management Work. In addition, we also find that both the Owner and the Supervision Engineer have personnel who are specialized in dealing with contract issues. These personnel constitute the Contract Management Personnel of the Owner, which shows how much the Owner and the Supervision Engineer attach importance to contract management. Among the Supervision Engineers, there are even engineers who specialize in handling contract claims. Therefore, in order to safeguard their own interests, the contract claim is one of the indispensable means.

In the Contract Management Work, one of our common work is the claim, under what circumstances will the claim event occur? According to the 2017 edition of FIDIC Red Book, in the process of project implementation, including the Owner to the Contractor Claim, if the Owner thinks it has the right to claim additional payment to the Contractor, or reduce the Contract Price, and extend the Project Defects Notification Period, so the Owner can according to the Contract, claim for compensation to the Contractor, the Claim is the Owner of the Claim.

In the same way, since there is the existence of the Owner to the Contractor claim, then, there is also a Contractor to Owner's claim for compensation, according to the Contract provisions, if the Contractor considers its reserves the right to claim to Owner time delay (and) or additional costs, so, the Contractor shall according to the Contract, claim for compensation to the Owners, these claims are the Contractor's claims. The Contractor's claim and the Owner's claim together constitute a Contract claim. Of course, not every project has claims, and in some cases, there may be no Contract claims after the completion of the project.

In addition to the above two cases, if either of the Owner or the Contractor considers that it is entitled to a relevant interest or release from the other, such benefits or discharges may be of any kind, including in connection with any certificate, decision, instruction, notice, opinion or evaluation of the Supervision Engineer, excluding any other interest related to the above two interests. In other words, in addition to the above two kinds of claims, the Owner and the Contractor may enjoy other aspects of the relevant interests or relief.

On the whole, making claim is a difficult thing. Actually both of the Parties are entitled to claims and the Employer may make counter-claim or defensive claims against the claims the Contractor raised. The reimbursement costs the Contractor claimed is often offset by what the Employer counterclaims for.

Besides, too many claims will cause the Contractor adverse effect, i. e. going into the blacklist and being classified as the type of claim - conscious. This may deprive the Contractors of chances to win other projects in tendering thereafter. Thus it's necessary to weigh the advantages and disadvantages properly when making claim decisions.

In accordance with the Contract, whether the Owner's claim or the Contractor's claim occurs, the corresponding claim and claim assessment shall be carried out in accordance with Sub-Clause 20.2 of the Contract. But if the third scenario happens, if the other Party or the Supervision Engineer does not agree to the rights or discharge of the claimant, or is deemed to disagree, or not responding within a reasonable period of time, that doesn't mean there's a dispute. The Party making the claim may give notice to the Supervision Engineer, who shall then carry out the relevant work in accordance with Sub-Clause 3.7.

According to the Contract, the Party making the claim becomes aware of the other Party's or the Supervision Engineer's disapproval, or after being deemed to disagree, notice shall be given as soon as practicable, and the relevant details, including the detailed claim event of the claimant, and the disapproval of the other Party or the Supervision Engineer, or deemed as disapproval, shall be submitted together to the Supervision Engineer. After receiving the relevant Materials, the Supervision Engineer shall make a fair and just decision in accordance with the Contract and within the time specified in the Contract.

Grounds for raising a claim:

①*instruction from the Engineer*;

②*correspondence*;

③*meeting minutes*;

④*construction site record*;

⑤*project financial information*;

⑥*site climate information*;

⑦*market information*;

⑧*legislation and policies*.

20.2   Claims For Payment and/or EOT

20.2.1   Notice of Claim

As the two Parties to the Contract, in the signing stage of the Contract Document, both Parties have no objection to the content of the Contract, after reaching an agreement, the Contract can be signed. Therefore, the Contract Document is legally binding on both Parties and is the basis of the contractual relationship between the two Parties. Therefore, if either the Owner or the Contractor considers that he or she is entitled to claim against the other in accordance with any of the terms of the Contract or any other document in connection with the Contract, the procedures prescribed in the Contract must be followed and the provisions of the Contract shall be strictly followed.

The first step in a Contract Claim is to issue a notice of claim. Regardless of whether the claimant is the Owner or the Contractor, the claimant shall, as soon as it becomes aware of the claim event or circumstance, give notice of claim to the Supervision Engineer in accordance with the Contract.

The Contract specifies a time frame for giving notice of the claim, which must be given within 28 days of becoming aware of the event or circumstance of the claim. The contents of the notice of claim shall also include a detailed description of the events or circumstances that gave rise to the claim and shall also indicate the terms of the Contract under which the claim was given.

We may ask, what are the consequences if we fail to give notice of the claim within 28 days of becoming aware of the claim event or circumstance? If this happens, the claimant loses its right to claim according to the Contract and the respondent is released from any liability for the event or circumstance resulting from the claim. Contract claim event or situation is very common in the daily Contract Management Process. As a claimant, one of the purposes of issuing a notice of claim is to remind the other Party and ask the other Party to resolve the existing problem as soon as possible.

From the processing of the claim notice, we can learn that no matter which Party is the claimant, the 2017 FIDIC contract conditions require both Parties to intervene from the initial stage of the claim to understand the claim event or situation in order to better resolve the claim event. In addition, if the claimant fails to give the notice of claim within 28 days as stipulated in the contract, it should explain in detail the reasons for the late notice of claim in the submission of the detailed claim report. It may also obtain the approval of the Supervision Engineer, so it can also carry out the claim. In other words, the 2017 FIDIC contract conditions do not apply one size fits all, because the actual situation is complex and changeable.

20.2.2　Engineer's initial response

In the event or circumstance of a claim, the Supervision Engineer shall act as an intermediary between the Owner and the Contractor and shall make a fair determination in accordance with the Contract. Upon receipt of the notice of claim, the Supervision Engineer shall immediately make a preliminary understanding of the claim event or situation, and make a preliminary response within 14 days after receipt of the notice of claim, formally issue a notice, and make clear whether the notice is sent within 28 days as stipulated in the Contract. This clause is a new clause in the FIDIC contract conditions of 2017 edition. The purpose of this clause is to require the Supervision Engineer to intervene in the claim from the initial stage of the claim.

If the Supervision Engineer does not give any reply within 14 days after receiving the notice of claim, the notice of claim shall be deemed to be valid. In such case, if the other Party does not agree with the opinion of the Supervision Engineer and does not recognize the notice of claim as a valid notice of claim, it shall formally notify the Supervision Engineer and state the detailed reasons for its disapproval. The Supervision Engineer shall carefully review this notice of disapproval at the stage of adjudicating claims according to the Contract. From this, we can see that both Parties begin to understand the claim event or situation at the initial stage of the claim.

In addition, if the claimant receives a reply from the Supervision Engineer within 14 days after sending the claim notice, the Supervision Engineer considers that the claim notice is not sent within 28 days after becoming aware of the claim event or circumstance, and the claim notice is invalid. If the claimant does not agree with the opinion of the Supervision Engineer and can justify its late notice of claim, the claimant shall, in the detailed claim report submitted, give detailed reasons for disagreeing with the opinion of the supervision or explain in detail the reasons for its late notice of claim.

20.2.3　Contemporary records

The claimant shall, after sending the notice of claim, make a contemporaneous record of the claim event or circumstance as required by the Contract. A contemporaneous record is a record prepared or generated at the same time as or immediately after the occurrence of a claim event or circumstance. That is, the claimant may make a record either at the same time as the event or circumstance of the claim occurs, as soon as it becomes aware of the event or circumstance of the claim.

The Supervision Engineer may deny the liability of the claimant, supervise the claimant to make records in the same period after the occurrence of the claim event, or instruct the claimant to make additional records. The claimant shall allow the Supervision Engineer to inspect the records during normal working hours and may also inspect the records during such other hours as may be agreed. The claimant can submit a copy of the corresponding record to the Supervision Engineer. However, the supervision, inspection or instruction of the Supervision Engineer does not imply acceptance of the accuracy or completeness of the claimant's records. That is, the accuracy or completeness of the claim record is the sole responsibility of the claimant.

20.2.4 Fully detailed Claim

After all Parties have a preliminary response, the claimant shall also be accordance with the requirements of the Contract, submit a detailed claim report, the details of the claim report should include the contents stipulated in the Contract, including detailed cause claim event or situation, a contract or legal basis of the claim, the claim records of all in the same period, a full explanation of the support claim additional amount, and detailed support for the duration claim. Detailed supporting instructions for reducing the contract price and extending the defect notice period in the case of the Owner's claim.

The above detailed claim report shall be submitted to the Supervision Engineer within 84 days after the claimant becomes aware of the claim event, or within such other period as the claimant proposes and the Supervision Engineer agrees. However, if the claimant is unable to submit the contractual or legal basis for the claim within this time period, the notice of claim will be deemed to have expired and will no longer be a valid notice of claim. At the same time, the Supervision Engineer shall give such notice to the claimant within 14 days after the expiration of the time for submitting the claim report stipulated in the Contract.

If the claimant fails to submit a detailed claim within the prescribed time, or if the claimant has submitted a detailed claim within the prescribed time, the Supervision Engineer fails to give such notice within 14 days, the claim notice issued by the claimant shall continue to be valid. If the other Party does not agree that the notice of claim is a valid notice, the Supervision Engineer shall be notified and a detailed statement of the disapproval shall be submitted. After that, the Supervision Engineer shall take the notice of the other Party into account in his decision in accordance with the Contract. In other words, the other side is also entitled to a different opinion.

If the claimant has received notice from the Supervision Engineer, in addition, the claimant does not agree with the opinion of the Supervision Engineer that it can provide detailed justification for the late payment of the claim. In the detailed claim report, the claimant shall include its detailed justification for the late payment of the claim, which shall be fully considered by the Supervision Engineer in the course of reviewing the claim report. However, if the claim event or circumstance has a continuous impact, then the claim will be opened and adjudicated in accordance with the provisions of a claim with a continuous impact.

20.2.5 Agreement or determination of the Claim

After receiving the detailed claim report submitted by the claimant, either the interim claim report or the final claim report, the Supervision Engineer shall, in accordance with the provisions of the Contract, stand in a neutral position to determine the additional cost and the extension time of the project before or after the expiration of the original period. In the case of a claim by the Owner, the amount to be reduced from the Contract Price and the period for which the Defects Notification Period is extended before or after the expiry of the Defects Notification Period shall be determined. Here, no matter the claim of the Owner or the claim of the Contractor, the Supervision Engineer should adjudicate fairly.

However, if the Supervision Engineer has made an initial reply to the claim notice sent by the claimant and given notice to the detailed claim report submitted by the claimant, the Supervision Engineer shall continue to adjudicate the claim submitted by the claimant in a fair and impartial manner in accordance with the provisions of the Contract. The Supervision Engineer's decision shall be combined with the detailed claim report submitted by the claimant and disagreement with the detailed description of the notice of the Supervision Engineer, giving full consideration to whether the notice of claim sent by the claimant is valid or how the late claim report is justified, in which case, the relevant provisions shall be given full consideration when making the decision.

If any of the above occurs, the Supervision Engineer shall give full consideration to relevant information, including whether or to what extent the other Party is affected by the late payment of the claim. If the claimant is unable to give notice of the claim within the time specified in the Contract, the claimant may include in the claim report evidence that it believes the other Party had prior knowledge of the event or circumstances of the claim. And if the claimant is unable to submit the claim report within the time specified in the Contract, the claimant may include in the claim report evidence that it believes the other Party had prior knowledge of the contractual or legal basis for the claim.

After receiving the detailed claim report from the claimant, whether it is the interim claim report or the final claim report, if the Supervision Engineer needs additional information, he shall immediately notify the claimant, describing in detail the additional information needed and the reasons for the need. Upon receipt of the request from the Supervision Engineer, the claimant shall submit the relevant additional information to the Supervision Engineer as soon as possible. The Supervision Engineer shall, within the time specified in the Contract, give a response to the Contract or legal basis of the claimant and give a corresponding notice to the claimant.

After the aforesaid matters are done, the Supervision Engineer shall proceed to adjudicate the claim in accordance with the Contract procedure.

The date on which the time for calculation of the award begins is the date on which the Supervision Engineer receives additional information from the claimant.

If the Supervision Engineer fails to give a final decision or remains silent after the expiration of the time specified in the Contract, it means that the Supervision Engineer rejects the claim and the claim becomes a dispute, and the claimant can directly submit it to DAAB for arbitration without the need to issue a notice of dissatisfaction.

20.2.6 **Claims of continuing effect**

The FIDIC contract conditions strictly stipulate the procedure of contract claim. In general, the claimant submits the claim directly according to the Contract. However, there are special cases where the claimant encounters a contract claim event or circumstance that has a continuous impact. In such a case, a contract claim cannot be opened in the manner of an event or circumstance that would normally have a one-off effect. Contract claims for events or circumstances of continuous impact are more cumbersome and, under the terms of the FIDIC contract, the contract claims procedures for such events or circumstances are consistent with those for general events.

The claimant shall also give notice of the claim within a specified period of time in accordance with the provisions of the Contract when it encounters a contract claim for events or circumstances of continuous effect.

After receiving the notice from the claimant, the Supervision Engineer shall make a preliminary response according to the Contract, and the other Party may also make its corresponding response according to the actual situation. It is important to note that this is a preliminary response and does not represent a rejection of the amount of the claim. In the detailed claim report, the claimant may provide its detailed arguments to the Supervising Engineer. In making the award, the Supervision Engineer shall give full consideration to the justifications of the Parties. The claimant shall also keep a contemporaneous record, which shall be kept synchronously at the occurrence of the contract claim event or circumstance, or immediately after the occurrence.

Here, keeping a record of the same period is not directly related to whether the notice of claim is issued or not. Even if no notice of claim is issued, the claimant has the obligation and responsibility to keep a record of the same period. The Supervision Engineer may provide supervision, guidance and inspection in this process, and these works do not mean that he accepts the record. The completeness and accuracy of contemporaneous records shall be the responsibility of the claimant. The Claimant shall submit a detailed claim report within 84 days after the claimant becomes aware of the contract claim event or circumstance. The report includes a detailed description of the events or circumstances of the claim, the contractual or legal basis for the claim, the contemporaneous records on which the claimant relied, and a detailed description of the calculation of additional costs and delays. In the case of the Owner's claim, it is a detailed description of the Contract Price reduction and the extension of the Defects Notification Period. Unlike a general contract claim, the claim report here becomes an interim claim report.

After receiving the first claim report submitted by the claimant in accordance with the provisions of the Contract, the Supervision Engineer shall, in accordance with the provisions of the Contract, send a notice to the claimant within a specified period of time, giving its response on the contractual or legal basis of the claim. After submitting the first interim claim, the claimant shall submit a further interim claim report on a monthly basis, showing the accumulated amount of claim, or the accumulated time of construction claim. If the claimant is the Owner, the cumulative amount of the contract price reduction or the extension of the Defects Notification Period shall be given.

Within 28 days after the end of an event or circumstance having a continuous impact, or by the claimant. Within other time periods agreed by the Supervision Engineer, the claimant shall submit the final claim report to the Supervision Engineer, providing the total claim amount and the total claim time for the construction period. If the claimant is the Owner, the amount of reduction in the total Contract Price and the extension of the total Defects Notification Period shall be given. From this, we can know that the claimant can only calculate the total claim amount and time after the continuous impact events or circumstances have ended. In fact, after the above analysis, we can find that claims with a continuous impact of events or circumstances are not very different from the average claim. For general claims, we can submit all claim data at one time and calculate the amount and time of claim at one time. For the claim events or circumstances with continuous impact, the claim report shall be submitted in multiple times. Each claim report shall contain the accumulated claim amount and time. The total claim amount and time can be calculated when the last detailed claim report is submitted.

Upon receipt of the notice of claim and up to the award of the completion of the claim, the Engineer shall place in each Interim Payment Certificate any substantiated amount of claim payable to the claimant. Here, we need to know that as long as the amount due to the claimant is verified, whether as a whole or in part, the Supervision Engineer shall put the verified part of the amount into the Interim Payment Certificate for measurement. Therefore, in the claim process, the claimant should confirm the relevant claim as soon as possible to protect their own rights and interests.

20.2.7　General requirements

By complying with Sub-Clause 20.2 of the Contract, the Owner shall only be entitled to claim any costs from the Contractor, or to extend the Defects Notification Period, or to make any deductions or deductions from any amounts due to the Contractor. It can be seen from this provision that the Owner shall have no claim against the Contractor unless he has complied with the provisions of Sub-Clause 20.2 of the Contract. The Owner shall have no right to unreasonably withhold any monies due to the Contractor. The Costs may only be set off or deducted from the Contractor by means of a contract claim in accordance with the provisions of the Contract.

※Vocabulary

1. specialize in 专门研究……
2. reimbursement *n.* 赔付,偿付,赔偿;赔偿金额
3. counterclaims *n.* 反诉;反对要求
   　　　　　v. 反诉;提起反诉
4. meeting minutes 会议记录
5. initial stage 原始期
6. intermediary *adj.* 中间的,过渡的

n. 调解人,中间人;媒介

7. contemporaneous *adj.* 同时期的;同时代的,同时发生的

8. contemporary *adj.* 当代的,现代的;同时期的,同时代的

n. 同时代的人;同龄人,同辈

9. completeness *n.* 完整;完全;完成;圆满;结束

10. expiration *n.* 到期,(一段时间的)结束;呼气,吐气

11. justification *n.* 正当理由,合理解释;证明为正当,辩护;齐行,整版;(上帝眼中的)称义

12. neutral *adj.* 中立的,不偏不倚的;中性的,不带感情色彩的;暗淡的,素净的;(化学中)中性的,非酸非碱的;不带电的

n. (车辆排挡的)空挡;中立者,中立国;素净色,中和色;不活动,停滞;不带电的接触点

13. prior knowledge 先验知识

14. continuous impact 连续冲击

15. the cumulative amount 累计金额

16. general requirements 一般要求;总要求;常规要求

21 Disputes and Arbitration

21.1 Constitution of the DAAB

In the implementation of overseas engineering projects, there will be contract claims. Under normal circumstances, both the Contractor and the Owner can handle the claims smoothly, either in accordance with the ruling of the Supervision Engineer or through friendly negotiation. However, when the two Parties cannot reach an agreement, the claim becomes a dispute. At this time, the dispute should be decided by the specified DRE, DAB or DAAB in accordance with the provisions of the Contract. In the terms and conditions of the FIDIC contract (2017), the dispute is decided by DAAB.

Most people are familiar with DRE, whose full name is Dispute Review Expert. There's also the DAB, which stands for Dispute Adjudication Board. In the 2017 FIDIC contract conditions, the aforementioned dispute resolution method is changed to DAAB, whose full name is Dispute Avoidance/Adjudication Board, also known as the Dispute Avoidance and Adjudication Board. Through its new name, one role of the DAAB is to help the Owners and Contractors avoid controversy.

After the completion of the project bidding, the Owner shall issue the letter of award to the winning bidder. According to the requirements of the Contract, the DAAB shall be jointly appointed by the Owner and the Contractor within the time specified in the Contract Data after the signing of the letter of award by the Owner. If there is no specified time, the joint appointment of DAAB shall be completed within 28 days after the signing of the letter of award by the Owner.

According to the Contract Data, DAAB members can be composed of 3 or 1 person. If the Contract Data does not specify, and the two Parties do not agree on the number, the DAAB members should be composed of 3 people.

Obviously, if the Parties agree that one person will form the DAAB, then the person chosen by the Owner and the Contractor will form the DAAB. If the Parties disagree about the formation of a DAAB by one person, the DAAB is formed by three people. Either one or three people should be selected from the list listed in the Contract Data, rather than someone else. However, in general, during the tender process, the Employer will not prepare the DAAB candidates in advance, so in practice, the procedure for appointing DAAB members will be different from that specified in the Contract.

Those with overseas project implementation experience may understand the role of DAAB. It is a real problem that not all DAAB personnel deal with disputes from a neutral perspective. The list of personnel prepared by the Owner may have a good relationship with the Owner. In the process of adjudicating the dispute, it is impossible to maintain a neutral position and may be biased to the Owner. This is not unprecedented in the implementation of projects, so in general, DAAB appointments are started after projects start and after problems are encountered, except for some aid projects.

DAAB consisting of one person is easy to understand, if the Owner and the Contractor agree that a person, can be appointed directly, the Contractor can provide its designated for the Owner to choose, the Owner can also provide the designated person for Contractor selection, if both of them don't agree with each other, to change, until both sides agree. If they do not agree, they may request the appointment of the contracted body, whose appointment is final and must be approved by both Parties before they sign a DAAB agreement with it.

The three-person DAAB appointment process is slightly more complicated, with the Owner and the Contractor each appointing one person first and each Party agreeing to the other's appointment. That is, the Owner shall agree to the members appointed by the Contractor, and the Contractor shall agree to the members appointed by the Owner. In this way, the DAAB members determine 2 people, and the Contractor and the Owner consult with them together, and then the two people jointly elect the third person, and the third person is the chairman of DAAB. DAAB is formally established after the signing of the DAAB Agreement by the Owner, the Contractor and a 1 person DAAB or 3 person DAAB.

Once a DAAB member has been appointed, it is not permanent or non-replaceable. At any time, by mutual agreement, it may appoint a suitable and qualified person to replace one or more DAAB members. Unless otherwise provided in the agreement with DAAB, if a member refuses to make a ruling or is unable to make a ruling due to death, illness, disability, resignation or termination of the appointment agreement, then the procedure for the appointment of the replacement of such member shall be the same as that for the appointment of this Article.

After the establishment of DAAB, how to bear its costs? In accordance with the Contract, the cost of consulting any expert, whether it be a 1 person or a 3 person DAAB, as well as any questions raised by DAAB by the Owner and the Contractor, shall be borne equally by the Owner and the Contractor. In general, after the establishment of DAAB, the Contractor and the Owner shall visit the project regularly to understand the implementation of the project according to the DAAB agreement. Any expenses related to the project inspection shall be borne by the Contractor and the Owner from the time when the DAAB member starts from home. If a dispute is submitted to the DAAB for adjudication, the adjudication fee will be 50/50 regardless of who wins or loses.

21.2 Failure to Appoint DAAB Member(s)

Therefore, in general, the appointment of DAAB is determined according to the implementation of the project after the formal signing of the project contract. If the project does not go well and there is a large number of claims or situations, the Contractor will ask the Owner to appoint DAAB on his own initiative so that DAAB personnel can intervene in the project early in the morning to understand the problems of the project. In the project contract claim, the earlier you intervene, the more you know and the closer you are to the real situation. Even in some cases, if the project goes well, the Contractor and the Owner will not consider appointing a DAAB.

However, the reality is complicated and changeable, and sometimes DAAB can not be appointed smoothly due to the reasons of the Owners and Contractors. To sum up, these causes fall into four categories.

In the first category, a DAAB is composed of one person. However, within the time specified in the Contract Data, the Owner and the Contractor cannot reach an agreement on the appointment, which leads to the failure to form a DAAB within the time specified. As we all know, the main role of DAAB is to adjudicate disputes. DAAB can get involved in the implementation of a project at the initial stage, which is conducive to timely understanding of the situation.

In the second category, a DAAB is composed of three people. Neither Party has nominated a candidate for approval by the other Party within the time specified in the Contract. Neither side agrees with the other's candidate; (and) or both Parties disagree on the appointment of a third candidate. In the DAAB appointment, we all know that if the DAAB consists of three people, each side appoints one person and then the other side approves. Then the two people recommend a third person, who is the chairman of DAAB, and the third person also needs the consent of both Parties. Therefore, the above problems will occur.

Thirdly, in the event that either a single DAAB or a three-person DAAB refuses to make a decision or is unable to make a decision due to death, illness, disability, resignation or termination of the appointment, neither Party has appointed a replacement within 42 days of such an occurrence. In accordance with the DAAB appointment procedure, within 42 days of the occurrence of the foregoing, the Parties shall appoint a replacement to take the place of the original and perform DAAB duties. In the actual implementation process, the two Parties may not agree on the replacement, leading to the failure to appoint a replacement within the specified time.

Fourthly, in the process of the appointment of DAAB personnel, it may appear that both Parties have agreed on the appointment or replacement of DAAB personnel. However, one Party may, for some reason, be unable to sign the DAAB agreement with DAAB personnel or replacement personnel, thus making the appointment of DAAB not effective. The other Party may request it in writing to complete the signing of the agreement as soon as possible, and if the agreement has not been signed within 14 days after receiving the request, then the appointment of the DAAB has failed. It's rare, but it's possible.

After the occurrence of the above four types of circumstances, both Parties or either Party may request in writing the agency named in the Contract Data to complete the relevant appointment, which agency, after consulting both Parties, will formally appoint the DAAB personnel or replacement personnel, and the appointment of such agency shall be final and binding upon both Parties. Moreover, upon completion of the appointment of this body, both Parties and DAAB will be deemed to have signed the DAAB Agreement and will be subject to this Agreement. DAAB's monthly service fee and daily fee shall be subject to the terms of appointment, and the same law governing DAAB agreements also governs the Contract between the Owner and the Contractor.

Upon completion of the DAAB appointment, the Employer and the Contractor shall be responsible for the remuneration of the appointed agency or officer. Each takes half. If the Contractor pays the full amount of remuneration, the Contractor shall include one half of the amount in the payment specification and the Employer shall pay the Contractor accordingly in accordance with the Contract. If the Employer has paid the whole remuneration, the Supervision Engineer shall deduct half from the payment statement. The same principle applies to the remuneration of DAAB members. The Employer and the Contractor shall pay half and half respectively. If one Party pays in full, the other Party shall return the payment accordingly in the interim bill.

Therefore, in the event that DAAB cannot be appointed on time due to the above circumstances, both Parties or either Party may request in writing the agency designated by the Contract to make the appointment, which is the right of either Party.

21.3 Avoidance of Disputes

After the appointment of the DAAB, the two sides can jointly request the assistance of the DAAB, or hold informal talks in the presence of the DAAB to try to resolve their differences. However, neither Party shall consult DAAB members alone. Any information provided to DAAB by either Party must be copied to the other Party. So unless due to project implementation, do not need to appoint DAAB, so, the two sides can not appoint, if a request for appointment, or double were required to be appointed, but cannot agree, can according to the Contract, a formal request for institutional appointment, the agency appointment is final, binding upon both Parties.

21.4   Obtaining DAAB's Decision

21.4.1   Reference of a Dispute to the DAAB

Under the terms of the FIDIC contract, if either Party is not satisfied with the decision of the Supervision Engineer, it may give notice of dissatisfaction to the other Party within 28 days after receiving the decision of the Supervision Engineer. Or after receiving the Contract Claim, the Supervision Engineer cannot make a decision within the specified time and keep silent. Then, either Party may submit the Contract Claim directly to DAAB for adjudication without the need to give notice of dissatisfaction. At this point, the nature of the Contract Claim existing in the project has changed into a Contract Dispute, which shall be handled in accordance with the Contract Provisions.

If the Dispute cannot be resolved amicably through negotiation, then either Party shall submit the Dispute to the DAAB within 42 days after the notification of the dissatisfaction is given or received. If the Dispute is not submitted to DAAB within 42 days, the notice of dissatisfaction is void and DAAB is no longer obligated to decide the Dispute. The Dispute Report submitted to DAAB shall indicate the terms of the Contract under which the Dispute has been submitted and shall state the relevant events. The Report shall be submitted in written form and shall be copied to the other Party and the Supervision Engineer.

21.4.2   The Parties' obligations after the reference

If the DAAB consists of 3 persons, the date on which the Dispute Report is received by the DAAB chairman shall be the date on which the DAAB receives it. Unless prohibited by law, a Dispute Report submitted to the DAAB for adjudication pursuant to this provision shall be deemed to break any limitation or limitation period of any applicable statute. Upon submission of the Dispute Report, the Parties shall immediately provide all information, access to the project Site and appropriate facilities as required by DAAB so that DAAB can make a decision accordingly. The Parties shall continue to perform their contractual obligations unless and until the Contract has been scrapped or terminated.

21.4.3   The DAAB's decision

DAAB shall give a decision within 84 days after receipt of the Dispute Award Report from the Parties, or such other time as DAAB proposes to be agreed upon by the Parties. However, if, at the end of this period, the invoice payment time of any DAAB member has expired and neither Party has paid. Then, DAAB is not obligated to make any ruling until the remaining payment has been made. In other words, after the expiration of the 84 days, or at the expiration of any other period of the agreement, if there is any unpaid payment from the DAAB, the DAAB may not make any award.

DAAB shall make a decision as soon as possible upon receipt of the remaining payment, which shall be in writing, logical and in accordance with the relevant terms of the Contract and shall send one copy to each Party and a copy to the Supervision Engineer. This award shall be binding upon both Parties and shall be executed immediately, and the Owner shall be responsible for supervising the execution of the award by the Engineer regardless of whether either Party is dissatisfied with the award. In other words, since DAAB has made a decision, one Party may not be satisfied with the decision, but the decision should be implemented immediately.

If a DAAB award requires one Party to pay a certain amount to the other Party, then, subject to the following conditions, the amount shall be paid immediately without any certificate or notice. At the request of the other Party, but only on a reasonable basis, if the award is overturned by arbitration and DAAB considers that the payee cannot return the payment, DAAB may require the payee to provide a suitable security. In other words, although DAAB makes an award, but the other Party has a reasonable basis for DAAB to think that the award may be overturned by arbitration, then the payee should provide security.

21.4.4　Dissatisfaction with DAAB's decision

The award of DAAB shall not be regarded as arbitration, nor shall DAAB act in the capacity of arbitration. If either Party is dissatisfied with the decision of DAAB, it shall give a notice of dissatisfaction to the other Party and copy it to DAAB and the Supervision Engineer. The notice shall state that the DAAB adjudication is a notice of dissatisfaction, detailing the incident in dispute and the reasons for the dissatisfaction. Finally, such notice shall be given within 28 days of receipt of the DAAB award. The process here is similar to the process of dissatisfaction with the award of the Supervision Engineer, which needs to be issued within the specified time. The notice of dissatisfaction may be in respect of the DAAB award as a whole or a part of the DAAB award and, in the case of the award as a whole, is required to be consistent with the above notice.

If it is a partial award, the unsatisfactory part shall be clearly indicated in the notice of dissatisfaction. This part, and the award of any other part affected by this part, or the integrity of the award of any other part dependent on this part, shall be deemed to be severed from the remaining award. If no notice of dissatisfaction is given to the remaining award, it shall be final and binding on both Parties.

However, if DAAB is unable to make a determination within the time specified in the Contract and DAAB has not given any explanation, then either Party may give the other Party a notice of dissatisfaction within 28 days after the expiration of the DAAB determination period, with the same requirements as above. Neither Party shall initiate arbitration without giving notice of dissatisfaction. In other words, the notice of dissatisfaction is a prerequisite for the initiation of arbitration. If no notice of dissatisfaction is given, the award of DAAB is deemed to be final and to be complied with by both parties.

If the Parties do not give notice of their dissatisfaction within 28 days from the date of receipt of the DAAB award, the award of DAAB shall be deemed final and binding upon both Parties and shall be binding upon both Parties. If a notice of dissatisfaction has been served, arbitration may proceed. In addition, if the Supervision Engineer fails to make a decision on the Contract Claim within the time specified in the Contract and the project does not appoint DAAB, then in such a case, the Contract Claim of the project becomes a Contract Dispute, and both Parties can also directly conduct arbitration without giving a notice of dissatisfaction.

21.5 Amicable Settlement

After a Contract Dispute occurs, both Parties can carry out friendly negotiation no matter whether either Party gives a notice of dissatisfaction or the Supervision Engineer remains silent. Especially after the verdict of the Supervision Engineer is over, both Parties can jointly request the assistance of DAAB and strive to settle the Dispute in a friendly negotiation way. At the same time, both Parties can prepare DAAB adjudication documents at the same time, and if the Dispute cannot be resolved amicably through negotiation. After all, the Dispute will be submitted to the DAAB within the time stipulated in the Contract.

21.6 Arbitration

According to the FIDIC contract conditions, if there is a Contract Dispute between the two Parties in an overseas project under the FIDIC contract conditions, there are three ways to resolve the Contract Dispute. The first is DAAB arbitration, the second is friendly negotiation between the two Parties, and the third is arbitration. Arbitration is the final way to resolve Contract Disputes. Therefore, the decision of arbitration is final binding on both Parties and should be executed by both Parties.

The reasons for arbitration mainly include four aspects. Firstly, As we all know, whether it is the Owner or the Contractor, the Contract Claim should be adjudicated by the Supervision Engineer first. If either Party is not satisfied with the decision of the Supervisor, or the Supervisor fails to make the decision within the time specified in the Contract. Then, the Contract Claim event escalates into a Contract Dispute. Either Party can refer the matter to the DAAB for adjudication. If either Party is not satisfied with the DAAB award, it may submit it to arbitration.

Secondly, after either Party brings the Dispute to the DAAB for adjudication, the DAAB makes a decision based on the Contract, but the other side refused to implement the DAAB ruling. Then, the other Party may submit the Dispute to arbitration directly without friendly negotiation between both Parties.

Thirdly, if either Party is not satisfied with the decision of the Supervision Engineer, or the Supervision Engineer fails to make the decision within the time specified in the Contract, and the project does not appoint a DAAB. According to the Contract, either Party may submit the dispute directly to arbitration.

Finally, after a notice of dissatisfaction has been given in accordance with the Contract, the Parties may settle the Dispute amicably, except in the second category above. However, the amicable negotiation must be reached within 28 days after the notice of dissatisfaction is given. If the Parties have reached an agreement on the existing Dispute, the Dispute may be deemed to have been settled and the arbitration shall cease. If the Parties fail to reach an agreement, arbitration shall commence on the twenty-eighth day after the notice of dissatisfaction or on the twenty-eighth day after the notice of dissatisfaction is given. In addition, arbitration shall commence within this time even if the Parties have not attempted to resolve the Dispute by amicable negotiation.

After the commencement of the arbitration, the arbitrators shall arbitrate the Disputes between the Parties in accordance with the arbitration rules of the international chamber of commerce. At this stage, the arbitrators shall have the right to review, display and modify any award of DAAB in relation to the Dispute, other than the final and binding award, and any changes, opinions, instructions, decisions and certificates made by the Supervision Engineer in relation to the Dispute, other than the final and binding decision. The arbitrators may also summon the supervision Engineer to provide any evidence related to the Dispute and may have the Supervision Engineer as a witness.

The arbitrators have no right to amend the awards and decisions of either DAAB or the Supervision Engineer if they are final and binding on both Parties. However, they may amend the decisions that are not final and binding on both Parties. It can be said that the arbitrators can review and modify any award related to the Dispute. In addition, the arbitrators can call the Supervision Engineer as a witness or require the Supervision Engineer to provide evidence. Here, the Supervision Engineer should be strictly neutral.

In making any award relating to fees, the arbitrators may consider either Party's failure to cooperate with the other Party in appointing a DAAB, (and) or inability to appoint a DAAB. In addition, before the arbitrators, neither Party shall be bound by the arbitration procedure with respect to the evidence and arguments previously submitted to DAAB, or the reasons for the dissatisfaction given to the Party in the notice of dissatisfaction, and any decision made by DAAB shall be accepted as evidence of the arbitration. Here, the Parties can submit their own reasonable evidence again to the arbitrators, including the DAAB decision.

Then, is there a time limit for arbitration? Arbitration may be initiated during the implementation of the project or after the completion of the project according to the provisions of the Contract, but if arbitration is initiated during the implementation of the project, the obligations of the Contractor and the Owner, the Supervision Engineer and the DAAB shall not change for any reason. That is to say, if the arbitration is carried out during the implementation of the project, the Contractor and the Owner, the Supervision Engineer and the DAAB still have to fulfill their contractual obligations during the process, which cannot be changed by arbitration.

After the conclusion of the arbitration, if the arbitration decides that one Party shall pay money to the other Party, then the money shall take effect and be paid immediately, without the need for any additional certificate or notice. In other words, whether the Owner or the Contractor, if the arbitration determines that one Party shall pay the other the appropriate amount, the payment shall be made immediately and without the need for a payment certificate or notice.

21.7   Failure to Comply with DAAB's Decision

If one Party refuses to implement the DAAB award, whether the DAAB award is final or binding on both Parties, the arbitrators have the right to require the other Party to implement the decision of the DAAB by way of summary, expedited procedure, order, either as interim measure, interim measure, or award.

Through the above explanation, we know that whether the Owner or the Contractor has a Contract Dispute, if the Dispute cannot be settled through DAAB and amicable negotiation, then the final way to settle the Dispute is arbitration, and the final decision shall be made in accordance with the arbitration rules of the International Chamber of Commerce.

21.8　No DAAB In Place

This Clause stipulated the situation when there is no appointed DAAB.

※ Vocabulary

1. Aforementioned *adj.* 上述的；前面提及的
2. formation *n.* 组成物；构成；形成，产生；编队，队形；(社会、政治等的)形态
3. designated person 指定人
4. mutual agreement 双方协定
5. resignation *n.* 辞职；辞职信，辞呈；顺从，听任；(棋)认输
6. intervene *v.* 干预，干涉；插话，打岔；干扰，阻挠；发生于其间，介于中间；调停，斡旋
7. remuneration *n.* 酬金，薪水，报酬；赔偿，补偿
8. half and half 一半一半；各占一半
9. governing *adj.* 统治的；控制的；管理的；治理的
  v. 统治；支配；控制；影响；抑制(情绪)；成为……的法律(govern 的现在分词)
10. in the presence of 在……面前；有某人在场
11. formal talks 正式会谈
12. obligated *adj.* 有义务的；责无旁贷的
  v. 使负义务(obligate 的过去式)
13. overturned *adj.* 倾覆的，倒转的
  v. 颠覆(overturn 的过去式)
14. in the capacity of 以……的资格
15. as a whole 总的来说
16. be resolved 被解决(resolved 是 resolve 的过去分词)
17. amicable negotiation 友好协商
18. arbitration rules 仲裁规则
19. binding award 约束性的仲裁裁决

Appendix 1

The Role of an Engineer

I Employment and authority of the Engineer/Owner's Representative in the new series of conditions of contract

The Engineer or the Owner's Representative is employed by the Owner. Article 3 [Engineer] of the Red Book provides for the appointment and commission, duties and authority of the Engineer/Owner's Representative.

(1)Appointment and entrustment of the Engineer/Owners' Representative

An engineer in the Red Book means a natural person or legal entity employed by the Employer who is contracted to perform management duties. When the Engineer appointed by the Owner is a legal entity, the Engineer unit shall issue a notice to both Parties and designate a natural person to take charge of the management work on its behalf. The Engineer may delegate certain of his duties and authority to his assistants. Sub-Clause 3. 4 [Delegation of the Engineer] provides for the delegation or removal of an assistant to the Engineer who is responsible for the exercise of the duties and authority delegated to him, but the Engineer shall not delegate to his assistant the two important functions and authority referred to in Sub-Clause 3. 7 [Agreement or Determination] and Sub-Clause 15. 1 [Notice to Correct].

Sub-Clause 3. 3 [The Engineer's Representative] provides for the appointment of the Engineer's Representative and requires the Engineer's Representative to be on the Site throughout the execution of the Contract and, if the Engineer's Representative is temporarily absent from the Site, the Engineer shall give notice to the Contractor specifying the person in charge. Qualification requirements for the Engineer's Representatives and custodians include two items: the first. industry qualification, relevant work experience and professional competence; the second is to be proficient in using the dominant language specified in Sub-Clause 1. 4 [Law and Language]. Other assistants should have the experience and professional ability to perform the delegated tasks specified in the delegated notice, and be fluent in the language of communication. Sub-Clause 3. 6 [Replacement of the Engineer] sets out the procedure for the replacement of the Engineer for two types of reasons. The first type is the replacement requested by the Employer, and if the Employer wishes to replace the Engineer, it shall be done not less than 42 days before the scheduled date of replacement.

The second category is an objective reason lead to replacement, if the Engineers for their death, disease, deformity, or resign cannot perform authority (or if the Engineer is a legal entity, the Engineer unit cannot or will not perform its functions and authorities, except the condition is caused by the Owner), the Owner should immediately replace specified personnel, but the specified personnel belongs to provisional designation. The formal replacement is still subject to acceptance by the Contractor.

(2) Responsibilities and authority of the Engineer/Owner's Representative

Sub-Clause 3.2 [Engineer's Duties and Authority] of the Red Book sets out the terms of reference of the Engineer and states that the Engineer has no right to modify the Contract to release either Party from contractual obligations. It may be stated in the Particular Conditions that the Engineer must obtain the Employer's approval before exercising certain functions and authority. However, in order to ensure that the Engineer remains neutral in procuring negotiations or decisions between the Parties under Sub-Clause 3.7 [Agreement or Determination], the Engineer shall not be constrained by the Employer in the exercise of his authority under Sub-Clause 3.7 [Agreement or Determination]. The specific work of the Engineer is set out in Sub-Clause 3.5 [Engineer's Instructions] and Sub-Clause 3.7 [Agreement or Determination]. Sub-Clause 3.8 [Meetings] of the Red Book requires the Engineer to make record and provide copies to both Parties.

Ⅱ Process for negotiation or decision by the Engineer/Owner's Representative in the new series of contract conditions

The Sub-Clause 3.7 [Agreement or Determination] clause is a very important Clause in the 2017 edition of the FIDIC series of contract conditions, and it is closely related to many other important Clauses. Using the Red Book as an example, this book summarizes and analyses the procedures used by the Engineer in accordance with Sub-Clause 3.7 [Agreement or Determination]. The Red Book requires that the Engineer shall be "neutral" in the implementation of Sub-Clause 3.7 and shall not be deemed to be acting on behalf of the Owner.

According to Section 3.7 of the Red Book, there are two types of events which require the Engineer to agree or determine: matters and claims. Among them, the Claims are further divided under Sub-Clause 20.1 [Claims] into Category I Claims (the Owner's Claims against the Contractor), Category II Claims (the Contractor's Claims against the Owner) and Category III Claims (any other right or remedy that the Claimant considers to be entitled to claim or assert).

The Red Book Sub-Clause 3.7 is not directly related to the alternation as it is an ex post fact implementation and the alternation is an active action, but it will also be used to determine the cost and duration alternations during the alternation process. At the same time, Sub-Clause 3.7 is also a prelude to the dispute settlement procedure if the issue of variation cannot be amicably resolved and then escalates into a dispute.

Figure 1, using the Red Book as an example, describes the Engineer's handling of the relevant incident in accordance with Sub-Clause 3.7.

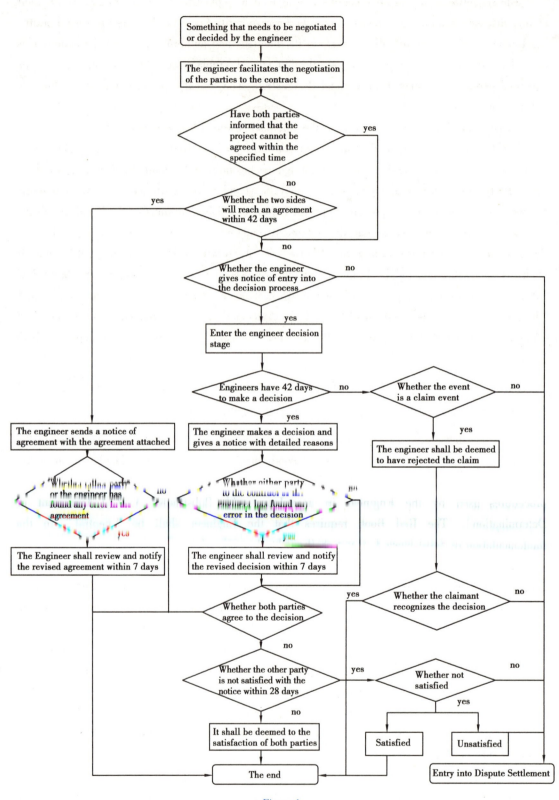

Figure 1

The basic procedures (Sub-Clause 3.7 in the Red Book are basically the same as those in Figure 1). The Claims and Dispute resolution procedures in Figure 1 have interfaces that are not present in this figure.

As shown in Figure 1, when there is an event (matter or claim) that needs to be "agreed upon or determined" by the Engineer, the Engineer is required to work together with both Parties as follows.

(1) Agreements

The Engineer shall immediately communicate fully with both parties to the Contract and make every effort to bring them to an agreement, if any, within 42 days (or such other period as may be agreed upon by the Parties), the Engineer shall issuse a consenual knowledge and agreement reached.

(If any minor error is found in the agreement within 14 days, the Engineer shall issue the revised agreement within 7 days after the discovery of the error).

(2) Decision

If the Engineer fails to reach an agreement between the Parties within 42 days, or if both Parties inform the Engineer that an agreement cannot be reached (whichever is earlier), the stage of the Engineer's discretion shall commence. The Engineer shall make a decision and issue it to the Parties within 42 days (or such other period as may be agreed upon by the Parties) after the decision has been entered into the decision stage (if any error is found in the decision within the 14-day period, the Engineer shall issue a revised decision within 7 days of the discovery of the error).

For decisions made by the Engineers:

①If a Party is dissatisfied with the Engineer's decision (or part of the decision), it shall, within 28 days after receiving the Engineer's decision, give notice of dissatisfaction (if only part of the decision is dissatisfied, the dissatisfied part shall be indicated in the notice of dissatisfaction). Either Party to the Contract may then submit a DAAB request for adjudication in accordance with Sub-Clause 21.4 [Obtaining DAAB's Decision].

②If the both sides of the Contract are satisfied with the Engineer's decision, or neither Party gives unsatisfactory notice within 28 days after receiving the Engineer's decision, the Parties are deemed to be fully satisfied with the decision, and the decision becomes a final binding decision (in case of partial dissatisfaction, the satisfactory part shall become final and binding).

If no agreement is reached between the Parties or the Engineer fails to make a decision within the prescribed time limit, then:

①If the event is a claim, the Engineer shall be deemed to have rejected the Claim.

②If the incident escalates into a dispute, either Party of the Contract can submit it to DAAB for decision.

(3) Time Limitation

The starting time of the 42 days (or such other period as the parties agree) for the Engineer to bring the Parties to an agreement or will vary depending on the type of event that needs to be dealt with:

①If the event is a matter and not a claim, the date on which Sub-Clause 3. 7. 3 [Time limites] is expressly applied in the relevant clause of these conditions is the starting time of the limitation.

②If the event is a Class III claim, the limitation shall start from the date on which the Engineer receives notice of the claim from the Claimant under Sub-Clause 20. 1 [Claims].

③If the event is a Category I or II claim, the time of limitation shall be the date on which the full and detailed claim report is received by the Engineer (if the event has a continuing effect, the date on which the interim or final full and detailed claim report is received by the Engineer).

(4)Execution

The agreement entered into by the Parties or the decision made by the Engineer shall be binding upon the Parties and the Engineer, unless there is an error correction, or the decision made by the Engineer is amended in accordance with the procedure of Article 21 [Disputes and Arbitration]. If a binding agreement or decision relates to payment, the Contractor may include such amount in the next payment request and the Engineer shall include such amount in the next payment certificate.

If the two sides reach an agreement, or the Engineer makes a decision and the decision becomes a binding final decision, however, a party of the Contract has not complied with the agreement reached or the final binding decision of the Engineer, then it shall be deemed as the party fails to comply with binding DAAB final decision, the other Party can submit this event to arbitration.

Ⅲ Analysis of relevant Clauses [Agreement or Determination] in the new series of contract conditions

The [Agreement or Determination] Clause is a typical "standard clause", which is directly or indirectly referenced by many other Clauses in the terms of Contract. "Standardization clause" is a common feature of international authoritative contract model.

This book has sorted out all other Clauses in the 2017 Red Book that refer to Clause 3. 7 [Agreement or Determination], which can be divided into three categories: the first is those that directly refer to "Agreement or Determination" and require action by the Engineer. The second is those that directly refer to Clause [Agreement or Determination] but does not require action by the Engineer. The third is the indirect reference to [Agreement or Determination] Clauses through the Variation, Claims and Disputes Clauses.

①direct reference "Agreement or Determinations" and need to take action to the terms of the Engineer direct reference in the Red Book [Agreement or Determination] Clause and the terms of the agreed or decision engineers need to act as shown in Table 1, some terms need the Engineer to make qualitative decisions (such as the fault reason analysis, ownership and responsibility, etc.), if need be, and then make quantitative decision through claim or change procedure. Some require the Engineer to make direct quantitative decisions on money, time, etc.

Table 1

Terms of Sub-Clauses	Name of Sub-Clauses	Type
1.9	Delayed by Drawings or Instructions	qualitative/ quantitative
4.7	Setting Out	qualitative/quantitative
4.7.3	Agreement or Determination of rectification measures, delay and/or Cost	qualitative/quantitative
10.2	Taking Over Parts	qualitative
11.2	Costs of Remedying Defects	quantitative
13.3	Variation Procedure	quantitative
13.3.1	Variation by Instruction	quantitative
13.5	Daywork	quantitative
14.4	Schedule of Payments	quantitative
14.5	Plant and Materials intended for the Works	quantitative
14.6	Issue of IPC	quantitative
14.6.3	Correction or Modification	quantitative
15.3	Valuation after Termination for Contractor's Default	quantitative
15.6	Valuation after Termination for Employer's Convenience	quantitative
18.5	Optional Termination	quantitative
20.1	Claims	qualitative/quantitative
20.2	Claims for Payment and/or EOT	quantitative
20.2.5	Agreement or Determination of the Claim	quantitative

②Citation of Terms [Agreement or Determination] without action by the Engineer. Table 2 lists the terms in the Red book which cite only [Agreement or Determination] terms without action by the Engineer.

Table 2

	Clause type	Clause number and name
"output" Clauses of the [Agreement or Determination] Clause	Unable to resolve according to [Agreement or Determination] Clause	21.4 [Obtaining DAAB's Decision]
	Execute as agreed or decided according to [Agreement or Determination] Clause	8.5 [Extension of Time for Completion] 14.3 [Application for Interim Payment] 14.13 [Issue of FPC]
	Failure to comply with an agreement or decision according to [Agreement or Determination] Clause	4.2 [Performance Security] 15.2 [Termination for Contractor's Default] 16.1 [Suspension by Contractor] 16.2 [Termination by Contractor] 21.6 [Arbitration]

Continued

	Clause type	Clause number and name
Others	Definition	1.1.29 [Dispute] 1.1.57 [Notice of dissatisfaction or NOD]
	Engineer's Rights according to [Agreement or Determination] Clause	3.2 [Engineer's Duties and Authority] 3.4 [Delegation by the Engineer]
	Time limits set by quoting [Agreement or Determination] Clause	20.2.6 [Claims of continuing effect]
	Can't be concurrent with [Agreement or Determination] Clause	21.3 [Avoidance of Disputes]

③Variation, claim and dispute settlement are the key and difficult issues to be dealt with by the Engineer/Owner's Representative during the implementation of the Contract. These three types of Clauses are inseparable from the [Agreement or Determination] Clauses. Red Book Sub-Clause 20.2 [Claims For Payment and/or EOT], Sub-Clause 13.3.1 [Variation by Instruction], Sub-Clause 21.4 [Obtaining DAAB's Decision] all refer directly to Sub-Clause 3.7 [Agreement or Determination], i.e., wherever the above three Clauses are directly referenced.

Other provisions refer indirectly to Sub-Clause 3.7 [Agreement or Determination]. Variation and Claim Clauses belong to the "input" Clauses of the [Agreement or Determination] Clauses, while Dispute Clauses belong to the "output" Clauses of the [Agreement or Determination] Clauses. Variation, claim and dispute are the most important application fields of the [Agreement or Determination] Clauses. Significant risk sharing and payment terms will also refer directly to Sub-Clause 3.7. Thus, the "Agreement or Determination" clause almost covers all important aspects of the whole system of conditions of the Contract. This also illustrates the importance of the [Agreement or Determination] Clause in the terms of the Contract.

Ⅳ Comparison of new and old FIDIC the Engineers/Owner's Representative

Compared with the 1999 version, the 2017 version of the FIDIC contract has made major revisions to the relevant provisions of the Engineer/Owner's Representative. The main changes are reflected in the following four aspects:

(1) The 2017 version of the contract is more explicit about the appointment and authorization of the Engineer/Owner's Representative. The 2017 version of the contract clearly states that the Engineer/Owner's representative is a natural person or legal entity who is employed by the Owner and is authorized by the Contract to perform management duties. When the Engineer/Owner's Representative employed by the Owner is a legal entity, a natural person shall be designated to take charge of the work on behalf of the legal entity. The 2017 version of the contract has more strict limits on the authority delegated by the Engineer/Owner's Representative. The 1999 version of the contract only requires that the authority delegated by Sub-Clause 3.5 [Engineer's Instructions] cannot be delegated to an assistant. Considering that the notice given in Sub-Clause 15.1 [Notice to Correct] is a warning signal to the Employer prior to termination of the Contract

and is a very serious issue, the 2017 version of the contract also limits the delegation of this authority by requiring that neither the authority in Sub-Clause 3. 7 [Agreement or Determination] nor the authority in Sub-Clause 15. 1 [Notice to Correct] can be delegated. The 2017 edition of Red Book added the Engineer Representatives and required them to be resident on site all the time.

(2) The 2017 version of the contract has significantly increased the number of [Agreement or Determination] Clauses, which are more detailed and more operable. The 1999 version of the contract has only a [Decision] Clause in the Engineer/Owner's Representative clause and does not explicitly state the concept of "agreement". The [Agreement or Determination] Clause has grown from two paragraphs in the 1999 edition to nearly three pages in the 2017 edition. The [Agreement or Determination] Clause clarifies the specific responsibilities and operating procedures of the Engineer/Owner's Representative when dealing with important matters or claims. It emphasizes the early involvement of the Engineer/Owner's Representative in the negotiation process with a view to facilitating an amicable settlement between the Parties. It adds time limit for the Engineers to respond. 2017 edition [Agreement or Determination] Clause and other related terms have more clear relationship between the interface, well-established "chain of procedures" for dealing with important matters in accordance with "agreed or decided" terms. The [Agreement or Determination] Clause is closely linked with important Clauses such as risk sharing, payment, change, claim and dispute settlement, so that the relationship between contract clauses is more systematic and rigorous, and becomes an organic whole.

(3) The 2017 version of the contract provides a clearer delineation of the basic concepts and handling procedures of changes, claims and disputes through the [Agreement or Determination] Clause. The 1999 version of the contract is less clear about the definition of variation and claim. The 2017 version of the contract separates the change from the claim through the [Agreement or Determination] Clause. If the Parties fail to reach an agreement on the change, it will directly rise into a dispute through the [Agreement or Determination] Clause, and either Party can submit to DAAB for its decision without going through the claim processing procedure. All Claims Clauses in the 1999 version of the contract refer to the [Determination] Clause, while the 2017 version of the contract adds a Sub-Clause 20. 2. 5 [Agreement or determination of the claim] to the claims processing procedure to embed the [Agreement or Determination] Clause in this Clause. Therefore, the terms of the Contract no longer refer to an [Agreement or Determination] Clause when they refer to Claims.

(4) The 2017 version of the contract strengthens and expands the status and role of the Engineer. The 1999 version only mentioned that the Engineer should make fair decisions, while the 2017 version of the Contract clearly states in the [Agreement or Determination] Clause that the Engineer should be neutral in the performance of his duties in relation to that Clause and should not be deemed to be acting on behalf of the Employer. "Neutrality" here should be understood as not taking sides with any Party to the Contract, understanding of the event is not biased, and uphold the spirit of fairness and justice of the Contract. The 2017 version of the contract will treat failure to comply with a binding agreement or a binding final decision under an [Agreement or

Determination] Clause in the same way as failure to comply with a DAAB decision. Although the 2017 version of the contract clearly separates the claim from the processing procedure of the change, it gives the Engineer the right to judge whether the incident occurred is a claim or a change. Although the claim processing procedure increases into two time limits, the judgment of whether the time limit is met is also made by the Engineer. All these treatments have greatly enhanced the status and function of the Engineer.

The Engineer or Owner's Representative and his team are the specific executors of the Owner's project management. Both the Owner and the Contractor should have a clear understanding of the role positioning, scope of authority, work content and work procedures of the Engineer/Owner's Representative. Compared with the 1999 version, the 2017 version of the FIDIC series contract strengthens and expands the status and role of the Engineer, and requires the Engineer to remain neutral in the implementation of the [Agreement or Determination] Clause. The significant upgrade of the status of the Engineer should be a decision made by FIDIC based on the basic practice of the current situation of international project contract management.

Ⅴ The 2017 Red Book expanded and enhanced the role and responsibilities of engineers.

(1)Qualifications (refer to Sub-Clause 3.1)

The 2017 Red Book puts forward higher professional qualifications and language ability requirements for engineers.

(2)Engineer's Representative (refer to Sub-Clause 3.3)

This Clause is added to the 2017 Red Book. The Engineers can designate representatives of engineers to exercise the power of the Engineers in accordance with Sub-Clause 3.4, and require the representatives of the Engineers to stay at the site, and the Engineers cannot change their representatives at will.

(3)Responsibility and authority of Engineers (refer to Sub-Clause 3.2)

The 2017 Red Book indicates that Engineer can make a decision according to Sub-Clause 3.7 without the approval of the Owner. Sub-Clause 3.4 of the 2017 edition of the Red Book adds the responsibilities that the Engineers cannot delegate to other engineers' assistants compared with the 1999 edition. In addition to the "Agreement or Decision" that engineers cannot delegate to their assistants, it also stipulates that the right to issue corrective notice in Sub-Clause 15.1 cannot be delegated to Engineers' assistants.

(4)Agreement or Decision (refer to Sub-Clause 3.7)

Unlike the 1999 Red Book, the 2017 edition requires the Engineers to remain "neutral" when dealing with contractual services using "agreed or decided" Clauses and should not be considered acting on behalf of the Owners. The 2017 Red Book stipulates the negotiation procedure for reaching an agreement centered on the Engineers. If the Parties are unable to reach an agreement on the matter within 42 days and the Engineer fails to decide the matter fairly within the next 42 days, the Parties may be deemed to have a dispute which may be submitted by either Party to DAAB without notice of dissatisfaction. If any Party objects to a decision, a notice of dissatisfaction must be given within 28 days, otherwise the decision will be considered final and binding. If either Party fails to comply with the agreement or binding final ruling, the other Party may submit the failure to perform the agreement directly to arbitration.

(5) Meeting (refer to Sub-Clause 3.8)

This is a new Clause added to the 2017 Red Book, which provides that the Engineers or Contractors may convene and arrange meetings on construction issues and that Owners may participate on their own.

※Vocabulary

1. legal entity 法人实体

2. entrustment *n.* 委托,托付;信托

3. proficient *adj.* 熟练的,精通的
   n. <古>专家,能手

4. constrained by 约束

5. be deemed 被视为;被认为

6. alternation *n.* 交替,轮流,间隔

7. decision stage 决策阶段

8. binding decision 约束性判决

9. applied in 应用于

10. authoritative *adj.* 专断的,命令式的;可靠的,可信的,权威的

11. sorted out 挑选出;分类

12. quantitative decision 定量决策

13. qualitative *adj.* 质量的,定性的,性质的

14. setting out 放线

15. application fields 应用领域

16. inseparable *adj.* (人)形影不离的;(东西)分不开的,不可分离的;(前缀)不可单独成
    词的,(德语)屈折变化时与词根不可分的
    n. 不能分开的人(或事物)

17. reflected in 反映在,体现在

18. more systematic 更加系统的

19. with a view to 着眼于;考虑到;以……为目的

20. delineation *n.* 描述;画轮廓

21. acting on 对……起作用;按照……行事

Appendix 2

The Contractor's Contractual Obligations and Rights

Ⅰ The Contractor's obligations under 1999 FIDIC version

(1) The most important contractual obligations of the Contractor

Project type: B. Q. , specification and drawings (deliverable)

Process type: design, construction, completion, maintenance;

The Contractor shall provide all necessary superintendence, labor, materials, work equipment and other goods in order to fulfill the obligations as stated above, and delegate to the site according to the requirements of the Engineer's Representative to supervise the whole process the project and any other personnel necessary to fulfill his contractual obligations.

Other obligations (environment, insurance, performance security, risk related, etc.)

The Contractor shall be abiding by the Contract unless impermissible in law or otherwise unenforceable (Figure 2)

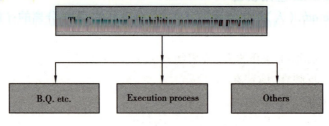

Figure 2

(2) Foundermental obligations

①Make interpretations on all relevant data in the Employer's possession on sub-surface and hydrological conditions at the Site.

②Be Responsible for environmental survey.

③Determine the construction scheme, and be responsible for the comprehensiveness, stability and safety of all relevant site works and the construction scheme.

④Besides, the Contractor shall also be responsible for the accuracy and comprehensiveness of the costs and quotations stated in the Letter of Tender and the Bill of Quantities. He is deemed to have completely accepted the adaptability and sufficiency of the agreed Contract Price.

While as to the risks which shall be undertaken by the Contractor for the above obligations, the limit shall be within the practicable scope of time and costs.

The Contractor is not encouraged to conduct the things above with too much stakes. The risks he has to undertake shall be relevant to and also be covered by the time(from the obtaining of the Letter of Tender to the completion of tendering) and incurred costs he spent before the tendering. It's unrealistic for the Contractor to spend a large amount of expenditure to conduct detailed environmental survey (i. e. archeological exploration), let not to say, devised plan and implementation scheme.

(3) All the activities and behavior of the Contractor shall be abiding by the applicable laws and regulations, so as to ensure that the Employer will be exempted from all relevant liabilities.

①The Contractor shall issue notice, pay taxes and incurred costs whatever in relevance to the implementation of the works and remedy of defects and enquire all necessary license;

②Be responsible for all the Contractor's equipment. Materials and infringed equipment patent and other rights entitled under the Contract either to be used or be relevant to the Works, and all claims and jurisdictions arose herein;

③Undertake all tonnage dues of various materials and royalties, rents and other costs in relevant to the Works;

④Be responsible for all the formalities and costs in relevance to custom clearance, import and export license, storage at the harbors of his own equipment, materials and other goods;

⑤Undertake all expenditures needed in order to obtain special or temporary accesses to and from the site, to provide at his afford the additional equipment used out of the site, the reconstruction or reinforcement of roads and bridges on the way to and from the site;

⑥Keep the confidentialities of the Works. Without the prior agreement of the Employer, the Contractor is not allowed to release any information related to the Works, either by publishing commercial or technical dissertation or in other circumstances.

(4) Unless otherwise stated in the Contract, two copies of the Contract and of each subsequent Drawing shall be supplied to the Contractor, who may make or request further copies at the cost of the Contractor. (Sub-Clause 1. 8)

Unless otherwise stated in the Contract, the Contractor shall supply to the Engineer six copies of each of the Contractor's Documents. The Contractor shall keep, on the Site, a copy of the Contract, publications named in the Specification, the Contractor's Documents (if any), the Drawings and Variations and other communications given under the Contract. The Employer's Personnel shall have the right of access to all these documents at all reasonable times. (Sub-Clause 1. 8)

If a Party (the Contractor) becomes aware of an error or defect of a technical nature in a document which was prepared for use in executing the Works, the Party (the Contractor) shall promptly give notice to the other Party (the Employer) of such error or defect. (Sub-Clause 1. 8)

As between the Parties, the Contractor shall retain the copyright and other intellectual property rights in the Contractor's Documents and other design documents made by (or on behalf of) the Contractor. (Sub-Clause 1. 10)

The Contractor may, at his cost, copy, use, and obtain communication of these documents for the purposes of the Contract. They shall not, without the Employer's consent, be copied, used or communicated to a third Party by the Contractor, except as necessary for the purposes of the Contract. (Sub-Clause 1. 11)

(5)The Contractor shall give notice to the Engineer and shall be entitled subject to Sub-Clause 20. 1 [Contractor's Claims] to:

①An extension of time for any such delay, if completion is or will be delayed, under Sub-Clause 8. 4 [Extension of Time for Completion]; and

②Payment of any such Cost plus reasonable profit, which shall be included in the Contract Price. (Sub-Clause 20. 1,Sub-Clause 1. 9,Sub-Clause 4. 7)

(6)If the Contractor suffers delay and/or incurs Cost as a result of a failure of the Engineer to issue the notified drawing or instruction within a time which is reasonable and is specified in the notice with supporting details, the Contractor shall give a further notice to the Engineer and shall be entitled subject to Sub-Clause 20. 1 [Contractor's Claims] to:

①An extension of time for any such delay, if completion is or will be delayed, under Sub-Clause 8. 4 [Extension of Time for Completion]; and

②Payment of any such Cost plus reasonable profit, which shall be included in the Contract Price. (Sub-Clause 1. 9)

(7)The Contractor shall disclose all such confidential and other information as the Engineer may reasonably require in order to verify the Contractor's compliance with the Contract. (Sub-Clause 1. 12)

(8)The Contractor shall give all notices, pay all taxes, duties and fees, and obtain all permits, licenses and approvals, as required by the Laws in relation to the execution and completion of the Works and the remedying of any defect. (Sub-Clause 1. 13)

(9)If the Contractor constitutes (under applicable Laws) a joint venture, consortium or other unincorporated grouping of two or more person, these persons shall be deemed to be jointly and severally liable to the Employer for the performance of the Contract, the Contractor shall not alter its composition or legal status without the prior consent of the Employer. (Sub-Clause 1. 14)

(10)The Contractor shall comply with the instructions given by the Engineer or delegated assistant, on any matter related to the Contract. (Sub-Clause 3. 3)

(11)The Employer shall not replace the Engineer with a person against whom the Contractor raises reasonable objection by notice to the Employer, with supporting particulars. (Sub-Clause 3. 4)

(12)The Contractor shall design (to the extent specified in the Contract), execute and complete the Works in accordance with the Contract and with the Engineer's instructions, and shall remedy any defects in the Works.

The Contractor shall provide the Plant and Contractor's Documents specified in the Contract, and all Contractor's Personnel, Goods, consumables and other things and services, whether of a temporary or permanent nature, required in and for this design, execution, completion and remedying of defects. (Sub-Clause 4. 1)

The Contractor shall be responsible for the adequacy, stability and safety of all Site operations and of all methods of construction. Except to the extent specified in the Contract, the Contractor shall:

①be responsible for all Contractor's Documents, Temporary Works, and such design of each item of Plant and Materials as is required for the item to be in accordance with the Contract, and

②not otherwise be responsible for the design or specification of the Permanent Works. (Sub-Clause 4.1)

If the Contract specifies that the Contractor shall design any part of the Permanent Works, then unless otherwise stated in the Particular Conditions: prior to the commencement of the Tests on Completion, the Contractor shall submit to the Engineer the "as-built" documents and operation and maintenance manuals in accordance with the Specification and in sufficient detail for the Employer to operate, maintain, dismantle, reassemble, adjust and repair this part of the Works. (Sub-Clause 4.1)

(13) The Contractor shall deliver the Performance Security to the Employer within 28 days after receiving the Letter of Acceptance, and shall send a copy to the Engineer. The Employer shall return the Performance Security to the Contractor within 21 days after receiving a copy of the Performance Certificate. (Sub-Clause 4.2)

(14) Unless the Contractor's Representative is named in the Contract, the Contractor shall, prior to the Commencement Date, submit to the Engineer for consent the name and particulars of the person the Contractor proposes to appoint as Contractor's Representative. The Contractor shall not, without the prior consent of the Engineer, revoke the appointment of the Contractor's Representative or appoint a replacement. (Sub-Clause 4.3)

Throughout the execution of the Works, and as long thereafter as is necessary to fulfill the Contractor's obligations, the Contractor shall provide all necessary superintendence to plan, arrange, direct, manage, inspect and test the Works. (Sub-Clause 6.8)

The Engineer may require the Contractor to remove (or cause to be removed) any person employed on the Site or Works, including the Contractor's Representative if applicable. (Sub-Clause 6.9)

The Contractor shall submit, to the Engineer, details showing the number of each class of Contractor's Personnel and of each type of Contractor's Equipment on the Site. (Sub-Clause 6.10)

The Contractor shall at all times take all reasonable precautions to prevent any unlawful, riotous or disorderly conduct by or amongst the Contractor's Personnel, and to preserve peace and protection of persons and property on and near the Site. (Sub-Clause 6.11)

(15) The Contractor shall not subcontract the whole of the Works. (Sub-Clause 4.4)

Unless otherwise stated in the Particular Conditions, the prior consent of the Engineer shall be obtained to other proposed:

Subcontractors:

①material supplier;

②such Subcontractor as being stated in the Contract (Sub-Clause 4.4)

The Contractor shall be responsible for the acts or defaults of any Subcontractor, his agents or employees, as if they were the acts or defaults of the Contractor (Sub-Clause 4.4)

(16) The Contractor shall set out the Works in relation to original points, lines and levels of reference specified in the Contract or notified by the Engineer. The Contractor shall be responsible for the correct positioning of all parts of the Works, and shall rectify any error in the positions, levels, dimensions or alignment of the Works.

The Employer shall be responsible for any errors in these specified or notified items of reference, but the Contractor shall use reasonable efforts to verify their accuracy before they are used. (Sub-Clause 4.7)

(17) The Contractor shall:

①Take care for the safety of all persons entitled to be on the Site.

②Use reasonable efforts to keep the Site and Works clear of unnecessary obstruction so as to avoid danger to these persons.

③Provide fencing, lighting, guarding and watching of the Works until completion and taking over under Article 10 [Employer's Taking Over]; and

④Provide any Temporary Works (including roadways, footways, guards and fences) which may be necessary, because of the execution of the Works, for the use and protection of the public and of owners and occupiers of adjacent land. (Sub-Clause 4.8)

(18) The Contractor shall institute a quality assurance system to demonstrate compliance with the requirements of the Contract. (Sub-Clause 4.9)

(19) The Contractor shall be responsible for interpreting all such data. To the extent which was practicable (taking account of cost and time), the Contractor shall be deemed to have obtained all necessary information as to risks, contingencies and other circumstances which may influence or affect the Tender or Works. To the same extent, the Contractor shall be deemed to have inspected and examined the Site, its surroundings, the above data and other available information, and to have been satisfied before submitting the Tender as to all relevant matters. (Sub-Clause 4.10)

The Contractor shall be deemed to:

①have satisfied himself as to the correctness and sufficiency of the Accepted Contract Amount (Sub-Clause 4.11)

②If the Contractor encounters adverse physical conditions which he considers to have been Unforeseeable, the Contractor shall give notice to the Engineer as soon as practicable. The Contractor shall continue executing the Works, using such proper and reasonable measures as are appropriate for the physical conditions. If and to the extent that the Contractor encounters physical conditions which are Unforeseeable, gives such a notice, and suffers delay and/or incurs Cost due to these conditions, the Contractor shall be entitled subject to Sub-Clause 20.1 [Contractor's Claims]. (Sub-Clause 4.12)

(20) The Contractor shall bear all costs and charges for special and/or temporary rights of-way which he may require, including those for access to the Site. The Contractor shall also obtain, at his risk and cost, any additional facilities outside the Site which he may require for the purposes of the Works. (Sub-Clause 4.13)

(21) The Contractor shall be deemed to have been satisfied as to the suitability and availability of access routes to the Site. The Contractor shall use reasonable efforts to prevent any road or bridge from being damaged by the Contractor's traffic or by the Contractor's Personnel. (Sub-Clause 4. 15)

(22) The Contractor shall give the Engineer not less than 21 days' notice of the date on which any Plant or a major item of other Goods will be delivered to the Site and the Contractor shall be responsible for packing, loading, transporting, receiving, unloading, storing and protecting all Goods and other things required for the Works. (Sub-Clause 4. 16)

(23) The Contractor shall be responsible for all Contractors' Equipment. The Contractor shall not remove from the Site any major items of Contractor's Equipment without the consent of the Engineer. (Sub-Clause 4. 17)

(24) The Contractor shall take all reasonable steps to protect the environment (both on and off the Site) and to limit damage and nuisance to people and property resulting from pollution, noise and other results of his operations.

The Contractor shall ensure that emissions, surface discharges and effluent from the Contractor's activities shall not exceed the values indicated in the Specification, and shall not exceed the values prescribed by applicable Laws. (Sub-Clause 4. 18)

(25) The Contractor shall be entitled to use for the purposes of the Works such supplies of electricity, water, gas and other services as may be available on the Site and of which details and prices are given in the Specification. The Contractor shall, at his risk and cost, provide any apparatus necessary for his use of these services and for measuring the quantities consumed. (Sub-Clause 4. 19)

(26) The Contractor shall be responsible for each item of Employer's Equipment whilst any of the Contractor's Personnel is operating it, driving it, directing it orin possession or control of it. The Contractor's obligations of inspection, care, custody and control shall not relieve the Employer of liability for any shortage, defector default not apparent from a visual inspection. (Sub-Clause 4. 20)

(27) The Contractor shall submit a detailed time program to the Engineer within 28 day safter receiving the notice under Sub-Clause 8. 1 [Commencement of Works]. The Contractor shall also submit a revised program whenever the previous programs inconsistent with actual progress or with the Contractor's obligations. Unless otherwise stated in the Particular Conditions, monthly progress reports shall be prepared by the Contractor and submitted to the Engineer in six copies. If, at any time:

①actual progress is too slow to complete within the Time for Completion; and/or

②progress has fallen (or will fall) behind the current program under Sub-Clause 8. 3 [Program me], then the Engineer may instruct the Contractor to submit, under Sub-Clause 8. 3, a revised program and supporting report describing the revised methods which the Contractor proposes to adopt in order to expedite progress and complete within the Time for Completion Goods, at the risk and cost of the Contractor. (Sub-Clause 4. 21, Sub-Clause 8. 6)

(28) The Contractor shall keep the Site clear during the execution of the Works. Upon the

issue of a Taking-Over Certificate, the Contractor shall remove from the Site all Contractor's Equipment, surplus material, wreckage, rubbish and Temporary Works. However, the Contractor may retain on Site, during the Defects Notification Period, such Goods as are required for the Contractor to fulfill obligations under the Contract. (Sub-Clause 4.23)

(29) All fossils, coins, articles of value or antiquity, and structures and other remains or items of geological or archaeological interest found on the Site shall be placed under the care and authority of the Employer. The Contractor shall take reasonable precautions to prevent Contractor's Personnel or other persons from removing or damaging any of these findings. (Sub-Clause 4.24)

(30) The Contractor shall not be under any obligation to employ a nominated Subcontractor against whom the Contractor raises reasonable objection by notice to the Engineer as soon as practicable, with supporting particulars. (Sub-Clause 5.2)

The Contractor shall pay to the nominated Subcontractor the amounts which the Engineer certifies to be due in accordance with the Subcontract. Before issuing a Payment Certificate which includes an amount payable to a nominated Subcontractor, the Engineer may request the Contractor to supply reasonable evidence that the nominated Subcontractor has received all amounts due in accordance with previous Payment Certificates, less applicable deductions for retention or otherwise. (Sub-Clause 5.4)

(31) Except as otherwise stated in the Specification, the Contractor shall make arrangements for the engagement of all staff and labour, local or otherwise, and for their payment, housing, feeding and transport. (Sub-Clause 6.1)

The Contractor shall pay rates of wages, and observe conditions of labour, which are not lower than those established for the trade or industry where the work is carried out. (Sub-Clause 6.2)

The Contractor shall comply with all the relevant labour Laws applicable to the Contractor's Personnel. The Contractor shall require his employees to obey all applicable Laws, including those concerning safety at work. (Sub-Clause 6.4)

No work shall be carried out on the Site on locally recognized days of rest, or outside the normal working hours stated in the Appendix to Tender. (Sub-Clause 6.5)

The Contractor shall not permit any of the Contractor's Personnel to maintain any temporary or permanent living quarters within the structures forming part of the Permanent Works. (Sub-Clause 6.6)

The Contractor shall at all times take all reasonable precautions to maintain the health and safety of the Contractor's Personnel. The Contractor shall appoint an accident prevention officer at the Site, responsible for maintaining safety and protection against accidents (Sub-Clause 6.7)

(32) The Contractor shall submit the following samples of Materials, and relevant information, to the Engineer for consent prior to using the Materials in or for the Works. (Sub-Clause 7.2)

The Contractor shall give the Employer's Personnel full opportunity to carry out these activities, including providing access, facilities, permissions and safety equipment. (Sub-Clause 7.3)

The Contractor shall provide all apparatus, assistance, documents and other in formation, electricity, equipment, fuel, consumables, instruments, labor, materials, and suitably qualified and experienced staff, as are necessary to carry out the specified tests efficiently. The Contractor shall agree, with the Engineer, the time and place for the specified testing of any Plant, Materials and other parts of the Works. (Sub-Clause 7.4)

The Contractor shall then promptly make good the defect and ensure that the rejected item complies with the Contract. (Sub-Clause 7.5)

The Engineer may instruct the Contractor to:

①Remove from the Site and replace any Plant or Materials which is not in accordance with the Contract.

②Remove and re-execute any other work which is not in accordance with the Contract. (Sub-Clause 7.6)

(33) Unless otherwise stated in the Specification, the Contractor shall pay all royalties, rents and other payments for natural Materials obtained from outside the Site. (Sub-Clause 7.8)

(34) The Contractor shall commence the execution of the Works as soon as is reasonably practicable after the Commencement Date, and shall then proceed with the Works with due expedition and without delay. (Sub-Clause 8.1)

(35) The Engineer may at any time instruct the Contractor to suspend progress of part or all of the Works. During such suspension, the Contractor shall protect ,store and secure such part or the Works against any deterioration, loss or damage. (Sub-Clause 8.8)

If the Contractor suffers delay and/or incurs Cost from complying with the Engineer's instructions under Sub-Clause 8.8 [Suspension of Work] and/or from resuming the Works, the Contractor shall give notice to the Engineer and shall be entitled subject to Sub-Clause 20.1 [Contractor's Claims]. (Sub-Clause 8.9)

The Contractor shall be entitled to payment of the value (as at the date of suspension) of Plant and/or Materials which have not been delivered to Site, if:

①the Works on Plant or delivery of Plant and/or Materials has been suspended for more than 28 days; and

②the Contractor has marked the Plant and/or Materials as the Employer's property in accordance with the Engineer's instructions. (Sub-Clause 8.10)

If the suspension under Sub-Clause 8.8 [Suspension of Work] has continued for more than 84 days, the Contractor may request the Engineer's permission to proceed. If the Engineer does not give permission within 28 days after being requested to do so, the Contractor may, by giving notice to the Engineer, treat the suspension as an omission under Article 13 [Variations and Adjustments] of the affected part of the Works. If the suspension affects the whole of the Works, the Contractor may give notice of termination under Sub-Clause 16.2 [Termination by Contractor]. (Sub-Clause 8.11)

(36) The Contractor shall take full responsibility for the care of the Works and Goods from the Commencement Date until the Taking-Over Certificate is issued. The Contractor shall be liable for any loss or damage caused by any actions performed by the Contractor after a Taking-Over

Certificate has been issued. The Contractor shall also be liable for any loss or damage which occurs after a Taking-Over Certificate has been issued and which arose from a previous event for which the Contractor was liable. (Sub-Clause 17.2)

(37) The Contractor shall indemnify and hold the Employer harmless against and from any other claim which arises out of or in relation to:

①the manufacture, use, sale or import of any Goods; or

②any design for which the Contractor is responsible. (Sub-Clause 17.5)

(38) Neither Party shall be liable to the other Party for loss of use of any Works, loss of profit, loss of any contract or for any indirect or consequential loss or damage which may be suffered by the other Party in connection with the Contract, other than under Sub-Clause 16.4 [Payment after Termination by Contractor] and Sub-Clause 17.1 [Indemnities]. (Sub-Clause 17.6)

(39) ① The insuring Party shall insure the Works, Plant, Materials and Contractor's Documents for not less than the full reinstatement cost including the costs of demolition, removal of debris and professional fees and profit.

②The insuring Party shall insure the Contractor's Equipment for not less than the full replacement value, including delivery to Site.

③The insuring Party shall insure against each Party's liability for any loss, damage, death or bodily injury which may occur to any physical propertyor to any person. (Sub-Clause 18.2, Sub-Clause 18.3)

The Contractor shall effect and maintain insurance against liability for claims, damages, losses and expenses (including legal fees and expenses) arising from injury, sickness, disease or death of any person employed by the Contractor or any other of the Contractor's Personnel. (Sub-Clause 18.4)

Whenever the Contractor is the insuring Party, such insurance shall be effected with insurers and in terms approved by the Employer. (Sub-Clause 18.1)

The relevant insuring Party shall, within the respective periods stated in the Appendix to Tender (calculated from the Commencement Date), submit to the other Party:

①evidence that the insurances described in this Clause have been effected; and

②copies of the policies for the insurances described in Sub-Clause 18.2[Insurance for Works and Contractor's Equipment] and Sub-Clause 18.3 [Insurance against Injury to Persons and Damage to Property].

If the insuring Party fails to effect and keep in force any of the insurances it is required to effect and maintain under the Contract, or fails to provide satisfactory evidence and copies of policies in accordance with this Sub-Clause, the other Party may (at its option and without prejudice to any other right or remedy) effect insurance for the relevant coverage and pay the premiums due. The insuring Party shall pay the amount of these premiums to the other Party, and the Contract Price shall be adjusted accordingly. (Sub-Clause 18.1)

Ⅱ Changes in 2017 FIDIC version

(1) General obligations of contractors (refer to Sub-Clause 41)

The 2017 Red Book simplifies the Contractor's core obligations and the Contractor shall perform the work in accordance with the Contract. At the same time, the 2017 edition of the Red Book expands the Contractor's obligation to be responsible for any design according to the Contract. The Contractor should ensure that the design and Contractor's documents meet the technical standards stipulated in the regulations and laws (effective at the time of receiving the project), and meet the documents constituting the Contract.

(2) Performance security (refer to Sub-Clause 4.2)

The 2017 Red Book provides that when the change or adjustment results in an increase or decrease of more than 20 percent in the Contract Price compared with the accepted bid price, the Owner may require the Contractor to increase the amount of the performance security, and the Contractor may also reduce the amount of the performance security. If the owner requests the Contractor to increase the cost, the change clause shall apply.

(3) Contractor documents (refer to Sub-Clause 4.1, Sub-Clause 4.4)

The 2017 Red Book provides that when the contractor is responsible for the design of any part of the permanent Works, construction cannot commence until the Engineer has (or is deemed to have) issued a notice of no objection to the Contractor's documents. In addition, the 2017 Red Book expanded the Contractor's obligation to provide completion records, operations and maintenance manuals.

(4) Key personnel of Contractors (refer to Sub-Clause 6.12)

The 1999 Red Book only puts forward specific requirements for the selection and replacement of Contractors' Representatives (i. e. project managers of Contractors), and the 2017 edition increases the requirements for other key personnel of Contractors, and clarifies the replacement of these key personnel.

(5) Taking-Over of the Works (refer to Sub-Clause 10.1)

The 2017 Red Book adds conditions for Taking-Over of the Works to the 1999 version, adding that the project can be completed unless the Engineer has issued (or is deemed to have been issued) no objection notice under Sub-Clause 4.4 with respect to completion records and operation and maintenance manuals and the Contractor has provided training in accordance with Sub-Clause 4.5.

(6) Cost of repairing defects (refer to Sub-Clause 11.2)

The 2017 edition of the Red Book increases the Contractor's cost of repairing defects compared with the 1999 edition: the Contractor is responsible for repairing the defects caused by the Contractor's responsibility (such as completion records, operation and maintenance manuals and training). The 2017 edition of the Red Book clearly divides the change into three automatic ways, indicative change, request for proposals and defects caused by improper maintenance.

(7) Change (refer to Sub-Clause 13.3)

The 2017 Red Book clearly divides the change into three methods: indicative change, request for proposals and contractor's requirements for valuable engineering and specified change.

The Contractor should submit detailed information, including the Works to be carried out, the resources and methods used; implementing the schedule of changes; proposal for amendments to the schedule and completion time; proposals for amendments to the Contract Price (supported by evidence); and any costs incurred as a result of the increase in the construction period that the Contractor considers appropriate. When requesting proposals, the Contractor may claim under Sub-Clause 20. 2 for additional costs incurred in submitting proposals. Changes of a valuable engineering nature initiated by the Contractor are dealt with in accordance with Sub-Clause 13. 2.

(8)Contractor design risk (refer to Sub-Clause 17. 4)

The 2017 edition of the Red Book adds an owner-free content: requiring the Contractor to protect the Owner's engineering interests from all errors in the Contractor's design (if any) and avoid any responsibility. The application of such risks to total liability limits the Contractor's liability in this regard.

(9)Limits of responsibility (refer to Sub-Clause 1. 15)

The liability limit clause stipulates that either Party shall not be responsible for any indirect or consequential losses that may be incurred by the other Party in connection with the Contract, except in some cases specified in the Clause. In the 2017 edition of the Red Book, the scope of such exceptions has increased: including the cases referred to in Sub-Clause 8. 8 [Delay Damages] and Sub-Clause 17. 3 [Intellectual and Industrail property rights], but the 2017 edition has not yet defined the concept of "indirect of consequential loss". The 2017 Red Book also added a case where the liability limit clause was not applicable, namely gross negligence.

※ **Vocabulary**

1. impermissible *adj.* 不允许的，不准可的

2. hydrological conditions 水文条件

3. adaptability *n.* 适应性；可变性；适合性

4. formalities *n.* 手续；礼节（formality 的复数）；拘谨

5. unless otherwise stated 除非另作说明

6. entitled *adj.* 有资格的

      v. 使享有权利；给……命名（或题名）（entitle 的过去式和过去分词）

7. jointly and severally 个别并连带负责

8. unincorporated *adj.* （公司等）无法人地位的；未被包括在内的；未正式成为某城镇一部分的

9. consumables *n.* 消耗品，消费品；耗材（consumable 的复数）

10. disorderly conduct 扰乱社会治安的行为，妨碍治安行为

11. precautions *n.* 防范；预防措施；预警（precaution 的复数）

12. alignment of 对准

13. assurance system 保障体系

14. effluent *n.* 污水；流出物；废气

      adj. 流出的，发出的

15. archaeological *adj.* 考古学的，考古的
16. nominated subcontractor 指定分包商
17. normal working hours 正常工作时间
18. expedition *n.* 远征，考察；探险队，考察队；动作敏捷，迅速
19. suspension of work 工作中断
20. suspended *v.* 悬挂；停止，暂停，中止；(因犯错而)暂令停职；暂令停学；暂令停止参加
    活动；悬浮，漂浮(suspend 的过去式和过去分词)
21. loss or damage 损失或损害
22. indemnify *v.* 赔偿；保护；使免于受罚
23. consequential loss 间接损失；从属的损失；后果性损失
24. reinstatement *n.* 恢复；复原；复职
25. satisfactory evidence 令人满意的证据
26. without prejudice to 不使……受损害
27. accepted bid 中标
28. request for proposals 提案申请；征询方案
29. amendments *n.* 修正(amendment 的复数)；修正案
30. liability limit 责任限额(指保险单上规定的最高赔偿金额)

Appendix 3

Claim List

I Provision list of Claim in 1999 FIDIC version

（1）Explicit claim provisions

Table 3

No.	Sub-Clause number	Sub-Clause name	Claims and Claimable Contents
1	1.9	Delayed Drawings or Instructions	C+P+T
2	2.1	Right of Access to the Site	C+P+T
3	3.3	Instructions of the Engineer	C+P+T
4	4.6	Co-operation	C+P+T
5	4.7	Setting Out	C+P+T
6	4.12	Unforeseeable Physical Conditions	C+T
7	4.24	Fossils	C+T
8	7.2	Samples	C+P
9	7.4	Testing	C+P+T
10	8.3	Programme	C+P+T
11	8.4	Extension of Time for Completion	T
12	8.5	Delays Caused by Authorities	T
13	8.8 & 8.9 & 8.11	Suspension of Work & Consequences of Suspension & Prolonged Suspension	C+T
14	9.2	Delayed Tests	C+P+T
15	10.2	Taking Over of Parts of the Works	C+P
16	10.3	Interference with Tests on Completion	C+P+T
17	11.2	Cost of Remedying Defects	C+P
18	11.6	Further Tests	C+P
19	11.8	Contractor to Search	C+P
20	12.4	Omissions	C
21	13.1	Right to Vary	C+P+T

Continued

No.	Sub-Clause number	Sub-Clause name	Claims and Claimable Contents
22	13.2	Value Engineering	C
23	13.5	Provisional Sums	C+P
24	13.7	Adjustments for Changes in Legislation	C+T
25	13.8	Adjustments for Changes in Cost	C
26	15.5	Employer's Entitlement to Termination	C+P
27	16.1	Contractor's Entitlement to Suspend Work	C+P+T
28	16.2 & 16.4	Termination by Contractor & Termination by Contractor	C+P
29	17.3 & 17.4	Employer's Risks & Consequences of Employer's Risks	C+P+T
30	17.5	Intellectual and Industrial Property Rights	C
31	18.1	General Requirements for Insurances	C
32	19.4	Consequences of Force Majeure	C+T
33	19.6	Optional Termination, Payment and Release	C
34	19.7	Release from Performance under the Law	C

Note: C—Costs; P—Profits; T—Time

(2) Implicit claim provisions

Table 4

No.	Sub-Clause number	Sub-Clause name	Claims and Claimable Contents
1	1.3	Communications	C+P+T
2	1.5	Priority of Documents	C+T
3	1.8	Care and Supply of Documents	C+P+T
4	1.13	Compliance with Laws	C+P+T
5	2.3	Employer's Personnel	C+T
6	2.5	Employer's Claims	C
7	3.2	Delegation by the Engineer	C+P+T
8	4.2	Performance Security	C
9	4.10	Site Data	C+T
10	4.20	Employer's Equipment and Free-Issue Material	C+P+T
11	5.2	Objection to Nomination	C+T
12	7.3	Inspection	C+P+T
13	8.1	Commencement of Works	C+T
14	8.12	Resumption of Work	C+P+T

Continued

No.	Sub-Clause number	Sub-Clause name	Claims and Claimable Contents
15	12. 1	Works to be Measured	C+P
16	12. 3	Evaluation	C+P

Note: C—Costs; P—Profits; T—Time

Ⅱ Provision list of Claim in 2017 FIDIC version

(1) Explicit claim provisions

Table 5

No.	Sub-Clause number	Sub-Clause name	Claims and Claimable Contents
1	1.9	Delayed drawings or instructions	T+C+P
2	1.13	Compliance with Laws	T+C+P
3	2.1	Rights of access to the site	T+C+P
4	4.6	Co-operation	T+C+P
5	4.7.3	Agreement or Determination of rectification measures, delay and/or Cost	T+C+P
6	4.12.4	Delay and/or Cost	T+C
7	4.15	Access Route	T+C
8	4.23	Archaeological or geological findings	T+C
9	7.4	Testing by the Contractor	T+C+P
10	7.6	Remedial work	T+C+P
11	8.5	Extension of time for Completion	T
12	8.6	Delays caused by Authorities	T
13	8.10	Consequences of Employer's Suspension	T+C+P
14	9.2	Delayed Tests	T+C+P
15	10.2	Taking Over Parts	C+P
16	10.3	Interference with Tests on Completion	T+C+P
17	11.7	Rights of Access after Taking Over	C+P
18	11.8	Contractor to Search	C+P
19	13.3.2	Variation Procedure	C+P
20	13.6	Adjustments for Changes in Laws	C+P
21	15.5	Termination for Employer's Convenience	C
22	16.1	Suspension by Contractor	T+C
23	16.2.2	Termination by Contractor	C+P
24	16.3	Contractor's Obligation After Termination	T+C+P
25	16.4	Payment after Termination by Contractor	T+C+P

Continued

No.	Sub-Clause number	Sub-Clause name	Claims and Claimable Contents
26	17.2	Liability for Care of the Works	C+P
27	17.3	Intellectual and Industrial Property Rights	C+P
28	18.4	Consequences of an Exceptional Event	T+C+P
29	18.5	Optional Termination	C
30	18.6	Release from Performance under the Law	T+C

Note: C—Costs; P—Profits; T—Time

(2) Implicit claim provisions

Table 6

No.	Sub-Clause number	Sub-Clause name	Claims and Claimable Contents
1	1.3	Notice and Other Communications	T+C+P
2	1.5	Priority of Documents	T+C+P
3	1.8	Care and Supply of Documents	T+C+P
4	3.4	Delegation by the Engineer	T+C+P
5	3.5	Engineer's Instructions	T+C+P
6	4.2	Performance Security	C
7	5.2.2	Objection to Nomination	T+C
8	4.10	Use of Site Data	T+C
9	4.19	Temporary Utilities	C+P
10	8.1	Commencement of Works	T+C+P
11	8.13	Resumption of Work	T+C+P
12	12.1	Works to be Measured	C+P
13	12.3	Valuation of the Works	C+P
14	17.5	Indemnities by Employer	C
15	19.1	General Requirments	C

Note: C—Costs; P—Profits; T—Time

※**Vocabulary**

1. value engineering 价值工程;工程经济学
2. interference with 干涉;妨碍,打扰
3. resumption of work 恢复工作
4. geological *adj.* 地质的,地质学的

Appendix 4

Counter Claim Provision List

Counter claim in 2017

(1) Explicit Claim Provisions

Table 7

(1)	Sub-Clause 1.13	Compliance with Laws	Additional costs incurred by the Owner as a result of the Contractor's failure to provide assistance and documentation to enable the Owner to obtain the relevant permit or as a result of the Contractor's failure to comply with the permit, license or approval obtained by the Owner.
(2)	Sub-Clause 4.2.2	Claims under the Performance Security	The Owner's claim for performance guarantee or other expenses based on the matters listed.
(3)	Sub-Clause 7.4	Testing by the Contractor	The Owner's loss caused by the Contractor's delay in a test.
(4)	Sub-Clause 7.5	Defects and Rejection	The Engineers require rejection or re-inspection of defective equipment, materials, contractor design (if any) or process to incur additional costs for the Owners.
(5)	Sub-Clause 7.6	Remedial Work	The Contractor failed to remove unqualified equipment and materials as instructed by the Engineer, and all costs incurred to the Owner for work that did not meet the contract requirements for repairs.
(6)	Sub-Clause 8.7	Rate of Progress	The Contractor need to speed up the Owners to pay additional costs for slow progress due to their own reasons.
(7)	Sub-Clause 8.8	Delay Damages	The Contractor fails to pay the Owner Compensation for Misdue Damages for Completion at the time specified in Sub-Clause 8.2.
(8)	Sub-Clause 9.2	Delayed Tests	Additional costs incurred to the Owners in self-testing due to delays in completion tests due to the Contractors.

Continued

(9)	Sub-Clause 9.3	Retesting	Applicable to Sub-Clause 7.5, the project or section fails to pass the completion test, so additional cost incurred to the Owner for re-examining the defective equipment, materials, contractor design (if any) or process.
(10)	Sub-Clause 9.4	Failure to Pass Tests on Completion	Failure of the project or section to pass the completion test specified in Sub-Clause 9.3 and reduction of performancedamage compensation or contract price payable to the owner upon request for transfer.
(11)	Sub-Clause 11.1	Completion of Outstanding Works and Remedying Defects	Applicable to Sub-Clause 7.5, the additional cost occurred to the Owners for defective equipment, materials, contractor design (if any) or process re-inspection.
(12)	Sub-Clause 11.3	Extension of Defects Notification Period	The Contractor does not conduct an investigation and the Owners may investigate by themselves and the additional costs incurred to their own
(13)	Sub-Clause 11.4	Failure to Remedy Defects	The Contractor fails to clean up the site as stipulated in the Contract, and the Owner may restore the site at his own expense.
(14)	Sub-Clause 11.8	Contractor to Search	The re-test according to the items listed in Sub-Clause 11.2 leads to additional costs for the Owners.
(15)	Sub-Clause 11.11	Clearance of Site	The Contractor fails to meet performance requirements and shall compensate the Owner for performance damage compensation.
(16)	Sub-Clause 13.6	Adjustments for Changes in Laws	When the legal change leads to the reduction of engineering costs, the Owner has the right to deduct the Contract Price.
(17)	Sub-Clause 15.4	Payment after Termination for Contractor's Default	In case of a serious breach, destruction or bribery by the Contractor, the Owner may terminate the Contract and claim to the Contractor the additional costs required for the completion of the Works, the resulting loss or damage compensation and compensation for overdue damages.

(2) Implicit Claim Provisions

Table 8

(1)	Sub-Clause 4.14	Avoidance of Interference	Any loss and additional costs caused by unnecessary and inappropriate interference by the Contractor to the Owner.

Continued

(2)	Sub-Clause 4.16	Transport of Goods	The Contractor losses and additional costs caused by cargo transportation of the Contractor.
(3)	Sub-Clause 4.18	Protection of the Environment	Loss of the Owners' benefits and additional costs due to environmental pollution by the Contractors.
(4)	Sub-Clause 4.19	Temporary Utilities	Facilities payable by the Contractor for the use of temporary facilities provided by the Owner.
(5)	Sub-Clause 14.2	Advance Payment	Payments that have not yet been paid before the issuance of the project acceptance certificate or before the termination of the Contract for other reasons.
(6)	Sub-Clause 17.4	Indemnities by Contractor	Within the scope of the guarantee provided by the Contractor, the losses and additional costs incurred by the Owner.
(7)	Sub-Clause 19.1	General Requiremnts	Additional costs incurred to the Owner caused by the Contractor for failure to comply with the relevant provisions.

※ Vocabulary

1. validity *n.* (法律上的)有效,合法,认可;真实性,正确性

2. workmanship *n.* 手艺,工艺;技巧

3. attributable to 由于,由……引起;可归因于;应得部分

4. omission *n.* 省略,遗漏;被省略(或排除)的人(或物);(尤指道德上或法律义务的)疏忽

5. request for transfer 请求调职,申请转职

6. acceptance certificate 验收证明书

Appendix 5

AIA and FIDIC

The American Institute of Architects (AIA), a professional organization for architects in the US, established AIA Middle East in 2010 to serve its members in the region.

As part of its remit, the AIA produces a comprehensive suite of standard form construction documents known as the AIA Contract Documents, which are widely used on construction projects in the US.

Despite their common usage in the US, the AIA Contract Documents are less well known in other international markets, particularly where the standard forms produced by the Fédération Internationale Des Ingénieurs Conseils (FIDIC) are in wide use. In order to promote their own documents, AIA members would have to show employers that the AIA forms are in line with current market positions in the region in relation to key construction risks.

The AIA General Conditions of Contract for Construction (A201-2007) is generally regarded as the most commonly used general conditions document on construction projects in the US. It is designed for use on projects where the design has been prepared by or on behalf of the Contractor, where the professional team is already in place. As such, it can be seen as the AIA equivalent to FIDIC's General Conditions of Contract (the Red Book), the best known of the FIDIC documents. It is useful, then, to look at how A201-2007 deals with certain of the key construction risks in comparison with the Red Book.

To take the example of liability for delay, Sub-Clause 8.4 of the Red Book sets out the entitlements of the Contractor to extensions of the time for completion. These entitlements arise from delays caused by variations, exceptionally adverse climatic conditions, unforeseeable labour or goods shortages caused by epidemic or government action and employer-caused delay. There are other entitlements enumerated throughout the remainder of the Contract, including delays caused by failure to be granted access to the Site and the occurrence of unforeseeable physical conditions.

Article 8.3.1 of A201-2007, on the other hand, sets out some arguably wider grounds for entitlement, including acts or neglect by the Owner (as A201-2007 identifies the Employer) and the architect (the Contract Administrator), causes beyond the Contractor's control and other causes the architect determines justify delay. The Employers used to the Red Book position may find these entitlements overly broad and seek to restrict them by way of amendment to the standard form.

A further point of difference emerges in the claims procedure. The claims procedure set out at Sub-Clause 20. 1 of the Red Book is generally considered to be onerous on the Contractor. Notice of a claim must be given within 28 days of the date the Contractor became, or should have become, aware of the relevant event. A further detailed claim must be made within 42 days of the same date. The submission of notice within 28 days is expressly set out as a condition precedent to entitlement under the claim. Depending on the applicable provisions of the governing law, this could lead to the Contractor losing any entitlement to relief.

Article 15. 1 of A201-2007 sets out an arguably more "contractor-friendly" position. Claims are required to be initiated within 21 days after the later of the date the event occurs or the date the Contractor recognises it. The time limit is, therefore, based on the Contractor's actual knowledge, rather than when it should have had such knowledge as in FIDIC. This requirement is not set out expressly as a condition precedent to a claim. In such circumstances, the Contractor under Article 8 of the Red Book is required to submit monthly interim claims and a final claim within 28 days of the event ceasing.

※ Vocabulary

1. key construction 重点建设,关键施工
2. remainder 剩余量
3. condition precedent 先决条件

Appendix 6

Contract Payment of 2017 FIDIC Contract Series

Ⅰ Types of Engineering Contract Price

Engineering Contracts can be divided into three types of Unit Price Contracts, Total Price Contracts and Cost Plus Fee Contracts.

The Unit Price Contract belongs to the re-measurement Contract. The Contract Price is calculated based on the unit price in the bill of quantities and the amount of actual settlement. The amount of engineering in the bill of quantities is only used as the basis for bidding quotation and evaluation, and is not used as the actual settlement amount.

At the same time, the Contractor undertakes the risk of unit price change, and the Owner undertakes the risk of engineering quantity change.

The Total Price Contract is also known as the fixed Total Price Contract. If the factors such as claims and changes are not considered, in the adjustment, the total price paid by the Owner to the Contractor shall be the Contract Price in the Contract Agreement, and the Owner shall pay in accordance with the agreed payment schedule. Under the Total Price Contract, the Contractor undertakes the risks of unit price change and engineering quantity change.

The Cost Plus Fee Contract is the type of actual reimbursement, and the total price paid by the Owner to the Contractor is the actual cost of the Contractor plus reasonable remuneration. In this type of Contract Price, the Owner undertakes the risk of unit price change and engineering quantity change. The final Contract Price has great uncertainty, and the risk of the Owner is large, which is rarely used in engineering practice.

The 2017 edition of Red Book basically belongs to Unit Price Contract, however, in practice, does not rule out that individual items of Red Book will use total price valuation and payment. There will also be a situation in which the Red Book is changed into a Total Price Contract. At this time, the Owner no longer bears the risk of engineering quantity change, and the corresponding risk-sharing clause should also be revised. The 2017 edition of the Yellow Book and the Silver Book belong to the Total Price Contract. Sometimes, part of the work of the Yellow Book may be re-measured, and the permanent engineering part of the general Silver Book will not be re-measured. When using the Yellow Book and Silver Book, claims, changes and other contents may be valuated by re-measurement or cost plus remuneration.

Ⅱ Bill of quantities

Bill of Quantities (BoQ) is the basis of project bidding quotation using unit Price Contract and the basis of unit Price Contract payment, claim and change pricing. There are a variety of engineering quantity list rules in the engineering industry. There are "Standard Method of Measurement" (SMM) certified by the Royal Institution of Chartered Surveyors (RICS) in the world. China's Ministry of Housing and Urban-Rural Construction issued the "Construction Engineering Quantity List Valuation Specification" which unified the preparation and measurement of the housing construction and decoration engineering quantity list. In addition, there are professional engineering bill of quantities measurement rules (such as highway engineering, water conservancy project, etc.) to unify specification of professional engineering bill of quantities preparation and calculation.

Under different bill of quantities rules, measurement methods may also be different.

BoQ is clearly included in the 2017 edition of the Red Book, and BoQ is defined specifically. BoQ is the basis of the Red Book pricing.

Under the 2017 Red Book, BoQ works only as bidding quotations and bid evaluation basis but not the actual implementation of the amount of work, nor is it the amount paid during the period. The unit price in BoQ is the basis of the Red Book pricing.

If the Yellow Book and Silver Book also include BoQ or other similar lists, the engineering quantity and unit price are only used for the purposes agreed in the Contract, and the engineering quantity in BoQ is not used as the engineering quantity of actual settlement.

Ⅲ Pricing and payment under FIDIC 2017 Red Book

The 2017 edition Red Book belongs to the Unit Price Contract of re-measurement. The Contract Price is calculated based on the unit price in BoQ and the actual settlement amount, and the actual settlement amount is calculated based on the approved drawings or the actual completion amount. When signing the Contract, the accepted contract amount is only temporary contract price.

1) Measurement methods and procedures

According to Article 12 of the general contract conditions of the 2017 edition of the Red Book [Measurement and Valuation], there are two types of measurement methods in the Red Book: the first type is field measurement in the engineering site, which should be carried out by the Contractor and the Engineer together; the second category is recorded and measured according to the specification.

In principle, the Unit Price Contract engineering measurement should generally adopt the first kind of way, there are also some works adopts the second kind of way, such as the general items in the bill of quantities (temporary engineering, design, HSE works, etc.), additives (need to be calculated according to the mix ratio), can be based on the approved drawings to determine the settlement of the amount of works (such as earthwork), these works cannot or does not need to carry out field measurement, but can be measured according to the record.

When an Engineer requests on-site measurement, the Engineer shall notify the Contractor at least 7 days in advance of the content, date and place of the measurement. The Contractor's Representative shall participate in or send another qualified representative to assist the Engineer to measure and try to reach agreement with the Engineer on the measurement results and provide the information required by the Engineer. If the Contractor fails to attend or send a representative according to the time and place of notification, the measurement implemented by the Engineer shall be regarded as completed in the presence of the Contractor and the Contractor has accepted the measurement results.

When measuring according to records, the Engineers are generally responsible for preparing records. Upon preparation of the records, the Engineer shall notify the time and place at least 7 days in advance of the Contract, requiring Contractor's Representative to examine and agree on records. If the Contractor's Representative fails to participate according to the time and place of notification or does not send representatives to participate, it shall be regarded as the Contractor has accepted the record results. If the Contractor has participated in the on-site measurement or record inspection, but the Contractor and the Engineer have not agreed on the measurement results, the Contractor shall notify the Engineer of the reasons for accurate records of on-site measurement or record inspection.

If the Contractor fails to participate in the on-site measurement or fails to notify the Engineer within 14 days after the record inspection, it shall be regarded as the Contractor has accepted the measurement results. After receiving such notice from the Contractor, the Engineer should agree or decide according to Sub-Clause 3.7 [Agreement or Determination]. At this time, the Engineer should temporarily estimate a project quantity for the Payment Certificate (IPC) during the issuance period.

2) Engineering valuation

After the completion of the project measurement, it is necessary to determine the unit price for the project evaluation. Unit price determination should follow the order and principle of "Same—Similar—Related—Cost Plus Profit", namely:

(1) Same

For each job, the unit price should first choose the unit price of the same work agreed in BoQ or other data tables.

(2) Similar

If BoQ or other data tables do not have the same work, the unit price of similar work should be selected.

(3) Related

When BoQ or other data tables do not have the same or similar work, and a new unit price need to be developed, BoQ or other data tables related work unit price should be referred to, and corresponding adjustments should be made.

（4）Cost Plus Profit

When BoQ or other datasheets are not available, the unit price shall be determined on the basis of a reasonable cost to carry out the work plus a certain percentage of profits（if not agreed at a profit rate of 5 percent）.

According to Sub-Clause 12.3［Valuation of the Works］of the 2017 Red Book, if any of the following conditions are met, a new unit price should be formulated:

①BoQ or other data tables do not include the work content, there is no unit price of the work, and there is no unit price of similar work in the Contract.

②When the change in the quantity of work results in a change in the cost sufficient to adjust the unit price, the change in the quantity of work shall meet the following conditions:

a. compared with the engineering quantity in BoQ or other data tables, the difference is more than 10%;

b. the engineering quantity difference multiplied by the unit price in the BoQ or other data sheet exceeded 0.01% of the accepted contract amount.

The engineering quantity difference leads to the cost change of the work exceeding 1%; and BoQ or other data tables do not agree that the unit price of the work is "fixed bill" "fixed fee" or other similar provisions.

③Change the work, and the above Article 1 or 2 applies.

If a work is included in the BoQ or other data tables, but the Contractor does not fill in the unit price, the value of the work should be regarded as being shared in the unit price of other work.

If the Engineer and the Contractor fail to agree on the unit price of a job, the Contractor shall notify the engineer to explain the reasons for disagreement, and the Engineer shall agree or decide the unit price according to Sub-Clause 3.7 after receiving the notification. Before unit price is agreed or decided, the Engineer should temporarily estimate a unit price for issuing IPC.

After the engineering quantity and unit price are determined, the amount of payment in the period can be determined, that is, the current project value of Sub-Clause 14.3［Application for Interim Payment］is determined, and then the payment certificate and payment process are entered.

Ⅳ Valuation and payment under 2017 FIDIC Yellow Book and Silver Book

The 2017 edition of the Yellow Book and the Silver Book are Total Price Contracts.

The payment in each period is not based on the unit price in the Contract and the actual completion of the project. The two Parties will agree on a payment plan to determine the amount of payment in each period, that is, the value of the current completion of the permanent project in Sub-Clause 14.3. There are three types of payment plans in Sub-Clause 14.4［Schedule of Payments］of the 2017 edition of the Guidelines for the Preparation of Specific Conditions for Yellow and Silver Book: the first is to pay in installments according to the agreed amount or proportion; the second is payment according to the agreed milestone; the third is according to the agreement of the permanent project main quantities list（BPQPW）payment. These three types of payment schedules are described and analyzed below.

1) Valuation and payment by installment according to agreed amount or proportion

The Contract Price shall be divided into a certain amount or proportion by period (monthly or other time interval) during the Contract period, and the cumulative amount per period shall be equal to the Contract Price or proportion of 100%.

The Contractor submits the interim payment application form according to the amount or proportion in each period, with supporting information to apply for payment of the corresponding amount. This approach is simple and clear, but it is likely that actual project progress is inconsistent with the schedule on which the payment plan is based in the implementation process. If the Engineers find that the schedule on which the payment plan is based is not consistent with the actual schedule, they have the right to adjust the payment plan, which may lead to frequent changes in the payment plan and thus generate many disputes. This method is more suitable for very simple engineering projects, large and complex engineering projects in reality seldom use it.

2) Valuation and payment by milestone

In the manner of milestone valuation and payment, the Contractor shall submit at the time of tender a schedule of milestone payments indicating the amount or proportion to be Paid for the completion of each milestone. After signing the Contract, but not before the start of the construction, the two sides can revise the milestone payment schedule.

During the project implementation period, the Contractor applies for the payment of the corresponding amount for each milestone (or each period), according to the interim payment application statement submitted by the milestone payment plan, and the corresponding supporting materials (including the information proving the completion of the milestone) are attached.

This method is suitable for projects that are easy to clearly determine the payment milestone. If the milestone is not easy to judge, the two sides are tend to dispute whether the milestone is completed. Sometimes, although the subject of the milestone has been completed, there may still be a very small part of the round-off work to be completed for a long time, the Contractor may not be able to get the corresponding schedule.

Due to the large amount of equipment, equipment orders, shipments and installation is clear, industrial projects are suitable for setting payment milestones, the Silver Book often this use.

Payment milestones should be set scientifically and reasonably according to the specific situation of the project, which should not be too coarse. Otherwise, it is easy to cause the Contractor to complete a lot of works, but it cannot be paid in time during the application period, resulting in a large cash flow pressure of the Contractor. It should not be too detailed.

Otherwise, the detailed design or design changes will cause changes in work content, which will easily lead to frequent changes in payment milestones, and both Parties may invest a lot of works in this regard.

3) Pricing and payment according to BPQPW

If the project's permanent works can be split into a number of simple partial works, you can use BPQPW pricing. Before the start of the project, the Contractor refines part of the project, selects the items in the BPQPW composed of the main work, and then calculates the expected completion quantity and unit price of these items. The total amount of the expected completion quantity multiplied by the unit price should be equal to the Contract Price, and each unit price should be the comprehensive unit price after considering the value of the temporary project, design and other works not included in the BPQPW, but the other works implemented to complete the works.

The BPQPW is submitted by the Contractor to the Engineer (or the Owner's Representative), with supporting materials and calculation process, and is used after the approval of the Engineer (or the Owner's Representative).

Before receiving the Taking-Over Certificate, BPQPW may be inconsistent with the actual situation due to design changes and the Contractor should resubmit and modify BPQPW.

During the implementation of the project, the Contractor shall calculate the amount of the interim payment according to the actual works completed in the current period and BPQPW, and prepare the interim payment application form, with supporting materials.

BPQPW is recommended in the 1999 edition of FIDIC Guidelines for the Preparation of Specific Conditions for the Yellow Book. However, only the first two valuation methods are recommended in the 1999 edition of the FIDIC Silver Book special conditions compilation guide.

The 2017 edition of FIDIC also includes the BPQPW valuation method in the Silver Book. It may be considered that the first two valuation methods are not sufficient to meet all the projects using the Silver Book, especially for projects with long duration and easy to be split by parts (such as highways and railway projects using the Silver Book), BPQPW is more conducive to valuation. Compared with the payment by milestone, the BPQPW method does not need to set a detailed payment milestone, and also avoids the difficulty of reaching an agreement on whether the milestone is completed.

In the practice of engineering contract management, BPQPW may have a variety of determinations. For example, after the Contract Price is divided according to the main works, the amount of each work is obtained. The value of the project completed in the current period is obtained by multiplying the percentage of each work completed in the current period by the value of the work. The percentage of each work completed in the current period is calculated on the basis of the actual amount of work completed in the current period and the expected amount of work completed. In addition, temporary works, design, thematic reports or data can be listed separately in BPQPW.

V Major differences in payment provisions between the FIDIC series contracts of the year 2017 and 1999

The provisions on payment in the 2017 edition of FIDIC contract conditions are roughly the same as the corresponding 1999 edition of FIDIC contract conditions. The main differences are as follows:

(1) There is a substantial increase in the length of the relevant provisions on payment in general contract conditions. The relevant provisions on payment in 2017 edition of contract terms are clearer, more possibilities are considered.

(2) Sub-Clause 2. 4 [Employer's Financial Arrangements] adds a payment guarantee for changing prices. If the single change price exceeds 10 percent of the Contract Price or the cumulative change price exceeds 30 percent of the original Contract Price, the Contractor may require the Owner to provide proof of the relevant financial arrangements to demonstrate its ability to pay for the change.

(3) Linkage with performance securitys is increased. Sub-Clause 4.2 [Performance Security] provides that a change or adjustment shall result in accumulation pursuant to Article 13 [Variations and Adjustments].

When the amount changes exceed 20% of the amount of the accepted Contract, the amount of the performance security should be increased or decreased accordingly.

(4) The interim report content is more accurate and comprehensive. In comparison with the 1999 contract terms, the interim statement at the time of the application for payment was increased from 7 to 10, with 1 amendment. The original "increase or decrease in the amount based on the Contract, including the amount determined in accordance with Article 20 [Claims, Disputes and Arbitration]" is modified to "increase or decrease in the amount based on the Contract, including the amount determined in accordance with Sub-Clause 3. 7 [Agreement or Determination]", because the claim amount will be agreed or decided in accordance with Sub-Clause 3.7, and the amount of disputes or arbitration should be paid immediately, not reflected in the interim statement. In addition, three additional amounts were added to the 2017 version of the interim statement of conditions of contract, namely, "provisional amount" "refund of retention money" and "contractor use of temporary facilities provided by the Owner".

(5) The Yellow Book details the IPC issuance procedures and increases the prerequisites for the issuance of IPC. The provisions of the 1999 edition of the Yellow Book on the issuance of IPC are less than half pages, and the 2017 edition of the contract conditions on the issuance of IPC is 1 page and half. The issuance of IPC, IPC detention and IPC modification have made detailed provisions, which are more operational. At the same time, "appointing the contractor representative" is added as the precondition of IPC.

(6) "Partially agreed final report" is added. Sub-Clause 14. 11 [Final Statement] provides that if there is still a disputed amount between the Parties after the issuance of the performance certificate, the Contractor shall prepare and submit a partial agreed final statement for temporary final payment. This change has more practical significance and is conducive to gradually solving problems.

(7) Interest payments for late payments are further explicitly simplified. According to Sub-Clause 14. 8 [Delayed Payment], if delayed payment occurs, the Contractor has the right to obtain the financing fee of the delayed payment, without providing a statement, without issuing a formal notice (including the claim notice in Sub-Clause 20. 2 and/or EOT), and without providing proof. Compared with the 1999 contract terms, the 2017 contract terms are clear and do not require notification to the Owners in accordance with the terms of the claim, which further demonstrates the naturality of the Contractor's right to receive financing fees for delayed payments and guarantees the fundamental rights of the Contractor.

※ Vocabulary

1. bidding quotation［金融］标盘
2. decoration engineering 装饰工程
3. field measurement 现场测量；实地量度；野外测量
4. fixed bill 定期汇票
5. milestone payments 按里程碑付款
6. proportion to 成比例
7. in the current 在目前
8. retention money 保留金
9. prerequisites n. 预备知识，先决条件（prerequisite 的复数）
10. the precondition 前提

Appendix 7

Analysis of Notification Requirements for Contractors in FIDIC 2017 Construction Contract

The notice clause is a key part of the international engineering contract. Its purpose is to ensure timely communication on matters that may lead to project delays or cost expansion in order to safeguard the interests of all Parties. Especially for the notification obligation imposed on the Contractor, timely notification can let the Owner timely investigate and understand the information and collect relevant evidence, quickly assess the impact of events on its investment, and start the decision-making process for rapid response. Especially in the context of the new coronavirus, the Parties to the Contract should carefully review the provisions on notification requirements in the Contract to ensure timely notification under the corresponding circumstances.

Many disputes in international works relate to the Contractor's failure to comply with the requirements of notice in the Contract, including the failure to give notice within a limited period of time, the failure to contain due details in the notice or the failure to comply with the formal requirements of the notice. In the case of disputes, the Contractor's failure to comply with the notification requirements may lead to the loss of relief for the extension of construction period or cost compensation.

While there was no consensus in the jurisprudence of different courts as to whether incomplete compliance with notification requirements was sufficient to constitute invalid notifications, some of the judgements supported strict compliance with notification requirements, while others preferred to less compliance.

However, in view of the importance of notification and the possible serious consequences of failure to comply with relevant requirements, it is necessary for the Contractor to pay attention to the notification requirements in the Contract.

For the notification obligation of the Contractor, at least the following matters need to be clarified in the Contract:

①what circumstances need the Contractor to give notice;

②timeliness requirements of notification;

③formative and content requirements of notification;

④whether effective notification is a prerequisite for obtaining certain compensation or relief.

Especially in the FIDIC 2017 version contract conditions, the notice (Sub-Clause 1. 1. 56) is specifically defined, and a Clause 1. 3 [*Notices and Other Communications*] is revised, notice and other forms of communication are distinguished, and the following specific requirements for notice are made clear:

①the notice shall be in writing;

②it should be the original copy signed by the Contractor Representative or the electronic original copy transmitted by the only electronic address assigned to the Contractor's Representative;

③should be clearly identified as a notification;

④if face-to-face or mail delivery is adopted, receipt should be obtained;

⑤should be delivered to the address of the recipient specified in the contract data table;

⑥when sending a notice to the Engineer (Owner), a copy should be copied to the Owner (Engineer) at the same time;

⑦no notice shall be unreasonably detained or delayed.

In addition, FIDIC 2017 version of the contract conditions also emphasizes the formal requirements of the notice, clearly stipulates that any content in the progress report does not constitute a notice under the terms of this contract (Sub-Clause 4. 20).

The content of the Contractor's notice can usually be divided into three categories: notice of action, notice of risk and notice of claim of rights (including notice of claim and notice of dissatisfaction). Based on the above three kinds of contents, this book sorts out the contents of the notice required by the Contractor in FIDIC 2017 edition construction contract conditions, and shows the terms and contents of the notice.

Table 9

Sub-Clause number	Content requirement	Time limit	Notification object
1. 9	If not issued within a reasonable specified time, as to details of the necessary drawings or instructions that may cause delays or interruptions in the project, detailed reasons and time to be issued and the specific nature and extent of any delay or interruption that may result shall also be issued		The Engineer
4. 1	Reasons for modifying design or Contractor's Documents submitted to the Engineers prior to review		The Engineer
4. 4. 1	Contractor's Documents are ready for review and are in Contractor's compliance with contract requirements		The Engineer
4. 16	The date on which the Goods will arrive at the Site	No less than 21 days	The Engineer

Continued

Sub-Clause number	Content requirement	Time limit	Notification object
4.17	Date of arrival of the Contractor's main equipment at the Site, indicating that the equipment is owned by the Contractor, Subcontractor or other Party and, if it is a lease, the lessor shall be specified	Within 7 days	The Engineer
5.1	Project expected commencement date and site commencement date of each Subcontractor	No less than 28 days	The Engineer
7.3	Time when materials, permanent equipment or works are ready for inspection by the Engineers		The Engineer
7.4	Time and place for specified inspection of any permanent equipment, materials and other parts of the project	Reasonanble time	The Engineer
8.12	Permission for continued construction		The Engineer
9.1	After a certain date the Contractor will be ready for each inspection	No less than 21 days	The Engineer
9.2	Time for delayed completion inspection determined by the Contractor	No less than 7 days	The Engineer
10.1	Application for Taking-Over Certificate	Within 14 days	The Engineer
11.5	Request the Owner to agree to remove the defective permanent equipment from the site for maintenance, with reasons. The notice should clearly identify each defective permanent equipment and specify, defect to be repaired, place to be repaired, mode of transport and insurance, pre-inspection and inspection on site, expected repair time, expected time for re-installation and inspection		The Employer
11.6	Describes repaired works, sections, partial or permanent equipment and recommended retesting	Within 7 days	The Engineer
11.7	Describes some pre-entry works, reasons for entry, and pre-selected entry times	Reasonanble time	The Employer
15.1	Upon receipt of the correction notice, describe the remedial measures to be taken by the Contractor and indicate the date of commencement of such measures	Immediately	The Engineer
16.1	Notice of suspension of work, and notes issued under Sub-Clause 16.1		The Employer
16.2.1	Notification of the Contractor's intention to terminate the Contract or of termination, indicating that it was issued under Sub-Clause 16.2.1		The Employer

Continued

Sub-Clause number	Content requirement	Time limit	Notification object
16.2.2	Notice of immediate termination of the Contract		The Employer
18.5	Notice of termination of Contract		The Employer

Table 10

Sub-Clause number	Content requirement	Time limit	Notification object
3.6	Indicate objection against substitution, and explain the reason	Within 14 days	The Employer
3.7.4	It clearly points out any printing, writing or calculation errors in the agreement or decision, and indicates that they are issued under Section 3.7.4	Within 14 days	The Engineer
3.7.5	Notification of dissatisfaction with the Engineer's decision shall be stated and reasons for dissatisfaction stated	Within 28 days	The Employer
5.2.2	Reasonable objections with supporting materials	Within 14 days	The Engineer
6.5	Explanation of reasons and description of work on site other than normal working hours specified in locally recognized rest days or contract data tables	Immediately	The Engineer
8.12	Some projects affected by prolonged suspension are regarded as a penalty reduction		The Engineer
10.2	It indicates that the part used in advance by the Owner is indicated as used		The Engineer
10.3	Description of the Owner's or Owners' reasons for Responsibility to Prevent Completion Inspection		The Engineer
11.2	Defects are caused by other reasons	Immediately	The Engineer
12.1	Explanation of reasons for the Contractor's belief that the measurement was inaccurate	Within 14 days	The Engineer
12.3	Clarifying the reasons why the Contractors disagree with rates and prices		The Engineer
13.1	Provide detailed supporting material instructions: change work is unpredictable; or the Contractor cannot immediately obtain the goods needed for change; or change will adversely affect Contractors' compliance with health and safety obligations and environmental protection obligations	Immediately	The Engineer

Continued

Sub-Clause number	Content requirement	Time limit	Notification object
14.6.3	The Contractor is dissatisfied with the full amount identified in the next Payment Certificate; the amounts identified do not include those determined under Sub-Clause 3.7		The Engineer
20.1	Notification of the claim submitted to the Engineer with a detailed description of the situation and details of the Owner or Engineer's dissent (or deemed dissent)	As soon as possible	The Engineer
20.2.1	Description of claim events	As soon as possible and within 28 days	The Engineer
20.2.2	Disagree with valid as the claim notice and elaborate on the reasons		The Engineer
21.4.4	It is indicated that the notice is not satisfied with the decision of DAAB, and the controversial issues and reasons for dissatisfaction are explained	Within 28 days	The Employer

Table 11

Sub-Clause number	Content requirement	Time limit	Notification object
1.5	Ambiguity or ambiguity in Contract Documents found	Immediately	The Engineer
1.8	Errors or defects found in specifications, drawings or Contractor's Documents	Immediately	The Employer
3.4	Query about instructions or notifications of engineer assistants		The Engineer
3.5	Holds that an engineer's order constitutes a change or non-compliance with applicable law, or a reduction in the safety of the project, or a technical infeasible, with reasons	Immediately, and before starting the Works of the instructions	The Engineer
4.7.2	Error of reference item	Within 28 days before construction; if feasible, as soon as possible	The Engineer
4.9.1	Problems in External Audit	Immediately	The Engineer

Continued

Sub-Clause number	Content requirement	Time limit	Notification object
4.12.1	Describe the material conditions encountered, state the reasons the Contractor considers that the material conditions are unpredictable, and explain how the material conditions adversely affect progress and increase costs	As soon as possible	The Engineer
4.23	Description of archaeological or geographical discoveries encountered	As soon as possible	The Engineer
13.6	Detailed supporting material indicating that legal changes make changes necessary	Immediately	The Engineer
17.2	Events occurred and resulted in damage to works, goods and Contractor's Documents	Immediately	The Engineer
18.2	Notify the abnormal events encountered and indicate which obligations are blocked or will be blocked	Within 14 days	The Employer
18.3	Notice of Cessation Impact of Abnormal Events	Immediately	The Employer
18.6	Notify the event		The Employer

※ Vocabulary

1. jurisprudence *n.* 法律体系;法学及其分支;法律知识;法院审判规程

2. original copy 原本,正本

3. assigned to 被分配给

4. notice of action[法] 诉讼通知

5. remedial measures 补救办法

Appendix 8

Understanding and Application of Force Majeure Clauses in Contracts

Ⅰ Evolution of force majeure clause

In the process of compiling contract conditions for each version of FIDIC, to some extent, it reflects the attempt to coordinate the universal application of force majeure clauses in common law and civil law.

In FIDIC 1987 *Conditions of Contract for Civil Engineering Construction* (hereinafter referred to as 87 Red Book), which is still being used in some projects, there is no definition of force majeure or a separate provision for force majeure incidents, but rather through the combined application of Sub-Clause 20. 4 [Owner's risk], Article 65 [Special risk] and Article 66 [Termination of Performance], the Contractor is able to obtain some protection similar to force majeure exemption.

The above provisions of the 87 Red Book are obviously insufficient, because it does not list specific events (such as plague and terrorist activities) as force majeure events, and there is no corresponding definition. Therefore, when the Contractor encounters such force majeure events, it may be difficult to invoke the provisions.

Compared with the 87 Red Book, FIDIC introduced the term " force majeure " in the series of rainbow book (FIDIC 1999 edition) compiled in 1999 through the arrangement of Sub-Clause 19.1 — Sub-Clause 19. 7, defined force majeure, and stipulated relevant procedures and consequences.

Based on the objective of improving the clarity and certainty of the terms of the Contract, the new editions of the Red, Yellow and Silver book (FIDIC 2017 edition) were prepared by FIDIC in 2017. The provisions on force majeure basically follow the relevant provisions of FIDIC 1999 edition. The more obvious modification is to change Article 19 of the latter to Article 18 of FIDIC 2017 edition, and to change the term "force majeure" to "exceptional event".

Ⅱ Definition of force majeure

In FIDIC 2017, "exceptional event" ("force majeure") is defined as a contract term, and the complete definition is arranged in the first paragraph of Sub-Clause 18. 1 [Exceptional Events] under Article 18 [Exceptional Events]. The exceptional event here refers to an event or situation, and needs to meet the following four conditions:

①one Party cannot control;

②the Party cannot reasonably prepare for the Contract before signing it;

③After occurrence, this Party cannot reasonably avoid or overcome;

④cannot be attributed mainly to others.

On the definition of the scope of force majeure itself, that is, the cause of performance is "event" or "situation", there are differences in the use of words in various judicial areas, such as the law in some judicial areas will force majeure be classified as "event", rather than "situation" into the provisions of force majeure.

In view of this, the FIDIC 2017 version defines force majeure as "event" or "situation", which to a large extent covers the definition of force majeure itself in various jurisdictions and matters that may arise in practice.

Based on the qualitative explanation of the first paragraph of Sub-Clause 18. 1, the second paragraph of Sub-Clause 18. 1 further lists the events or situations that (a) to (f) may constitute exceptional events in an unrestricted manner. In summary, subparagraphs (a) to (e) are "man-made", such as wars, insurrections, riots, strikes, etc. Subparagraph (f) is natural disasters, such as earthquakes, tsunamis, volcanic activities, hurricanes or typhoons. Different from FIDIC 1999, the strikes or shutdowns covered in Subparagraph (iii) are listed separately as Subparagraph (d) of the new version, and tsunami events are added in Subparagraph (f) of natural disasters, which should be adjusted according to the actual situation of international projects.

Ⅲ Obligations of the Parties after force majeure incidents

Paragraphs I and II of Sub-Clause 18. 2 of the 2017 edition of FIDIC [Notice of Exceptional] provide for procedural requirements for the affected Party following the occurrence of an exceptional event or situation - notification to the other Party within 14 days of the occurrence of an exceptional event and an indication of the fulfillment of an obligation that has been or will be hindered. The notification of exceptional events should not directly claim the duration or cost, but require the affected Party to describe the exceptional events and situations so that the other Party can take corresponding measures in time, and it is also the necessary basis of the claim procedure in Sub-Clause 18. 4 [Consequences of an Exceptional Event].

Different from the FIDIC 1999 edition, it is stipulated here that if the affected Party issues an exception notice after 14 days, the part of the affected Party that can be exempted from fulfilling its obligations is limited to the part of the obligation calculated from the date on which the other Party receives the notice. If the affected Party delays the issuance of notices of exceptional events, it is not entitled to claim exemptions for some obligations during the delay based on exceptional events.

It should be noted that the first paragraph of Sub-Clause 20. 2 [Claims for Payment and/or

EOT] requires the 28-day limitation of the claim notice. Combined with the provisions of Sub-Clause 18.4 quoted in Sub-Clause 20.2, the Contractor must meet the limitation requirements of the two notifications in Sub-Clause 18.2 and Sub-Clause 20.2 at the same time, in order to propose a complete and effective claim for the impact of exceptional events.

The first paragraph of Sub-Clause 18.3 of FIDIC 2017 [Duty to Minimize Delay] is basically consistent with the spirit of the "rule of mitigation" under the common law system and the civil law system. However, the reduction obligation of both Parties in this Clause focuses on the "delay" of the construction period of the project, and does not further provide the consequential provisions that violate the provisions here. Therefore, it is necessary to note that, even if the terms of the Contract are not clear, in practice, based on the "mitigation of loss rules" which are widely used in various judicial fields, if an event of force majeure occurs, the parties should consciously take reasonable measures to reduce any loss caused by force majeure.

IV Possible claim of the Contractor after force majeure event

As to whether the Contractor has the right to file a claim for the cost of force majeure, according to the arrangement of the Clause, in the matters listed in Sub-Clause 18.1, the natural disaster category (f) cannot file a claim for the cost; (a) items of war, hostilities (whether declared war or not), invasion and foreign hostile acts, whether or not occurred in the country where the project is located, can file claims for costs; the items listed in Sub-Clause 18.1, namely, the items listed in Sub-Clauses (b) to (e), should occur in the country where the project is located before the cost claim can be filed; other matters not listed and defined as exceptional events pursuant to Sub-Clause 18.1 are not entitled to claim costs but are entitled to claim duration. Therefore, the above claim arrangement means whether the exceptions need to be clearly listed, and which one is listed, is crucial to the Contractor's ability to claim costs.

V Contract termination caused by force majeure

The first paragraph of Sub-Clause 18.5 of FIDIC 2017 [Optional Termination] gives the Owners and Contractors the right to terminate the Contract due to exceptional events, and enters into force after 7 days of the issuance of the termination notice. It is divided into two situations:

①The exceptional events in the notice lead to the continuous obstruction of engineering implementation in all progress in essence for 84 days (the situation needs to be considered in essence is the continuity of obstruction, not limited to a single exceptional event, that is, at the same time, the continuity of various exceptional events hinders the implementation of 84 days).

②A cumulative period of 140 days is intermittently hindered by exceptional events in the same notice (this case is limited to cases in the same notice).

Finally, according to the provisions of Sub-Clause 18.6 of FIDIC 2017 [Release from Peformance under the Law], the following two extreme situations that cannot be controlled by both Parties may directly lead to the exemption of contractual obligations regardless of whether they constitute an exception:

①This situation makes one Party unable or unable to perform its contractual obligations legally.

②According to the applicable law, all Parties have the right to terminate the further performance of the Contract.

These two cases are extremes and need to be discussed according to the applicable legal rules, such as the rules of force majeure under the continental law system, the rules of change of circumstances or the rules of contract frustration under the common law system. This provision is more difficult to apply in practice and should be resorted to legal analysis according to specific circumstances.

※Vocabulary

1. the universal application 普遍应用

2. terrorist activities 恐怖活动

3. force majeure[保险]不可抗力

4. hereinafter *adv.*（正式声明、文件等中）在下文中（等于 hereafter）

5. to a large extent 在很大程度上

6. unrestricted *adj.* 自由的；无限制的；不受束缚的

7. procedural requirements 程序上的要求

8. take corresponding measures 采取相应措施

9. violate the provisions 违反了规定

10. consequential *adj.* 随之而来的，作为结果的；<法律>间接发生的，间接引起的；重要的，意义重大的

11. file a claim 提出索赔

12. intermittently *adv.* 间歇地

13. in essence 本质上，其实，大体上

14. continental law 欧洲大陆法

Appendix 9

Claim Procedures and Related Issues of New FIDIC Contract Conditions

I Definition of Claim in provision 1. 1. 6 of FIDIC series of contract conditions in 2017

The definition of Claim is "one Party asks or advocates the other Party's right or relief under any terms of the Contract Conditions, or related to the implementation of the Contract or the project."

As can be seen from the above definition, the Claim is based on law and Contract and is a normal and reasonable act. Claim has the following characteristics:

(1) Legitimacy

Its determination must be based on Contract Documents and relevant laws and regulations.

(2) Compensatory rather than punitive

It is set to compensate the loss of the non-fault Party.

(3) No fault

It is caused by non-self reasons, the Claim Party has no fault.

(4) Objective

When the actual economic interests or interests are indeed lost, the injured Party can file a claim with the other Party.

Claims are clearly divided into three categories in Article 20 [Employer's and Contractor's Claims] of the 2017 edtion of FIDIC:

(1) Category I: The Owner's claim for additional costs (or contract price deduction) and/or Defects Notification Period (DNP) extension.

(2) Category II: The Contractor's claim for additional costs and/or extended duration (EOT).

(3) Category III: Rights or remedies required or asserted by one Party to the Contract to another Party in any other respect, including claims for any certificate, decision, direction, notice, opinion or valuation given by the Engineer (Owner), other than those relating to categories I and II above.

Ⅱ Difference between new and old FIDIC contract conditions on claims provisions

Compared with the 1999 edition of FIDIC series contract conditions, the 2017 edition of FIDIC series contract conditions have made substantial changes to claims related issues. The relevant provisions on claims procedures and claims content have increased significantly, and the definition and classification of Claims have become clearer. However, Claims procedures have become more complex and cumbersome. The main changes in the 2017 series of contracts with respect to claims include:

(1) The Claims are clearly defined and classified. The 2017 edition of FIDIC series of contract conditions gives a clear definition of the concept of Claims, and the Claims are divided into three categories, and the third category of Claims is introduced for the first time.

(2) The Claims of the Owners and Contractors are treated equally. The Owner's Claim and the Contractor's Claim related content are unified in Article 20 [Employer's and Contractor's Claims] to make provisions, and higher requirements are put forward on the Owner's Claim.

(3) The time restriction for submission of claims reports ("basis of claims") is added. The FIDIC series contract terms of 1999 only stipulate that if the Contractor fails to issue a claim notice within 28 days after the claim event, it will lose the right to receive cost compensation and duration extension. Based on the 2017 edition of FIDIC series contract conditions, the time limit for filing the "claim basis" in the claim report is further introduced, improving the requirements on claimant's.

(4) Flexibility in Claims processing is increased. The Engineer / Owner's Representative has greater discretion in handling Claims. The 2017 edition of the FIDIC series contract conditions introduced "Invalid claims notice" and the relevant provisions for its processing, making the processing of the limitation of Claims more flexible. When the claimant fails to issue a claim notice or submit the basis for the claim within the time specified in the Contract, the Engineer (the Silver Book is the Owner's Representative) is given greater freedom and space to deal with the Claim, and the Engineer/Owner's Representative will determine the amount and time extension of the claim in accordance with Sub-Clause 3.7 [Agreement or Determination] on a case-by-case basis.

(5) The contents that should be included in the claim report are clearly stipulated. Detailed provisions are made on the specific content of the claim report to be submitted by the claimant, including the cause of the Claim. A detailed description of the events or circumstances of the Claim, the Contract or other legal basis of the Claim ("the basis of the claim"), the simultaneous records on which all claimants are based and detailed supporting documentation supporting the Claim, etc.

In the revision process of the 2017 edition series of contract conditions, FIDIC takes Claims and Disputes as important issues to consider, hoping to deal with Claims reasonably and timely, so as to avoid Claims upgrading to Disputes. FIDIC believes that the Claim is only one Party's claim based on compliance or claiming its own rights, which does not necessarily rise to Disputes. Only when the Claim is partially or completely rejected can Disputes be formed.

※ **Vocabulary**

1. the injured party 受害方
2. compensatory *adj.* 赔偿的；弥补的，补偿的
3. defect notification 缺陷通知期限
4. put forward on 提出
5. invalid claims 无效要求
6. discretion *n.* 自行决定权，判断力；谨慎，慎重

Appendix 10

Care and Guarantee Analysis of the Works of New FIDIC Contract

I Duty and responsibilities of care of the works in FIDIC series of contract conditions in 2017 edition

Under the Contract, the Contractor and the Owner shall be responsible for the care of the Works, Goods and Contractor's Documents at different stages to protect them from damage. In the event of damage, responsibility will be divided and assumed according to the different care responsibilities and sources of damage.

(1)Care responsibilities for the Works, Goods and Contractor's Documents

In accordance with Sub-Clause 17.1 [Responsibilities for Care of the Works] of the general terms of contract of the 2017 edition FIDIC book, the Contractor shall be responsible for the care of the Works, Goods and Contractor's Documents from the commencement date of the project to the completion of the project. After the completion of the Works, the care responsibility for the Works is transferred to the Owner.

If the Engineer (or the Owner) has issued a Taking-Over Certificate for a certain part of the project, the care responsibilities of the project will be transferred to the Owner accordingly. After the project, care responsibilities are transferred to the Owner, the Contractor shall still be responsible for the unfinished round-off work at the completion of the project until the round-off work is completed. If the Contract is terminated during the execution of the Contract, the Contractor will no longer be responsible for taking care of the project from the date of termination.

(2)Restoration responsibility after damage to the Works, Goods and Contractor's Documents

During the care of the Contractor, if any loss or damage occurs to the Works, Goods or Contractor's Documents, the Contractor shall be responsible for repairing the Works, Goods or Contractor's Documents to meet the requirements of the Contract, and bear the risk and cost of repairing, except for the following six categories. In addition, in accordance with Sub-Clause 17.2 [Liability for Care of the Works], any damage or loss to any Works, Goods or Contractor's Documents occurred after the issuance of the Taking-Over Certificate resulting from the Contractor's cause or from the Contractor's liability before the issuance of the Taking-Over Certificate shall also be liable to the Contractor.

Pursuant to Sub-Clause 17. 2 [Liability for Care of the Works], the Contractor shall not be liable for loss or damage to the Works, Goods or Contractor's Documents arising from the following six types of events (unless the Works, Goods or Contractor's Documents have been rejected by the Engineer under the Contract prior to the following events):

①According to the contract implementation of the project on road traffic rights, light, air, water or other inevitable interference (except by the Contractor construction method).

②The Owners use any part of permanent works, unless otherwise stipulated in the Contract.

③Any errors, defects or omissions in the design that are responsible by the Owner or in Owner's requirements in (an experienced Contractor in the bidding site inspection and when he check the Owner's requirements still fails to find even after pay due attention to), except for the design part which is responsible by the Contractor in accordance with the provisions of the Contract.

④The natural force that are unforeseen or an experienced Contractor cannot reasonably foresee and take adequate preventive measures (except the risks assigned to the contractor in the contract data table).

⑤The events or situations listed in Sub-Clause 18. 1 [Exceptional Events].

⑥Any act or default by an Owner or other Contractor.

The first type of events above is inevitable in project implementation. Categories 2, 3 and 6 are caused by the Owner's actions. Events in categories 4 and 5 are caused by objective reasons. The above six types of events belong to the risks that the Owner should bear.

If the above six types of events cause damage to the Works, Goods or Contractor's Documents, the Contractor shall immediately notify the Engineer, and the Contractor shall repair the loss or damage according to the instructions of the Engineer. This instruction should be regarded as made by the Engineer according to Sub-Clause 13. 3. 1 [Variation by Instruction] and will be processed according to the change procedure. Contractor losses arising from exceptional events will be dealt with in accordance with Sub-Clause 18. 4 [Consequences of an Exceptional event].

If the loss or damage of the Works, Goods or Contractor's Documents is caused by the above six types of events and the reasons for the Contractor's responsibility, and the Contractor suffered delays and/or incurred additional costs for repairing the loss or damage, the Contractor has the right to obtain the compensation of corresponding proportion according to the provisions of Sub-Clause 20. 2 [Claims For Payment and/or EOT], and the extension of the construction period caused by the above six types of events.

On the third type of events, there are differences in the contract conditions of the three editions of 2017, in which the Red Book does not have the document concerning Owner's requirements but only technical specifications and drawings. The risks of errors, defects or omissions in the requirements of the Owner of the Silver Book are borne by the Contractor after signing the Contract. The third type of event in the Silver Book only refers to errors, defects or omissions in the design work that the Owner is responsible for.

Ⅱ 2017 edition FIDIC series contract conditions under the contract of mutual protection between the Parties

The Contractor and the Owner shall, in addition to taking care of the Works, Goods and Contractor's Documents under the Contract, indemnify the other Party against claims arising from third Parties as a result of his own conduct or breach of the contract, and the Contractor shall indemnify the Owner's losses as a result of his own mistakes in the design part.

(1) The Contractor's indemnities for the Owner

According to Sub-Clause 17.4 [Indemnities by Contractor], the Contractor shall indemnify the Owner, the Owner's personnel and their respective agents against claims, damages, losses and expenses from third Parties (including legal costs and expenses) resulting from:

①the personal injury, illness, illness or death of any person arising from the execution of the Works by the Contractor, other than the negligence, wilful act or breach of the Contract of the Owner, the Owner's personnel or any of their respective agents.

②damage or loss to any property, real or personal (other than works) caused by:

(a) the Contractor's implementation of the Works;

(b) the fault, willful act or breach of the Contract caused by the Contractor, Contractor's Personnel, any of their respective agents or any of their directly or indirectly employed persons.

Pursuant to Sub-Clause 17.4 [Indemnities by Contractor], the Contractor shall also protect the Owner from any loss or damage resulting from the failure of the completed Works (including production equipment) to meet the intended purpose of the contract resulting from the Contractor's performance of the design obligations, errors or omissions.

(2) The Owner's idemnities for the Contractor

According to Sub-Clause 17.5 [Indemnities by Employer], the Owner shall indemnify the Contractor, the Contractor's Personnel and their respective agents from claims, damages, losses and expenses (including legal costs and expenses) from third Parties caused by:

①Personal injury, illness, illness or death as a result of negligence, wilful conduct or breach of the Contract by the Owner, the Owner or any of their respective agents, or loss or damage to any property other than Works.

②The loss or damage to any property, real estate or movable property (except for the project) caused by the six types of exclusion events under Sub-Clause 17.2 [Liability for Care of the Works].

(3) Intellectual property rights and industrial property rights infringement protection

The Owners and Contractors should also indemnify the two sides from intellectual property and industrial property rights (such as patent, trademark, copyright, etc.) infringement caused by the third Party claim losses or damage.

Pursuant to Sub-Clause 17.3 [Intellectual and Industrial Property Rights], the Contractor shall idemnify the Owner from any loss or damage (including legal costs and expenses) incurred by the Contractor in carrying out the Works or by the Contractor in using construction equipment. The Owner should idemnify the Contractor from any loss or damage (including legal costs and expenses) caused by infringement claims:

①inevitable results caused by the Contractors' compliance with the Owners' requirements and/or any changes; or

②the results of the Owner's use of the Works:

a. the use is for purposes other than the Contract (express or implied); or

b. the use is used together with any article provided by a Non-Contractor unless otherwise stipulated in the Contract or the Contractor is informed before the base date.

When one Party to the Contract receives a third-party claim, it shall immediately give notice to the other Party. If one Party fails to give such notice within 28 days of receiving a third-party claim, it shall be deemed to have waived any guaranteed rights stipulated in this Article.

If a Party is entitled to be indemnified under this Sub-Clause, the indemnifier may (at its own expense) undertake negotiations for third-party claims and any proceedings or arbitration that may arise therefrom. When the indemnifier requests and undertakes the cost, the other Party should assist in processing the Claim. Unless the indemnifier fails to participate in third-party Claims negotiations in a timely manner, the other Party (and its personnel) shall not make any commitments that may prejudice the indemnifier.

The protection of intellectual property rights and industrial property rights infringement is a very important issue, and the infringement problem can not be transferred through insurance risk, and there is no maximum liability limit for compensation. Maybe because of its particularity, intellectual property rights and industrial property rights infringement protection in Sub-Clause 17.4 [Indemnities by Contractor] and Sub-Clause 17.5 [Indemnities by Employer] are separately listed as a clause.

(4) Common guarantee under cross responsibility

According to Sub-Clause 17.6 [Shared Indemnities], if both Parties are responsible for the occurrence of the event, the Contractor's indemnity of the Owner under the Contract should consider the impact of the six types of exceptions under Sub-Clause 17.2 [Liability for Care of the Works] on the loss or damage in proportion to reduce.

Ⅲ Differences in Relevant Provisions of 2017 FIDIC Contract Conditions

The provisions of the 2017 edition FIDIC series contract conditions on engineering care, security and exceptional events are basically consistent with the principles and concepts of the 1999 edition series contract. However, there are great differences in terms of terms and arrangements, as follows:

①Article 17 has made great changes in structure: putting the indemnity clause behind, and dividing the mutual indemnity between the Owner and the Contractor into two equivalent clauses.

②Sub-Clause 17.3 [Employer's Risks] and Sub-Clause 17.4 [Consequence of Employer's Risks] of the 1999 edition are deleted, and Sub-Clause 17.2 [Liability for Care of the Works] is added. Through Sub-Clause 17.2, the six types of risk events that the Owner should bear responsibility for engineering damage are clarified, and the concept of "Employer's Risks" is no longer used, which avoids the misunderstanding of the concept of "Employer's Risks" (mistaking that the "Employer's Risks" refers to all risks of the Owner under the Contract) and is clearer and more accurate. In addition, categories 1 and 6, particularly category 6, have been added compared to the 1999 edition to make it clear that the risks arising from the conduct or breach of contract of the Owner-related person are borne by the Owner and are more comprehensive.

③A new Sub-Clause 17.6 [Shared Indemnities] is added, which clarifies the indemnities under the events caused by the reasons for the joint responsibility of both Parties, facilitates the separation of responsibilities and facilitates the handling of problems.

④The 1999 version of Sub-Clause 17.6 [Limitation of Liability] has been moved to Sub-Clause 1.15 [Limitation of Liability], because the limitation of liability is not only the responsibility in Article 17, but also includes other contractual liability, such as compensation for damages in the wrong period, so it has become more comprehensive.

※Vocabulary

1. restoration *n.*（对艺术品、建筑等的）修复；（做法、权利、惯例或情况的）恢复，重新实施；归还，返还；（软件程序的）恢复，还原

2. be liable for loss 对损失负责

3. arising from 由……引起，起因于

4. intellectual property［专利］知识产权；著作权

5. infringement *n.*（对他人权益的）侵犯，侵害；（对法律、规则等的）违反，违背

6. inevitable results 必然结果

7. commitment *n.* 忠诚，献身；承诺，保证；奉献，投入；热情，决心；义务，责任；花费，使用（资金、时间、人力）；需要定期支付的款项

Appendix 11

Analysis of the New FIDIC Series Contract Conditions Changes

Ⅰ Engineering changes

The 2017 edition of FIDIC Red Book classifies engineering changes into the following six types:

①the change of quantities of any work in the Contract (but the change of such quantities does not necessarily constitute a change);

②changes in the quality or other characteristics of any work;

③changes in elevation, position and/or size of any part of the project;

④the deletion of any work, except that it is implemented by others without the consent of both Parties;

⑤any additional work, production equipment, materials or services required for permanent projects, including any relevant completion test, drilling, other test or survey work;

⑥changes in the order or timing of the implementation of the project.

Ⅱ Right to change

Whether the change is initiated by the Owner or the Contractor, the Owner should issue a change instruction after confirming the change, that is, the Owner shall have the right to decide the change, and the Owner decides whether or how to change. However, for a change initiated by the Owner, the Contractor may reasonably refuse to accept the change or to submit a change proposal. These reasons are as follows (the Red Book does not have Articles 4 and 5):

①considering the scope and nature of the project, the change is unpredictable;

②the Contractor shall not be able to obtain the material necessary to implement the change;

③the change would seriously affect the fulfillment by the Contractor of its obligations under Sub-Clause 4.8 [Health and Safety Obligations] and Sub-Clause 4.18 [Protection of the Environment];

④the change will seriously affect the performance assurance value;

⑤the change may adversely affect the Contractor's obligation to complete the project, resulting in the project can not meet the expected purpose of the project described in Sub-Clause 4. 1 [Contractor's General Obligations].

Upon receipt of the notice of rejection by the Contractor, the Owner may cancel, confirm or modify the change instruction.

Ⅲ Differences between the Yellow Book and Red Book and Silver Book on changes

In the provisions of the FIDIC series of contract conditions on the terms of change in the 2017 edition, the Silver Book is consistent with the Yellow Book except that the Owner replaces the role of Engineer in the Yellow Book. There are some differences between the Red Book and Yellow Book, including:

①In the Red Book, two grounds were deleted for the Contractor's refusal to change or submit the proposal, namely that the change would seriously affect the performance assurance value of the project and might affect the objective of meeting the intended purpose after the completion of the project. The reason for this difference is that the Contractor in The Yellow Book, as the general Contractor, needs to ensure the performance of the project and meet the expected purpose of the project, while the Contractor in the Red Book, as the construction unit of the project, does not have such obligations according to the construction plan.

②The Red Book classifies the changes, but the Yellow Book does not describe them in detail.

③The Red Book provides that if the Contractor initiates a change, the Owner will approve.

If the proposal of the Contractor is approved and the change is issued, the Contractor is responsible for the relevant design of the change unless the two Parties agree otherwise.

The Yellow Book does not specify this, the main reason is that the Contractor is responsible for the design under the Yellow Book, so if there is no special description of the design change, it is also undertaken by the Contractor. In the Red Book, the Contractor is generally only responsible for the construction according to the drawings, and the design is completed by other Parties. However, because the change is initiated by the Contractor according to the value engineering, and the Contractor has prepared a proposal for the change, the Contractor can better understand and implement the change (including design and construction), which is also in line with the general principle of risk distribution of FIDIC.

④In terms of the valuation of the change, the Red Book sets the price of the change in accordance with Article 12 [Measurement and Valuation], i. e. multiplied by the quantities of the Works by the applicable unit price, and in Sub-Clause 12. 3 [Valuation of the Works]. However, the Yellow Book is the total price contract, and Article 12 [Measurement and Valuation] in the Red Book is modified to the post-completion test in the Yellow Book. The modified pricing is processed according to whether the price rate table is included in the Contract. If a price rate statement is included in the Contract, the pricing is dealt with in reference to Sub-Clause 12. 3 of the Red Book (the relevant content is extracted in the Yellow Book). Otherwise, pursuant to Sub-Clause 3. 7 [Agreement or Determination], the price is agreed by both Parties or determined by the Owner/Engineer.

Ⅳ Difference between the new and old versions of contract conditions on the change provisions

Compared with the old version, the 2017 version of FIDIC contract terms amends Article 13 [*Valuations and Adjustments*] as follows:

(1)The process of change is combed and explained step by step according to the progress of change to make it clearer and easier to operate.

(2) Under the condition of clear change, the Contractor naturally enjoys the time limit extension and price adjustment, no claim notice is required under Sub-Clause 20. 2 [Claims For Payment and/or EOT].

Although this content may be regarded as a "implicit provision" or practice in old contracts, there is a dispute between the Owners and Contractors in practice due to the lack of explicit written provisions.

(3) In the case of the Owner's request for change of proposal, the Contractor's cost of preparing the change proposal clearly stipulates that if the Owner decides not to change, the Contractor may claim. Although the 1999 contract does not provide that the contractor is unable to claim, that is, if the Contractor considers that it has incurred additional costs for this purpose, it may initiate a claim under Sub-Clause 20. 1 [Contractor's claim].

However, due to the relevant content is not clearly defined, difficulties are caused to the Contractor Claims.

(4) In cases where the Contractor may refuse to change or submit a change proposal, the addition of:

a. a change would seriously affect the Contractor's performance of health, safety and environmental protection obligations; and

b. the change is unpredictable in relation to the scope and nature of the original Works.

At the same time, the Yellow Book and Silver Book of 2017 revise the 1999 edition of "reducing the safety and applicability of the project " to " possibly affecting the project to meet the expected goal ".

(5) The Contract Duration, Price and Payment Schedule are adjusted according to the changes. The 2017 edition of the Contract is determined by negotiation between the two Parties or the Owner/Engineer according to Sub-Clause 3. 7 [Agreement or Determination] (1999 edition is Section 3. 5 [Determinations]). Since the 2017 edition of the Contract has refined and modified the "determination" on the basis of the 1999 edition, it also has a corresponding impact on the decision made on the basis of the clause, which is manifested in:

a. the first is to limit the time for consultations or decisions, i. e. the adjustment of the Contract Period, Price and Schedule of Payment for the change shall be decided by consensus or Owners/Engineers within a certain period of time;

b. the second is for the Owners/Engineers to make decisions, if the Contractor objects and issues within the prescribed time dissatisfaction notice, then the DAAB procedure or arbitration procedure shall be entered.

In the 1999 edition contract, Article 20 [Claim, Disputes and Arbitration] applies only after the notification of dissatisfaction is issued. Generally, it's widely believed that it is necessary to start Sub-Clause 20.1 [Contractor's Claims] to claim the Owner, and then enter the subsequent DAB or arbitration procedure after the Claim is disputed.

(6) In terms of determining the price of the change, the 2017 edition of the Yellow Book and the Silver Book draws a lesson from the relevant contents of the 1999 edition of the Red Book, that is, if the Contract contains the price rate table, the price of the same or similar items in the price rate table shall be adopted, or the new price is formulated by the Owner/Engineer according to the relevant price. If the Contract does not contain a price rate statement, it is priced in the form of cost plus remuneration.

V Other adjustments

In addition to the modification of Article 13 of the 2017 edition FIDIC series contract conditions, some relevant provisions have also been adjusted as follows:

①In Sub-Clause 2.4 [Employer's Financial Arrangements], a price payment guarantee for the change is added. If the single change price exceeds 10% of the amount of the accepted contract price or the cumulative change price exceeds 30% of the amount of the accepted contract price, the Contractor may require the Owner to provide proof of the relevant financial arrangements to demonstrate its ability to pay for the change.

②Performance security is associated with changes. Section 4.2 [Performance Security] stipulates that when the change leads to the cumulative increase or decrease of the Contract Price by more than 20% of the amount of the accepted Contract Price, the guarantee amount needs to be adjusted accordingly if the Owner requests.

③Some adjustments have been made to the specific terms of application changes. Particular attention is required to specify in Sub-Clause 8.7 [Rate of Progress] that the measures taken by the Contractor to compensate for the loss of construction period under Sub-Clause 8.4 [Extension of completion time] (including catch-up measures), as required by the Owner/Engineer, shall apply in Sub-Clause 13.3.1 [Variation by Instruction], i.e. catch-up is a change.

※ Vocabulary

1. without the consent 未经同意
2. survey work 测量工作
3. unpredictable *adj.* 无法预测的,不定的;(人)善变的,难以捉摸的
       n. 不可预言的事
4. risk distribution 风险分布
5. modified *adj.* 改进的,修改的;改良的
       v. 修改;缓和(modify 的过去式和过去分词)
6. in line with 符合;与……一致
7. in terms of 依据;按照;在……方面;以……措词

8. schedule of payment 付款清单
9. manifested *adj.* 证明的;已显示的;显然的
　　　　v. 显示;证明(manifest 的过去分词)
10. extension *n.* 延伸,扩展;展期,延长期;扩建部分,延伸部分;(电话)分机;扩展名;(为非全日制学生开设的)进修部;牵伸(术);外延;广延(性)
11. directive *n.* 指示;指令
　　　　adj. 指导的;管理的

Appendix 12

Keywords Listed

Table 12

No.	Keywords	Enterpretation
1	Contract	合同
2	Contract Agreement	合同协议书
3	Letter of Acceptance	中标函
4	Letter of Tender	投标函
5	Specification	规范
6	Drawings	图纸
7	Schedules	明细表
8	Tender	投标书
9	Appendix to Tender	投标函附录
10	Bill of Quantities	工程量表
11	Daywork Schedule	计日工表
12	Assignment	转让
13	Delayed Drawings or Instructions	延误的图纸或指令
14	Compliance with Laws	遵守法律
15	Definitions	定义
16	Dates, Tests, Periods and Completion	日期、检验、期间和竣工
17	Base Date	基准日期
18	Commencement Date	开工日期
19	Time for Completion	竣工时间
20	Tests on Completion	竣工检验
20	Taking-Over Certificate	接收证书
21	Tests after Completion	竣工后检验
22	Performance Certificate	履约证书

Continued

No.	Keywords	Enterpretation
23	Money and Payments	款项与支付
24	Accepted Contract Amount	中标合同金额
25	Contract Price	合同价格
26	Cost	费用
27	Final Statement	最终报表
28	Foreign Currency	外币
29	Local Currency	当地币
30	Payment Certificate	支付证书
31	Provisional Sum	暂定金额
32	Retention Money	保留金
33	Statement	报表
34	Works and Goods	工程与货物
35	Contractor's Equipment	承包商的设备
36	Goods	货物
37	Materials	材料
38	Permanent Works	永久工程
39	Plant	永久设备
40	Section	区段
41	Temporary Works	临时工程
42	Contractor's Documents	承包商的文件
43	Employer's Equipment	业主的设备
44	Laws	法律
45	Performance Security	履约保证
46	Site	现场
47	Unforeseeable	不可预见
48	Variation	变更
49	Communications	通信联络
50	Law and Language	法律与语言
51	Joint and Several Liability	共同的及各自的责任
52	The Employer	业主
53	Right of Access to the Site	进入现场的权利
54	Permits, Licences or Approvals	许可证、执照或批准

Continued

No.	Keywords	Enterpretation
55	Employer's Personnel	业主的人员
56	Employer's Financial Arrangements	业主的财务安排
57	Employer's Claims	业主的索赔
58	Engineer's Duties and Authority	工程师的职责和权力
59	Instructions of the Engineers	工程师指令
60	Replacement of the Engineer	工程师的更换
61	Determinations	决定
62	The Contractor	承包商
63	Contractor's General Obligations	承包商的一般义务
64	Subcontractors	分包商
65	Assignment of Benefit of Subcontract	分包合同权益的转让
66	Cooperation	合作
67	Setting Out	放线
68	Safety Procedure	安全措施
69	Quality Assurance	质量保证
70	Site Data	现场数据
71	Sufficiency of the Accepted Contract Amount	中标合同金额的充分性
72	Unforeseeable Physical Conditions	不可预见的外界条件
73	Rights of Way and Facilities	道路通行权与设施使用权
74	Avoidance of Interference	避免干扰
75	Access Route	进场路线
76	Transport of Goods	货物运输
77	Contractor's Equipment	承包商的设备
78	Protection of the Environment	环境保护
79	Electricity, Water and Gas	电、水和燃气
80	Progress Reports	进度报告
81	Security of Site	现场安保
82	Contractor's Site Operations	承包商的现场作业
83	Fossils	化石
84	Nominated Subcontractor	指定分包商
85	Staff and Labour	职员与劳工
86	Plant, Materials and Workmanship	工程设备、材料和工艺材料

Continued

No.	Keywords	Enterpretation
87	Commencement，Delay and Suspension	开工、延误及暂停
88	Commencement of Work	开工
89	Extension of Time for Completion	竣工时间的延长
90	Delays Caused by Authorities	当局引起的延误
91	Rate of Progress	进展速度
92	Delay Damages	拖期赔偿费
93	Suspension of Work	暂停工作
94	Prolonged Suspension	持续的暂停
95	Tests on Completion	竣工检验
96	Employer's Taking Over	业主的接收
97	Taking Over of the Works and Sections	工程和区段的接收
98	Defects Liability	缺陷责任
99	Measurement and Evaluation	计量与估价
100	Works to be Measured	工程计量
101	Method of Measurement	计量方法
102	Evaluation	估价
103	Omissions	删减
104	Variation and Adjustment	变更与调整
105	Right to Vary	有权变更
106	Value Engineering	价值工程
107	Variation Procedure	变更程序
108	Payment in Applicable Currencies	以适用的货币支付
109	Provisional Sums	暂定金额
110	Daywork	计日工
111	Adjustment for Changes in Legislation	因立法变动而调整
112	Adjustment for Changes in Cost	因费用波动而调整
113	Contract Price and Payment	合同价格与支付
114	The Contract Price	合同价格
115	Advance Payment	预付款
116	Application for Interim Payment Certificate	申请期中支付证书
117	Schedule of Payments	支付计划表
118	Issue of Interim Payment Certificates	期中支付证书的签发

Continued

No.	Keywords	Enterpretation
119	Payment	支付
120	Delayed Payment	延误的付款
121	Payment of Retention Money	保留金的支付
122	Statement of Completion	竣工报表
123	Discharge	申结清单
124	Issue of Final Payment Certificate	最终支付证书的签发
125	Cessation of Employer's Liability	业主责任的终止
126	Currencies of Payment	支付货币
127	Termination by Employer	业主提出终止
128	Valuation at Date of Termination	终止日的估价
129	Termination by Employer	发包商提出终止
130	Cessation of Work and Removal of Contractor's Equipment	停止工作以及撤离承包商的设备
131	Risks and Responsibility	风险与责任
132	Indemnities	保障
133	Contractor's Care for the Works	承包商对工程的照管
134	Employer's Risks	业主的风险
135	Consequences of Employer's Risks	业主风险的后果
136	Intellectual and Industrial Property Rights	知识产权和工业产权
137	Limit of Liability	责任限度
138	Insurance	保险
139	General Requirements for Insurers	保险的总体要求
140	Insurance for Contractor's Personnel	承包商人员的保险
141	insurance policy	保险单
142	deductible	免赔额
143	joint insured	联合被保险人
144	insured	被保险人
145	insurance applicant	投保人
146	Construction All Risks	施工一切险
147	Erection All Risks	安装一切险
148	Employer's Liability Insurance	雇主责任险
149	Third Party Liability Insurance	第三方责任险
150	Optional Termination, Payment and Release	可选择的终止,支付以及解除履约

Continued

No.	Keywords	Enterpretation
151	Claim, Disputes and Arbitration	索赔、争端与仲裁
152	Contractor's Claims	承包商的索赔
153	Amicable Settlement	友好解决
154	Arbitration	仲裁
155	EPC Turnkey	全过程总包合同
156	Design service	设计服务合同
157	Procurement service	咨询服务合同
158	Construction or Erection	施工或安装承包合同
159	fixed lump-sum price	固定总价合同
160	fixed unite price	固定单价合同
161	Guaranteed maximum price	限定最高价格合同
162	Main Contract	总承包合同
163	Construction Subcontract	分包合同
164	Labor Subcontract	劳务分包
165	EM Subcontract	设备材料供应分包
166	Transportation Subcontract	运输分包

Typical Sequence of Events in Agreement or Determination under Sub-Clause 3.7

Scenario 1[1]

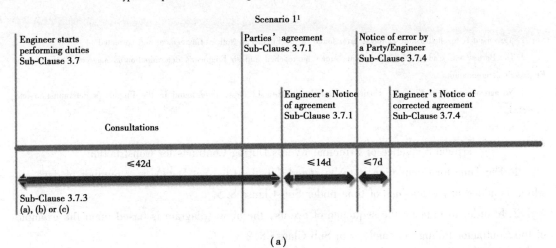

(a)

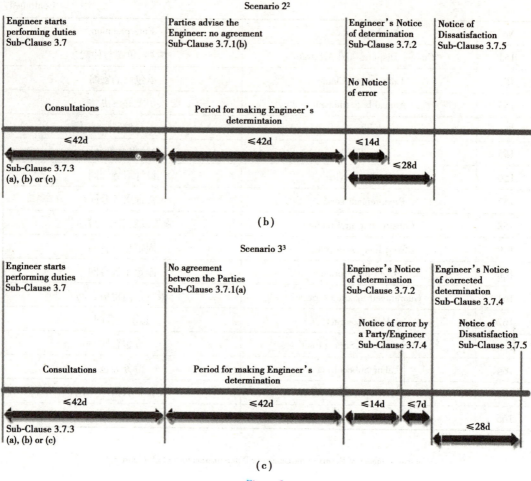

(b)

(c)

Figure 3

1. Agreement is reached within 42 days, error found in the Engineer's notice of agreement and corrected.

2. The Parties' early advice that agreement cannot be reached and so Engineer's determination is necessary, no error in Engineer's determination.

3. No agreement within 42 days, Engineer determines within 42 days, error found in the Engineer's determination and corrected.

Typical Sequence of Principal Events During Contracts for Construction

1. The Time for Completion is to be stated (in the Contract Data) as a number of days, to which is added any extensions of time under Sub-Clause 8.5.

2. In order to indicate the sequence of events, the above diagram is based upon the example of the Contractor failing to comply with Sub-Clause 8.2.

3. The Defects Notification Period is to be stated (in the Contract Data) as a number of days, to which is added any extensions under Sub-Clause 11.3.

4. Depending on the type of Works, Tests after Completion may also be required.

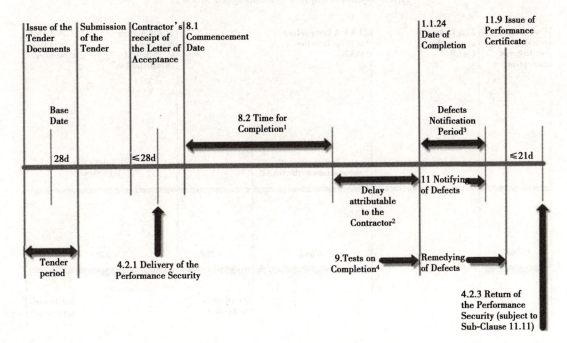

Figure 4

Typical Sequence of Payment Events Envisaged in Article 14

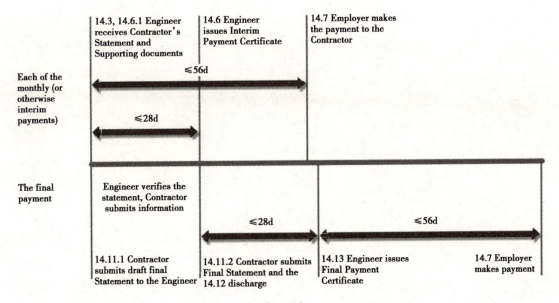

Figure 5

Typical Sequence of Dispute Events Envisaged in Article 21

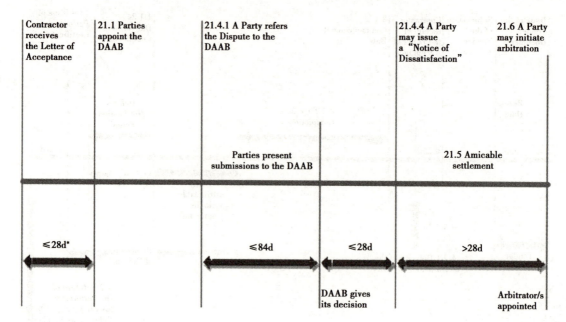

Figure 6

* If not stated otherwise in the Contract Data (Sub-Clause 21. 1)

References

[1] 田威. FIDIC 合同条件应用实务[M]. 北京:中国建筑工业出版社, 2009.

[2] 田威. FIDIC 合同的索赔条件——一个成功案例的分析[J]. 国际经济合作, 1993(3): 26-28+1.

[3] 田威. FIDIC 合同的进度计划条款[J]. 国际经济合作, 1993(6):27-29.

[4] 陈新元. FIDIC 施工合同条件与应用案例[M]. 北京:中国水利水电出版社, 2009.

[5] 尼尔 G. 巴尼 FIDIC 系列工程合同范本:编制原理与应用指南[M]. 北京:中国建筑工业出版社, 2008.

[6] 国际咨询工程师联合会, 中国工程咨询协会. 菲迪克(FIDIC)合同指南[M]. 北京:机械工业出版社, 2003.

[7] 张水波, 何伯森. FIDIC 新版合同条件导读与解析[M]. 北京:中国建筑工业出版社, 2008.

[8] 侯晓暾, 温文弛, 苏晓英. 浅谈 FIDIC 合同多种货币报价时价格调整公式中的权重系数[J]. 山西水利科技. 2000(4): 92-94.

[9] 王贤光. FIDIC 合同的索赔程序——某项目油料关税的索赔案例分析[J]. 经贸实务, 2003(2): 39-41.

[10] 周正宇. FIDIC 合同条件在北京城市道路建设中的运用[J]. 北京建筑工程学院学报, 2001, 17(4): 32-39+15.

[11] 李红苹, 王领. FIDIC 合同条件下的工程计量和支付管理在小浪底大坝工程的实践[J]. 西北水电, 2001(1): 7-10.

[12] 王卉. FIDIC 合同框架下的中国工程项目管理研究[D]. 大连:东北财经大学, 2007.

[13] 程建, 张辉璞, 胡明. FIDIC 合同下的国际工程索赔管理——非洲项目索赔案例实证分析[J]. 国际经济合作, 2007(9):4.

[14] 王守清. 国际工程项目风险管理案例分析[J]. 施工企业管理, 2008(2): 42-45.

[15] 赵凤茹. 国际工程承包项目合同管理与 FIDIC 合同条件应用研究[D]. 北京:对外经贸大学, 2007.

[16] 陈香宏. 国际工程合同管理实践与菲迪克施工合同条件案例解析[D]. 北京:清华大学, 2009.

[17] 韦锋. 探讨"案例模拟教学"在《建设工程招投标》课程中的应用[J]. 价值工程, 2012, 31(7): 1.

[18] 周天恩. 小浪底国际工程业主方合同管理案例分析[D]. 大连:大连理工大学, 2005.

[19] 宋高丽. 透过案例看固定总价合同纠纷[J]. 建筑经济, 2008(S2):3.

[20] 韩周强, 刘胜明, 杨俊杰. 投标世行贷款项目应注意的细节及其建议——某世界银行贷款项目案例分析[J]. 建筑经济, 2005(3):3.

[21] Warrender A . Contract interpretation[J]. Contract Journal, 2007, 438(6625): 34.

[22] Anonymous. New tunnel ensures safe water for rural KwaZulu-Natal[J]. Civil Engineering, 2002(10):4.

[23] Cotton A P, Sohail M , Scott R E . Towards improved labour standards for construction of minor works in low income countries [J]. Engineering Construction & Architectural Management, 2005, 12(6):617-632.

[24] Corbett E C., FIDIC 4th-a Practical Legal Guide: A Commentary on the International Construction Contract[M]. Sweet & Maxwell, 1991.

[25] Corbett, E. C. FIDIC's New Rainbow, The Red, Yellow Silver and Green 1st Editions [M]. Corbett & Co. , 1999.

[26] Harris F, Mc Caffer R., Modem Construction Management(5th edition)[M]. Blackwell Science Ltd. , Oxford, 2001.

[27] Kwakye A A. Construction project administration in practice[M]. Longman [co-published with] the Chartered Institute of Building, 1997.

[28] Guo Z L, Zhang H. Study of Natural Disasters Contract Conditions Based on the FIDIC Criteria[C]//Applied Mechanics and Materials, Trans Tech Publications Ltd, 2012, 238: 558-561.

[29] Wen Z, Zhou Q L. Some Suggestions for China Construction Project Investment Control Present Situation Based on FIDIC Contract[C]//Applied Mechanics and Materials. Trans Tech Publications Ltd, 2012, 209: 1294-1297.

[30] Zhou Y H, Tan W. Study on construction claim for international project based on contract status analysis[C]//Applied Mechanics and Materials. Trans Tech Publications Ltd, 2012, 174: 3356-3359.

[31] 张水波,姜丰军,刘小睿.新版 FIDIC 系列合同条件之合同终止与当事人权利[J].国际经济合作,2019(3):124-131.

[32] 张水波,匡伟.FIDIC 2017 版施工合同条件中工程师角色职能分析[J].天津大学学报(社会科学版),2021,23(6):481-487.

[33] 陈勇强,张水波,吕文学.2017 年版 FIDIC 系列合同条件修订对比[J].国际经济合作,2018(5):47-52.

[34] 张水波,董家广,仉乐.新版 FIDIC 合同条件保险条款应用分析[J].国际经济合作,2006(5):44-46.

[35] 陈勇强,姚洪江,谢爽.新版 FIDIC 系列合同条件之工程师/业主代表问题[J].国际经济合作,2019(1):127-136.

[36] 陈勇强,金梦夏,张帅军.新版 FIDIC 合同之工程照管、保障及例外事件分析[J].国际经济合作,2018(11):73-77.

[37] 高原,金梦夏,陈勇强.2017 年版 FIDIC 系列合同条件保险问题解析[J].国际经济合作,2018(11):78-82.

[38] 陈勇强,张帅军.2017 年版 FIDIC 系列合同条件支付问题之比较[J].国际经济合作,2018(10):73-77.

[39] 朱星宇,陈勇强,张玲,等.新版 FIDIC 合同条件之索赔条款分析[J].国际经济合作,

2018(9):87-91.

[40] 赵雅新,康飞,花园园. FIDIC2017 版合同条件对承包商的索赔通知要求分析[J]. 国际工程与劳务,2021(7):72-74.

[41] 赵雅新,康飞,花园园. FIDIC2017 版施工合同中对承包商的通知要求分析[J]. 国际工程与劳务,2021(6):62-65.

[42] 叶万和,张自为. 国际工程合同中不可抗力条款的理解与适用以 FIDIC 合同条件为主要视角[J]. 项目管理评论,2020(3):17-21.

[43] 邱佳娴. FIDIC 合同条件下不可抗力特殊性研究[D]. 南京:东南大学,2020.

[44] 万江山,王永刚,刘剑锋. FIDIC 合同黄皮书中价值工程案例分析——以保加利亚 EPK 铁路项目投标为例[J]. 国际工程与劳务,2021(7):75-77.

[45] 赵华. FIDIC 合同条件中业主便利解约条款研究[D]. 南京:东南大学,2020.

[46] 曹建. FIDIC 合同条件下的合同终止条件分析及策略研究[J]. 建筑科技,2020,4(4):68-70+75.

[47] 宋宜军,崔敏捷. FIDIC 合同体系中的不可抗力和承包商索赔[J]. 国际工程与劳务,2020(5):27-29.

[48] 宋宜军. 2017 版 FIDIC 合同体系介绍及与中国合同体系比较[J]. 国际工程与劳务,2019(10):58-62.

[49] 崔军. FIDIC(2017 年第二版)合同条件的主要变化[J]. 国际工程与劳务,2018(3):68-70.

[50] 高原,金梦夏,陈勇强. 2017 年版 FIDIC 系列合同条件保险问题解析[J]. 国际经济合作,2018(11):78-82.

[51] 焦文平. 2017 版与 1999 版 FIDIC 合同条款对比分析应用[J]. 建筑与预算,2019(6):34-36.

[52] 莫俊睿. FIDIC 2017 版合同条款中进度管理问题分析[J]. 工程建设与设计,2019(16):243-244.